Children and Youth in a New Nation

CHILDREN AND YOUTH IN AMERICA
General Editor: James Marten

Children in Colonial America
Edited by James Marten

Children and Youth in a New Nation
Edited by James Marten

Children and Youth in a New Nation

EDITED BY

James Marten

FOREWORD BY PAUL S. BOYER

NEW YORK UNIVERSITY PRESS

NEW YORK AND LONDON

NEW YORK UNIVERSITY PRESS
New York and London
www.nyupress.org

© 2009 by New York University
All rights reserved

Library of Congress Cataloging-in-Publication Data
Children and youth in a new nation / edited by James Marten ;
foreword by Paul S. Boyer.
p.   cm. — (Children and youth in America)
Includes bibliographical references and index.
ISBN-13: 978-0-8147-5742-0 (cl : alk. paper)
ISBN-10: 0-8147-5742-1 (cl : alk. paper)
ISBN-13: 978-0-8147-5749-9 (pb : alk. paper)
ISBN-10: 0-8147-5749-9 (pb : alk. paper)
1. Children—United States—History—18th century. 2. Children—United
States—History—19th century. 3. Youth—United States—History—18th
century. 4. Youth—United States—History—19th century. 5. Child
welfare—United States—History.   I. Marten, James Alan.
HQ792.U5C424 2008
305.230973—dc22   2008032763

New York University Press books are printed on acid-free paper, and
their binding materials are chosen for strength and durability. We
strive to use environmentally responsible suppliers and materials
to the greatest extent possible in publishing our books.

Manufactured in the United States of America

C   10 9 8 7 6 5 4 3 2 1
P   10 9 8 7 6 5 4 3 2 1

Contents

Acknowledgments

My greatest thanks go to the collegial and hardworking contributors to this book who made it possible to deliver the manuscript to the publisher on time and to Paul S. Boyer for agreeing to write the Foreword—and for his gracious and timely words. The anonymous readers provided helpful comments that strengthened the individual essays as well as the editor's introductions to the book's five sections, while Kristen Foster offered useful suggestions for the general introduction. Eric Zinner, Despina Papazoglou Gimbel, Ciara McLaughlin, and the rest of the staff at NYU Press deserve thanks for continuing to support the Children and Youth in America series and for their help in pushing this volume through the publication process.

Extracts from the diaries of Louisa Jane Trumbull and the journals of Louisa Clap Trumbull are published with permission of the American Antiquarian Society. Excerpts from the *Narrative* by William Wells Brown are printed courtesy of the Documenting the American South project at the University Library of the University of North Carolina at Chapel Hill (http://docsouth.unc.edu/neh/brown47/brown47.html).

Foreword

Paul S. Boyer

The best way to know a society, it has been said, is to examine how it treats its most vulnerable members. As a corollary, one might further suggest that how a society treats its children and how it perceives this early stage of life provide valuable clues for understanding that society. *Childhood and Youth in a New Nation* makes this point convincingly as the essays and primary sources offer many perspectives on childhood in America from the Revolution through the 1840s.

Just as "American history" is not a seamless whole but rather is segmented by multiple distinctions of gender, region, ethnicity, social class, occupation, and religion, so "the history of childhood" is not homogenous but must be built up from the historical experience of many diverse groups. This work conveys that diversity, and the editor has wisely avoided forcing the material into a single procrustean interpretive framework.

Even to note some of the most obvious differences among various groups of children in the early republic is to underscore this heterogeneity of experience. As thousands of native-born families migrated to cities seeking economic opportunity, their children faced the dangers and temptations of urban life, while also embodying the promise of upward mobility through education and white-collar employment. For the more than 2.4 million immigrants who arrived from Germany, Scandinavia, Ireland, and elsewhere from 1820 through the 1840s, children represented an essential source of labor and income. While many of these immigrants moved on to midwestern farms, many others, particularly the Irish, arriving in great numbers after 1840, settled in cities. Crowded into slums, urban immigrant children daily confronted the lure and hazards of the city streets. Immigrant parents worried as their offspring forgot the Old

Country and become "Americanized" in speech, dress, diet, and world-view. As for enslaved African Americans, their children could be sold and disappear overnight at the owner's whim. Native American children, together with their families and communities, faced the prospect of displacement as white settlers pushed ever westward and into southeastern lands occupied by the Cherokee, Creek, and other settled tribes.[1]

Even farm children of the Northeast and Midwest, seemingly insulated from the social changes of the period, proved restless, drawn by the lure of the city and the frontier. New England farm girls flocked to the region's textile mills. As one wrote to her father, "I want you to consent to let me go to Lowell if you can. I think it would be much better for me than to stay about here."[2] With what mixture of apprehension and hope did rural parents watch their children depart for the West, the mills, or the burgeoning cities?

But if no single narrative encompasses the history of childhood in America in the early national era, certain demographic patterns and large-scale social trends do emerge. First of all, it is important to emphasize that the social realities addressed in this book concern the historical experience of *half* the U.S. population in these years. The median age in 1820 was 16.7 years: fully half of all citizens were under seventeen years of age. In 1860, the median age was still only 19.4. (In 2004, it stood at thirty-six.)[3] In terms of numbers alone, to neglect the historical experience of children and youth in these years is to ignore 50 percent of the population.

But this age cohort invites our attention not only because of its size but also because these young lives were so often disrupted as premodern folkways gave way to upheavals associated with immigration, urban growth, nascent industrialization, and internal population movements. The essays and documents that follow convey this turbulence while also gesturing toward the larger social processes that produced it.

The essays also address the debates *about* children that marked these decades. Optimistic reformers, influenced by the romantic movement's view of childhood innocence and purity, idealized children as the shining hope of the future. As the fertility rate declined (the average married white woman bore seven children in 1800, 5.4 in 1850) and as home and workplace grew more distinct for urban middle-class families, the nurture of children drew more attention. Childhood increasingly came to be viewed as a distinct life stage to be closely monitored, with exemplary behavior rewarded and undesirable traits nipped in the bud. Middle-class mothers were viewed as especially crucial in this process of shaping future citizens, but ministers, educators, book authors, and magazine editors all offered prescriptions for the moral guidance of middle-class youth.[4]

Other observers, however, focused on the children of the urban poor and those on the frontier (typically stereotyped as violence-prone and lawless), warning of the grave threat they posed. In an alarming 1849 report, New York police chief George Matsell described the city's ten thousand "idle and vicious children" as a "corrupt and festering fountain" polluting the wellsprings of urban life. For Protestant reformers and educators, the younger generation represented the best hope for molding the urban masses and turbulent frontier dwellers into a sober, law-abiding citizenry. Charles Loring Brace's Children's Aid Society (1853), intent on transporting New York's street urchins to midwestern farms, expressed a social-control impulse already well established in discussions about children and youth.[5]

Voluntary organizations such as the American Sunday-School Union (1824), the American Tract Society (1825), and the Young Men's Christian Association (1855) struggled to reach the nation's children and youth, especially in the cities, before it was too late. "A moral desolation broods over the scene of our exertions," lamented a Philadelphia Sunday school leader in 1826. The only hope, added another in 1830, was to influence children "before vice has confirmed its habits, while the heart is tender, and sensitive to any impression."[6]

These cross-currents of hope and anxiety emerge in the essays and documents that follow. Remote as this world seems today, readers may also experience a shock of recognition. The details differ, but many of the underlying concerns remain recognizable. Contemporary middle-class parents worry about drugs, Internet pornography, violent video games, and alcohol-fueled driving accidents. Black and Hispanic parents in the inner cities fear for their children's very survival. As Richard Rodriguez's *Hunger of Memory* reports, immigrant parents (now typically from Latin America or Asia) still grieve as their offspring drift away into the larger currents of American life. Peter Stearns, Paula Fass, and others have explored the contemporary concerns about children, from abusive baby-sitters and tainted Halloween candy to pedophilia, kidnapping, and school violence. Evangelical parents fear their children's exposure to "secular humanism" in the public schools.[7]

This volume explores a distinct era in this long history of intergenerational worry and apprehension—an era when the effort to fulfill the promise of the Revolution and to create a public school system and other institutions of social oversight while grappling with issues of expansion, sectional conflict over slavery, and the early stages of urbanization and industrialization added layers of complexity and urgency to concerns about the young. The essays range widely, from the Revolutionary War's impact on children to the ideas of educators, public health workers, and child welfare advocates. Other essays examine childhood and child nurture among Creek Indians on the frontier, in new religious movements, and in French and American families in St. Louis. Still others explore how the printed word, including schoolbooks, was mobilized to shape children's worldview and historical understanding. We also get fascinating glimpses into the childhood experience itself, as recalled in adulthood, recorded in youthful diaries, and articulated in the orations of graduates of a Philadelphia academy for young ladies.

Overall, these rich and diverse materials not only deepen our understanding of childhood and youth in the early republic but also offer new vantage points from which to reassess the larger contours of American history in these years. And, in the end, they remind us of continuities, as well as discontinuities, in the American historical experience.

NOTES

1. *Encyclopedia of American History,* 7th ed., ed. Jeffrey B. Morris and Richard B. Morris (New York: HarperCollins, 1996), 638 (immigration chart); Paul Boyer, *Urban Masses and Moral Order in America, 1820–1920* (Cambridge, MA: Harvard University Press, 1978), 3–4; Herbert G. Gutman, *The Black Family in Slavery and Freedom, 1750–1925* (New York: Pantheon Books, 1976); Angie Debow, *And Still the Waters Run: The Betrayal of the Five Civilized Tribes* (Princeton: Princeton University Press, 1940).

2. Quoted in Paul Boyer, *The American Nation: Annotated Teachers Edition* (Austin, TX: Holt, Rinehart and Winston, 2003), 257.

3. Bureau of the Census, U.S. Department of Commerce, *World Almanac and Book of Facts 2006* (New York: World Almanac Books, 2006), 485.

4. Carole Haber, "Life Cycle: Childhood and Adolescence," in *Encyclopedia of the United States in the Nineteenth Century,* 3 vols., ed. Paul Finkelman (New York: Charles Scribner's Sons, 2001), 2:193–95 (fertility statistics, 193); Margo Horn, "Childhood and Children: The Nineteenth Century," in *Encyclopedia of American Social History,* 3 vols., ed. Mary Kupiec Cayton, Elliot J. Gorn, and Peter W. Williams (New York: Charles Scribner's Sons, 1993), 3:2026–28; Bernard Wishy,

The Child and the Republic: The Dawn of American Child Nurture (Philadelphia: University of Pennsylvania Press, 1968); Linda K. Kerber, *Women of the Republic: Ideology and Intellect in Revolutionary America* (Chapel Hill: University of North Carolina Press, 1980); Mary P. Ryan, *Cradle of the Middle Class: The Family in Oneida County, New York, 1790–1981* (New York: Cambridge University Press, 1981).

5. Boyer, *Urban Masses*, 96–104 (Matsell quote, 96).

6. Ibid., 25, 34, 113; quoted passages, 35, 38.

7. Richard Rodriguez, *Hunger of Memory: The Education of Richard Rodriguez* (Boston: D. R. Godine, 1981); Peter Stearns, *Anxious Parents: A History of Modern Childrearing in America* (New York: New York University Press, 2003); Paula Fass, *Kidnapped: Child Abduction in America* (New York: Oxford University Press, 1997); David A. Noebel, J. F. Baldwin, and Kevin J. Bywater, *Clergy in the Classroom: The Religion of Secular Humanism* (Manitou Springs, CO: Summit Ministries, 1995).

Introduction

James Marten

The first children's magazine published in the United States was called, appropriately enough, the *Children's Magazine*. Appearing early in 1789—two months before the first session of the first U.S. Congress met in New York City—it lasted only a few issues. *Calculated for the Use of Families and Schools*, as its subtitle declared, the magazine was intended to supplement the books already in use by American teachers and parents. Although the magazine failed to attract a critical mass of subscribers, it nevertheless marked the beginning of a new sensibility about the place of children in American society.

Modern readers would not recognize the language and sentiments of the *Children's Magazine* as particularly child-friendly. But its promise to offer articles in a "style and manner . . . expressly calculated for children," in a cheap but pleasing format and on subjects "children can mostly comprehend," signified a recognition of the unique interests and special needs of children that few Americans a generation earlier would have thought important. The editors intended to address the apparently long-standing complaint that most educational materials consisted of long, boring books in which the "subjects become familiar and cease to command the attention" of students. They also promised to engage children at their own level, both in the subjects covered and in the language used. The writing would be "reduced" to the readers' "capacities," and the "variety of subjects" would "gratify and keep alive the passion of *curiosity*, which prompts the young mind to exertions." Youngsters' "desire for *novelty* would be satisfied with the arrival of a *new book* every month."[1]

Nearly fifty years later, the first issue of the legendary *Youth's Companion* appeared. Dedicated to the eternal salvation of its many readers, the

Youth's Companion would survive for over a century. But the "prospectus" published in the first issue highlighted the importance its editors placed on the development of new Americans in the new nation. "*This is a day of peculiar care for Youth*," they declared. "Christians feel that their children must be trained up for Christ. Patriots and philanthropists are making rapid improvements in every branch of education. Literature, science, liberty and religion are extending in the earth. The human mind is becoming emancipated from the bondage of ignorance and superstition." In the midst of all this progress, it was equally clear that "our children are born to higher destinies than their fathers; they will be actors in a far advanced period of the church and the world." As a result, it behooved parents, educators, public men, and even editors of children's magazines to ensure that children's "minds be formed, their hearts prepared, and their characters molded for the scenes and the duties of a brighter day."[2]

Despite its excessively didactic tone—at least to twenty-first century tastes—*The Children's Magazine* reflects in its own small way the commitments to democratizing education and civic engagement inspired by the American Revolution. Although tracking the proliferation of magazines for children measures a very narrow set of developments, the impressive production from the children's publishing industry during the years between the American Revolution and the 1840s suggest something of the evolving conceptions of childhood and youth during that time. The appearance, intent, and content of the first American journals intended for children and youth all highlight the seriousness with which parents, educators, and writers in the new nation took the processing of "Americanizing" children. Between the publication of the *Children's Magazine* in 1789 and the last issue in 1844 of *Parley's Magazine*, a precursor of the post–Civil War journals that were published during the "golden age" of "juvenile" periodicals, more than one hundred different magazines intended for children and youth appeared. Although many were narrowly conceived Sunday School magazines, some reflected an expanding concept of childhood. *The Youth's Cabinet; Devoted to Liberty, Peace, Temperance, and Religious, Moral, Intellectual, and Physical Education* offered an ambitious menu of purposes in the late 1830s, while the *Juvenile Gazette* was, according to its subtitle, an *Amusing Repository for Youth*—and was edited during its several months of publication in the late 1820s by a fifteen-year-old New Englander. The *Slave's Friend*, published from 1836 to 1839, combined moral instruction with abolitionism, while the *Cold Water Army* guided youngsters toward the temperance movement in the early

1840s. Some magazines lasted for a generation, some for only a few volumes, but clearly much had changed during the half-century since the brief life of the *Children's Magazine*.[3]

The table of contents for the last volume of *Parley's Magazine* demonstrates how the limited, provincial magazine world of the late eighteenth century had opened up by 1844. Fourteen illustrative medallions leaped from the frontispiece, providing portholes to the wide world: they featured an astronomer, a church, a farmer, an ostrich, a lion, an elephant, a sailing ship, a globe, and other pictures displaying the exotic and the mundane. The articles listed in the three-page table of contents for volume 12 ranged from "Advertising in Norway," "Alligators and Crocodiles," and "American Climate" through "Green Spectacles," "Hypochondriac," and "Lady Jane Gray," and all the way to "Origin of Lynching," "Rose—How to Increase Fragrance," "Something about Cats and Dogs," and, appropriately, "Yankee Doodle, Origin of."[4]

Although it remained highly moralistic and American-centric, *Parley's Magazine,* compared to the earliest magazines for children, offered its readers a wide array of cultural references, sketches of faraway places, natural history, amusing anecdotes, and descriptions of exotic foods, animals, and customs. The democratization of knowledge articulated by the editors of the *Children's Magazine* had been expanded, as had the mission to seize and keep young readers' loyalty with articles speaking to their interests and their attention spans. The world of children—at least the world presented to the middle-class children who read *Parley's Magazine*—had become more open, more complex, more exciting. The magazine was also bigger, with perhaps three hundred articles, travelogues, puzzles, anecdotes, and excerpts, along with about a hundred illustrations, in each four hundred-page volume (figure 1).

The expanding scope of children's magazines reflected in a small way the massive changes sweeping the United States and the opportunities they presented. As the political system became more democratic—at least for white men—the importance of creating an educated, committed citizenry rose. As a free-market system replaced the imperfect mercantilism of the British era, the opportunity for success and the danger of failure were enhanced, and a nascent class system developed. As established churches were disestablished and the Second Great Awakening brought Protestants into closer communion with their God, alternative routes to salvation appeared. As Americans migrated into Tennessee and Kentucky, into the Ohio country and the Mississippi Valley, and into Texas and even

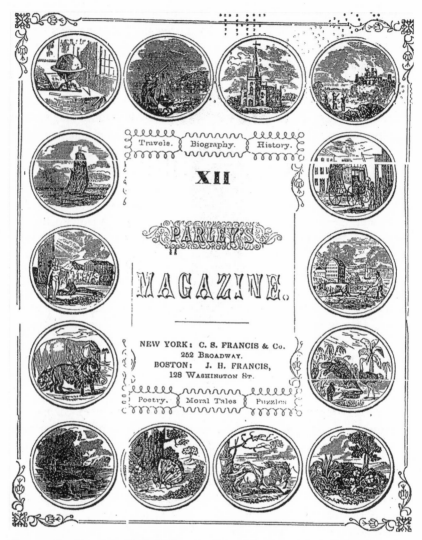

Figure 1 The title page of *Parley's Magazine* showed the natural, historical, and geographic worlds to which young readers would be exposed. *Parley's Magazine* 12 (January 1, 1844).

Oregon, new lifestyles, shaped by economic necessity and climate, arose. Not surprisingly, the ensuing contact with other cultures, including Hispanic, French, and Native American, accelerated the process of intercultural exchange.

Joyce Appleby has argued that "the egalitarian spirit promoted by the Revolution might have remained a patriotic sentiment had not the rush to new lands, the religious revivals, and the prosperity that brought the accoutrements of refinement to an ever-widening circle of families strengthened the hand of those who longed for comprehensive social change." Although historians are still divided about whether the Revolution was truly revolutionary, the material results of war and expansion in the decades afterwards clearly instituted changes that had deep ramifications for family structure and children's lives. Appleby argues that equality—or at least the rhetoric of equality—lessened apparent social differences, while at the same time economic and geographic expansion and mobility (both up and down) provided wider opportunities for success and failure. And ethnic homogeneity among the nonenslaved portion of the population ensured that, at least until Roman Catholic and non-English-speaking immigrants began arriving in large numbers late in the period, Americans could take comfort in a basic racial equality.[5]

As a result, new choices and opportunities emerged in virtually every facet of life during the years between the American Revolution and the 1840s. And as Americans tried to determine what it meant to be an American, they also wondered what it meant to be an American *child*. Colonial Americans had certainly worried about their children. Puritans, for instance, feared that their experiment in communal religion would be threatened if children were not brought up in a way pleasing in the eyes of God. That rather defensive, even fearful approach to childhood and youth gave way after the Revolution to a more optimistic campaign to integrate young Americans into the republican experiment.

Moreover, the development of what we would recognize as "modern" ideas about children and youth began during the period immediately following the American Revolution. As the forms and assumptions of the new nation sprang to life and evolved, certain ideas about childhood emerged. Although these ideals were not necessarily realized during this period—nor would ever be realized for all American children—they became powerful symbols of and even models for childhood and youth. Hints of what it meant to be "middle class" began to emerge during this time, including assumptions about caring for and educating children.

These concepts included the nurturing potential of the nuclear family, the connection between child-rearing practices and citizenship, the optimistic notion that education was a right rather than a privilege, and the belief (or at least the kernel that by 1900 would grow into belief) that society had a responsibility to children whose families were unable to care for them.

There is much that the larger history of the early republic can tell us about the lives of children, and much that the experiences of children can reveal about the nature of the early republic. As Jacqueline S. Reinier has written, the rise of the United States and the struggle by the founders and their successors to make a workable definition of republicanism led directly to "the staggering notion that one could mold the human personality in a desired direction," which, in turn, "generated optimism that a truly new affectionate and voluntary society could emerge." Few human institutions were untouched by this confidence and optimism. "In a general revolt against tyranny and patriarchy," Reinier writes, "philosophers, physicians, journalists, and printers championed and publicized the affectionate nuclear family"; this conception of the family, along with the new notion of companionate marriage, stressed "voluntary ties" and made the family "a kind of school for citizenship." Enlightenment notions of the "malleable child" led to the belief that youngsters could be "shaped by affectionate parents and educators" into "material for the virtuous, autonomous adult." All would help create and sustain the republican experiment. "Republican virtue"—the moral center of the republican ideology that fueled the revolution and inspired the government of the new nation—depended on a disinterested, engaged, and incorruptible citizenry, and Americans consciously defined assumptions and built institutions devoted to shaping their children into young republicans.[6]

Reinier stresses several influences that shaped attitudes about and the lives of children in the new republic: Enlightenment child-rearing advice and revolutionary ideology; the "democratization" of medicine and increasing awareness that children required separate treatment; the evolution of Protestant theology and the creation of Sunday schools and other institutions that highlighted "character" as an American trait; the development of public schools as a laboratory for republican behavior; and the integration of children into the free-market workplace as yet another way to instill the values of hard work, modesty, independence, and other necessary traits that combined to form "character."

Like virtually all works on the history of children and youth, this anthology deals with both aspirations and reality, with how adults believed children should live and how children actually lived, with the sometimes conflicting points of view of parents and their offspring. Children have always been seen as the embodiment of the future, and to that extent their well-being and education and nurturing have always been important. But the successful eruption of democracy combined with the rise of romantic visions of childhood suggested somewhat sternly by John Locke and popularized by Rousseau a century and a few decades prior to the nineteenth century, respectively, called for new approaches to rearing and appreciating children. This "newfound significance of children for the future republic," as Steven Mintz calls it, took on even greater importance as the proportion of the population under the age of sixteen rose to half and stayed there during the first part of the nineteenth century. The growing percentage of the population composed of children and the increasing seriousness with which adults thought about them gave rise to a generation of child advice books. "When the republic was young," writes Anne Scott MacLeod, "and national feeling ran high, concern for the future of the new nation and for the children who would soon be its active citizens became thoroughly intertwined." Advice books guided parents and educators in their efforts to build character in future republicans. Children were everywhere, and Americans were inspired to integrate them into the ideology of the republic and the future of its political and economic systems. *Children and Youth in a New Nation* contributes to our understanding of this conflation of national purpose and child development.[7]

Although this book roughly covers the seventy years after 1776, it is less about a specific time period than it is about a state of mind, as economic, geographic, and cultural developments forced Americans to continually define and redefine what it meant to be an American and what it meant to be a child in a new republic. There is no unifying argument as such, although all of the authors seek to answer the question: How can integrating the histories of the first decades of the United States and of American childhood enrich our understanding of both?

Although this is decidedly not a general history of childhood during this period, the authors introduce a number of the many versions of childhood that existed in parallel in the new nation, from the old colonies of Massachusetts and Virginia to the developing states along the Mississippi River. Where possible, they have explored the effects of race, class, and gender on the lives of American children. Taken together, the essays offer a sampling of ideas and experiences related to childhood during a formative period in American history.

The thirteen selections are divided into five parts. Part I begins with the Revolution itself and explores how American children and youth participated in and learned from the revolt and its aftermaths. Part II examines "ideal" childhoods as they were theorized by emerging religious denominations and by competing ethnic groups on the frontier. Part III shows how educators struggled to determine how the society that came out of the Revolution could best be served by its educational systems. Part IV foreshadows future "child-saving" efforts by reformers committed to constructing adequate systems of public health and child welfare institutions. Finally, Part V's three chapters contain lengthy excerpts from primary documents, both diaries and memoirs, that expand on the themes and arguments introduced in the essays and offer the points of view of children or of adults reflecting on their childhoods. Throughout, the authors introduce aspects of the "interior" lives of children and the ways in which society acted on them, creating the potential for conflict between public and private practices and values. They also consider the ways in which the democratization of politics, the establishment of religious freedom, the rise of the rule of law, and the devotion to property rights—all central components of the ideology that fueled the Revolution and shaped the new constitution—carried over into the lives of children. The emphasis on *rights* emerged alongside an emphasis on *duty*, as responsible child rearing evolved during this period from a personal choice to a civic duty; being a good parent and a good child became a patriotic duty. Finally, several of the essays show that children and youth in the new nation, as in all times and in all places, insisted on shaping their environment and exerting agency in their own upbringing.

Although the present volume focuses on the ways in which the development of the Republic and the emergence of new conceptualizations of childhood and youth were inextricably connected, it also shows that virtually all the issues raised by the authors transcend this period. Indeed, the ways in which Americans remembered and defined the Revolution continued to evolve; the ethnic, religious, and economic distinctions between groups of children would play—and continue to play—a huge role in American childhoods; the appropriate values to be reflected in educational institutions and school curricula are still hot-button topics; and the care of youngsters who fall outside the mainstream ethnic and economic groups has never been absent from the conversation about public policy and children. The issues raised during the age of the early republic continue to animate discussions about children and youth in our society and remain central questions in the quest by historians to better understand the historical processes that have shaped our nation.

Lucy Larcom's gentle and detailed *A New England Girlhood: Outlined from Memory* is a priceless if romanticized source for understanding the lives of children in the early nineteenth century. Published in 1889, it described a rather hardscrabble upbringing. Larcom's father died when she was quite young, forcing her mother to take in boarders and Larcom and her sisters to take their places among the famous "Lowell girls" in the mills of Lowell, Massachusetts. Larcom would later teach school in Illinois and gain fame as a public speaker, essayist, poet, and editor of *Our Young Folks*, perhaps the best magazine for children produced in the nineteenth century.

Larcom consciously explored the shifting contours of New England life as traditional customs slowly gave way to "modern" ways. Her loving descriptions of her little village and its people, like the essays in this anthology, indicate that the conversion from colonies to new nation was not instantaneous and that some traditions changed slowly or were simply covered with layers of new assumptions and laws.

"We were rather a young nation at this time," she wrote of her girlhood. She was born in 1824, two years prior to the fiftieth anniversary of the Declaration of Independence, and, in effect, grew up with her country. Because the country was so young, she could say that her generation's "republicanism was fresh and wide-awake." George Washington's legend had not dulled, and Larcom's hometown of Beverly still buzzed about the visit several years earlier of the Marquis de Lafayette, the French hero of the Revolution. Children still turned out for the excitement of watching the militia drill and parade on "training day," when Americans celebrated their amateur soldiers and renewed their vows to defend it with their blood. She recalled the Fourth of July (with Thanksgiving, the only major holidays "that we made much account of") as "a far more well behaved festival" than when she wrote late in the nineteenth century. Church bells rang all day, and cannons were fired first thing in the morning and at noon. Fireworks, apparently too expensive, played little part in the celebration. Rather, "somebody delivered an oration; there was a good deal said about 'this universal Yankee nation'; some rockets went up from Salem in the evening; we watched them from the hill, and then went to bed, feeling that we had been good patriots."[8]

Although she never married or bore children and although, unlike most women of the time, she made her living very publicly, in most ways

Larcom grew into the kind of patriotic, responsible, pious, and modest person that good republican children were supposed to become. Her thoughtful memories and observations will help introduce the several sections of this anthology.

Those five sections are followed by a set of study questions that will help readers explore the themes presented by the essays, documents, and illustrations. Finally, a brief historiographical essay and a selected bibliography of crucial secondary sources can be found in the "Suggested Readings."

NOTES

1. "Preface," *Children's Magazine* 1 (January 1789): [1–2].

2. "Prospectus," *Youth's Companion* 1 (April 16, 1827): 1.

3. Pat Pflieger, "American Children's Periodicals, 1789–1872," October 2006, www.merrycoz.org/bib/1820.htm. Although she focuses largely on books, an excellent survey is Gail S. Murray's *American Children's Literature and the Construction of Childhood* (New York: Twayne, 1998); see 23–50 for children's literature in the new republic.

4. *Parley's Magazine* 12 (January 1, 1844): v–vii.

5. Joyce Appleby, "The Social Consequences of American Revolutionary Ideals in the Early Republic," in *The Middling Sorts: Explorations in the History of the American Middle Class,* ed. Burton J. Bledstein and Robert D. Johnston (New York: Routledge, 2001), 31–49, quote on 34.

6. Jacqueline S. Reinier, *From Virtue to Character: American Childhood, 1775–1850* (New York: Twayne, 1996), xi–xii.

7. Steven Mintz, *Huck's Raft: A History of American Childhood* (Cambridge, MA: Harvard University Press, 2004), 71; Anne Scott MacLeod, "Child and Conscience," in *American Childhood: Essays on Children's Literature of the Nineteenth and Twentieth Centuries* (Athens: University of Georgia Press, 1994), 99.

8. Lucy Larcom, *A New England Girlhood: Outlined from Memory* (Boston: Houghton Mifflin, 1889), 97–99. The only modern biography of Larcom is Shirley Marchalonis, *The Worlds of Lucy Larcom, 1824–1893* (Athens: University of Georgia Press, 1989).

III

No Greater Distinction
American Children and the Revolution

The Revolution never seemed far away to Lucy Larcom. On chilly days, she and her sisters would cozy up on the "settle" built into their chimney corner "and toast our toes on the andirons" made in the shape of "two Continental soldiers in full uniform, marching one after the other." More substantively, they personally knew a living, breathing, veteran of the Revolution: the only one of their grandparents who still lived. He was a lovable old man of French descent, "piquant, merry, exceedingly polite, and very fond of us children." They loved him because he always rewarded their good behavior with raisins and peppermints. They loved that he was sexton of their church and was responsible for winding up the town clock and for ringing the church bell to mark the time on weekdays and Sundays. But his most impressive accomplishment was to have fought in the Revolution, "the greatest distinction we could imagine." His good nature, combined with his demonstrated patriotism and bravery, caused his granddaughter to write, "I did not believe that there was another grandfather so delightful as ours in all the world."[1]

Larcom's grandfather may well have been one of the boy soldiers described in the essay by Caroline Cox that leads off the first section of this anthology. Together, these three pieces reveal a broad spectrum of ways in which American children experienced the American Revolution and then remembered those experiences as adults. Cox and Vincent DiGirolamo show how blurred was the line between child and adult in revolutionary America as young boys fought alongside their older brothers, uncles, and fathers and as other teenagers—and a few preteens—carried the news of their battlefield exploits to isolated towns and hamlets. Martha "Patsy" Jefferson—the oldest child of Thomas and Martha Jefferson—experienced a very different revolution. As Cynthia A. Kierner shows, the wartime life of this daughter of a governor and founding revolutionary was both more sheltered and, at times, more exposed than most children's. All three essays indicate the extent to which children of this time—like children in all times and places—have been integrated into their countries' armed conflicts, sharing the sacrifices and the glory and the bittersweet memories inspired by wars in every participant. Cox and Kierner also show the extent to which the memories of childhood and youth for the first generation of young republicans were shaped by their roles in the dramatic events of the 1770s and 1780s.[2]

Those young soldiers and postboys were old men by the time Lucy Larcom wrote of her village's devotion to the revolutionary past, and Patsy Jefferson would live for only a few years (until 1836) after Larcom's birth. The transition from colonial backwater to revolutionary republic was, however, still in progress as Larcom's generation came of age fifty years later.

NOTES

1. Lucy Larcom, *A New England Girlhood: Outlined from Memory* (Boston: Houghton Mifflin, 1889), 22, 26.

2. For a sampling of the ways in which children have been victims and actors of wars all over the world during the last two centuries, see James Marten, ed., *Children and War: A Historical Anthology* (New York: New York University Press, 2002).

Boy Soldiers of the American Revolution
The Effects of War on Society

Caroline Cox

In 1776, Josiah Brandon of North Carolina volunteered for militia duty just before he turned sixteen, determined to join his neighbors fighting against the Cherokee Indians. Over the next three years he served multiple short tours in the militia, although the target of those expeditions eventually changed to local Tories. His decision indicated an independent spirit, as his father was a staunch loyalist and often away from home serving as an officer alongside the British. However, in 1780, Josiah's father reasserted his authority and took his son, still "a minor, under his absolute control," into the loyalist forces with him. Both father and son fought with the British at the Battle of Kings Mountain, South Carolina, in October 1780. His father was killed in the fierce fighting and Josiah was taken prisoner, although he was released shortly thereafter when his mother came to take home her sick and exhausted son. Free from his father's control, Josiah went on to serve three more terms with the North Carolina patriot militia. Decades later, Josiah was granted a pension in recognition of his service over the objection of neighbors who remembered his brief switch of sides. Josiah and his family excused his loyalist service on the grounds that, as a dependent youth, he had been obliged to obey his father.[1]

Josiah Brandon's experience indicates that legal and social dependence constrained the actions even of older boys of an independent mind. However, Josiah hinted in his recollections of the war that his father's authority had been less than absolute. On one occasion, he referred to his switch to the loyalist side as "an indiscreet act of my youth," implying that he had had some choice in the matter and had been perhaps responding to his father's persuasion rather than coercion.[2]

The nuances of Josiah's story remind us that it is hard to generalize about what it meant to be a dependent youth and that the journey to independence was uneven and complicated. This was as true for the new nation as it was for individuals. The United States was born in a political struggle over authority and when and under what circumstances those under it could negotiate. Historian Holly Brewer has argued that as the society moved to a political system based on consent, children, particularly older children, had to be more clearly excluded and came to be categorized by age rather than understanding. Josiah Brandon's story and others from Revolutionary War veterans who were boys when they served put faces on this transition and bring into focus the internal dynamics of revolutionary families. In this larger political context, the experiences of boy soldiers allow us to take a fresh look at such subjects as the possible agency of children, what it meant to be a dependent youth, the texture of family life, the nature of patriarchal authority, and indeed citizenship itself.[3]

Scholars previously addressing these questions have been frustrated. Extant primary sources from children are in short supply, and historians seeking to understand the essence of childhood and youth have been forced to examine institutional histories, prescriptive literature, or observations from parents and other adults. Few scholars working on these topics have considered the experiences of young soldiers. This is partly because military history, even so-called "new" military history that examines military service from a social or cultural perspective, has remained a very separate academic field and partly because letters and diaries from boy soldiers are almost nonexistent. Few boys had the literacy skills, access to pen and paper, or the opportunity—even if they had the inclination—to send anyone a letter or to keep a diary.[4]

However, the few published memoirs and the Revolutionary War pension applications from men who served when they were boys help us understand childhood in this era. These sources, both written decades after military service, must of course be used with caution. Memories become confused and are colored by adult experiences. Shifting cultural and political attitudes toward events and ideas further alter people's recollections. Published memoirs can be especially problematic. Authors may want to present themselves in a particular way to a public audience. Even testimony for a pension application had an audience of a local jurist, the pension commissioner, and sometimes family and friends.

But read with care, pension applications and published memoirs can still be valuable sources. Both have military service as the focus of the testimony. Any discussions of the journey toward enlistment and other details of family life were often incidental and thus less subject to exaggeration. In applying for a pension, available on the basis of financial need after 1818 and on the basis of service alone after 1832, every veteran had to offer proof that he had served. This was complicated, as few had any written record of their enlistment. Local officials taking depositions tried to elicit information about the service years, such as the date and location where a man had signed on, the names of officers under whom he had served, the battles in which he had fought, or any other information that might locate him in place and time so that the information might be corroborated by the few extant muster rolls. All of this highlighted the importance of military events and diminished the importance of the soldier's background story. Thus details about the family context such as those mentioned by Brandon are all the more compelling.[5]

Veterans had also to provide depositions from family or friends who could testify to their service, and those people were often able to offer other glimpses of family life that show the tension between growing lads and their fathers. Young Samuel Aspenwall of Connecticut, for example, who at fifteen had joined the Continental army, the regular army in the Revolutionary War, had his service confirmed by his sister, Mary Truman. She remembered that Samuel had had "a strong desire to enlist" but that their father, Asa Aspenwall, had thought it was too risky. However, he gave way and arranged for Samuel to be inoculated against smallpox "for the purpose of joining the army with more safety." Their father was also not going to allow his son to enlist with just any group of people. Mary remembered how he had accompanied her brother to the muster in Windham, Connecticut, to make sure Samuel enlisted "in a company agreeable to my father's mind." She also could pinpoint the date of his return a year later, as it was the time of "the birth of a sister." Thus a careful reading of the voluminous pension records illuminates many details of the family negotiations that took place around the transition from childhood to adulthood that would remain otherwise hidden.[6]

These carefully gleaned stories of boy soldiers can take us inside their families. Drawing their experiences out from the confines of military history, we can learn much more detail about their relationships with their parents or guardians, tensions surrounding their financial dependence, and their attempts to be masters of their own fates. Their complex and uneven journeys to maturity and independence help us understand the larger journey of the nation itself.

In the modern era, many people recoil in horror at the thought of boys serving as soldiers. After all, war is brutal, bloody, and relentless. Enlistment is seen as an adult responsibility, one that requires maturity to commit to the potential sacrifice and to deal with the horrors and hardships. It requires a leap of historical imagination to take us back to the eighteenth century in our own society, when soldiering was only loosely connected to citizenship and for many was simply another kind of job. Although it was one that came with somewhat greater risk than civilian life, the pay was steady. Fighting was indeed a bloody affair, but battles were relatively brief and happened only occasionally. The greater misery of wartime for soldiers was often the exhausting weeks spent on the march, the continuous foraging for fresh food to augment the poor-quality food that was supplied, the discomfort of sleeping on the ground, and the diseases that preyed on tired, undernourished soldiers in camps. Mortality statistics confirm the harsh conditions of military life. In the Revolutionary War, a total of about twenty-five thousand patriot soldiers died, but about eighteen thousand died of disease rather than in battle. This ratio of disease to combat deaths was comparable to the wartime experiences of many European armies of the era and, indeed, better than many of them.[7]

Americans have particular trouble imagining boy soldiers in the story of the American Revolution, a war in which supposedly outraged citizens, voters and taxpayers, rose up against British attempts to impose taxation without representation. The presence of boys in military service in that period has to be understood in the context of military life of the time and shifting ideas about childhood and the age at which one could assume mature responsibilities.

Just as in our own era there are inconsistent ideas about the age of mature decision making with regard to voting, sexual activity, smoking, drinking, and military service, among other things, so there were inconsistencies in the eighteenth century. However, just before and during the eighteenth century, ideas about child development and maturity underwent a significant change. The age at which adults felt that children could participate meaningfully in a wide range of activities had risen dramatically. For example, at the beginning of the century, jury service in most colonies was open to those who were at least fourteen years old (and who met some sort of property requirement), but by the end of the century it was largely restricted to property-owning voters over twenty-one. In the seventeenth century, Puritans in New England had accepted that children under five had the necessary understanding to enter into covenants with the church. However, over time religious leaders put greater emphasis on comprehension and questioned whether children so young could undergo conversion in any meaningful way. Religious leaders could not agree on what the right age was, but in practice few children under fourteen came to be allowed to covenant with the church. The age for militia obligations rose similarly. In the Elizabethan era, English militia laws included any "man childe" over seven. However, by the time of the American Revolution, militia duty had been restricted in Britain and its colonies to free men of at least sixteen. Society was grappling with new thinking about child development and the resulting realization that the journey to adult maturity was a long and individual one. Consequently, legislators and a variety of civic and religious leaders tried to come up with general rules to accommodate these new ideas.[8]

There was a close connection between militia service and citizenship for many political theorists of the era. Drawing on the perceived virtues of the ancient world, writers from Machiavelli onwards saw citizen soldiers as the best defense against enemies abroad and tyranny at home. As the age for militia service trended higher over this period, though, the connection between military service and the other rights of citizenship was either vague or unstated. The debates about suitable age for jury service, for example, centered on property ownership and analytical ability. As to voting, only Pennsylvania at the beginning of the Revolutionary War briefly offered voting rights without an age restriction to men who served in the militia, but that provision was soon removed. So even though the political rhetoric connected the citizen and the soldier, it did not extend yet to a unified conception of citizenship.[9]

In Britain, its colonies, and the new United States, the militia was conceptualized legally and socially very differently from any regular army. The militia ideally consisted of citizen soldiers, and the regulations that governed them were separate from those laws that governed other troops that were raised. The militia was to be called out only for local emergencies of short duration, often ranging from two weeks to three months. Troops serving for longer periods and traveling farther from home in earlier colonial wars were organized as so-called provincial armies and, during the American Revolution, the Continental army. These soldiers were recruited from wherever they might be found, and there was no mention of citizenship or age in any rules or laws that governed them. Many of the enlisted men who served in these forces were of a lower social status than the militiamen.

Boys in military service, then, were part of this shifting and variegated landscape. People at the time were rarely clear about the age of a person when they called him "boy" or "youth." A boy could be as old as in his late teens but of slight build, and a youth might be someone who was even older but immature or simply unmarried even though in his twenties. In this study, *boy* particularly means those soldiers who began their military service when they were under sixteen. That age had become a common benchmark in revolutionary society. It was the demarcation between children and productive adults for many colonial census takers, and it was the minimum age that states repeated in their wartime militia and draft legislation. Continental recruiting parties, even though working with no legal minimum, were often directed by high-ranking officers to enlist only soldiers sixteen and over. Legislators and Continental generals may have considered sixteen to be an appropriate age for military service in terms of assuming the burdens of citizenship and mature decision making, but militia and Continental recruiting officers were more concerned with who had the physical stamina to work. A "stout lad" of fourteen was a more desirable recruit than a slight boy of sixteen, and a blind eye was usually turned to the actual age of a suitable lad. Young boys who were eager to serve out of financial need, a desire for adventure, a wish to get away from a bad home situation, or enthusiasm for the cause could usually find someone willing to take them. Thus military participation by boys under sixteen captures the contradictions in revolutionary society between political rhetoric, legislation, and social policy on the one hand and practical familial and military realities on the other.[10]

Earlier, in the French and Indian War (1755–63), boys had rarely made an appearance on the provincial muster rolls. A few accompanied their officer fathers as servants—often called "waiters"—but few lived the hard life of a soldier. Mortality rates were high from disease and short supplies. The fact that the war began with the shocking and bloody defeat of British General Edward Braddock and his forces in the backcountry probably gave pause to even the most adventurous youth and caused many a parent to find some other work for their teenage sons. In Virginia, not one lad under sixteen appears on Colonel George Washington's muster rolls for the Virginia provincials, and there were only a few youths under eighteen. Similarly, there were only a few boys under eighteen among New York provincials.[11]

In the Revolutionary War, the Continental army was eager for recruits of any age who might do a soldier's work. In 1775, recruits included men of all ages and social ranks who were enthusiastic about the revolutionary cause and believed that the war would be short. But after a year or so, disease, harsh conditions, tough discipline, and no end in sight to the fighting caused many men who had other ways of making a living to go home. Many of them preferred to continue to serve the cause through militia service rather than longer-term enlistments in the army. This left the army struggling for recruits, and by 1777 many states had introduced draft legislation to fill the ranks. In these circumstances, any boy who could physically handle the hardships of the service was an attractive recruit.[12]

As the war progressed, more boys appeared on the muster rolls as military service became a more familiar work option. Young American men had a range of short-term service options, and that meant that boys could try out army life and revisit their decision at regular intervals. Unfortunately, incomplete records make it impossible to come up with exact numbers. Pension records and memoirs indicate that boys either enlisted independently or did so as substitutes for drafted fathers, neighbors, older brothers, or strangers in both the militia and the Continental army. There was no shame in either hiring a substitute or serving as one.

The substitution system indicates the loose nature of the connection between service and citizenship. While the two were firmly connected in the political theory of the era, service was an obligation that could be met by simply supplying someone to perform it. The cost of hiring a substitute was privately negotiated and dependent on the exigencies of the moment. One sixteen-year-old who went as a substitute, Joseph Plumb Martin, could not recall as an old man what he had been paid but remembered that it had been "perhaps enough to keep the blood circulating during the short space of time I tarried at home after I had enlisted." Another young man, Absalom Hughes, substituted for a man whose family was so anxious to keep him home that they offered Hughes a hundred acres of land to serve in his place, an offer he could not refuse. More commonly, though, substitution was a mechanism by which families shifted the burden of service among themselves without any money changing hands. If a father's or older brother's labor could not be spared from the farm or business when he was drafted into the Continentals or the militia, then a younger son might go in his place. In these ways, the citizenship obligation of a parent, neighbor, or stranger was met.[13]

Thus in 1779 fourteen-year-old Simeon Hewitt of Stonington, Connecticut, eagerly volunteered to go in his father's place into the militia. Simeon's father was hesitant, but the boy's enthusiasm, combined with the fact that both father and son knew the men who would be his officers, led his father to agree that Simeon could go if the captain allowed it. Father and son went off to the muster at New London, and Simeon recalled that the captain "agreed to take me on trial, with an agreement on the part of my father to return if I did not answer the purpose." The boy answered the purpose and served the required two months. Before he was seventeen, Simeon had served a year in the army and another two months in the militia as a substitute for a Stonington neighbor, a service for which either he or his father would have received a fee.[14]

To "answer the purpose," Simeon must have been a well-built lad. Soldiering was hard physical labor, and boys were useful only in limited ways. The smooth-bore musket soldiers carried weighed about ten pounds, and soldiers in the field carried around many more pounds of gear. Physical strength was also required for the militia, who carried the same burdens, though over shorter distances. Even drummer boys needed stamina. Pre–Revolutionary War British army instruction manuals advised that "boys much under fourteen, unless they are remarkably stout, are rather an incumbrance to a regiment (especially on service) as they are in general unable to bear fatigue, or even carry their drums on a march."[15]

Continental army and militia officers never changed their minds about the need for older soldiers, but the escalating need for recruits meant they could not be picky. Senior American military officers bemoaned the number of boys appearing in the ranks, but recruiting officers anxious to meet their quotas continuously turned a blind eye to extreme youth. By 1781, General Edward Hand complained about the number of boys among his soldiers who were too small to be useful, and the following year Baron von Steuben, the senior American officer in charge of training the troops, organized some boys into a special unit to be taught reading and writing. But most company and regimental officers preferred to hang on to their boy soldiers, no matter how young and useless, in order to keep their rosters at maximum strength. While some functions could be found for them, such as playing music, waiting on officers, chopping firewood, and preparing ammunition, the army had a limited need for these tasks.[16]

Despite the complaints of senior officers, as the war dragged on there was a steady stream of boys into the service as families and boys themselves came to see that the family's service obligation could be as easily met by one person as another. There was considerable variation in the pace of enlistment by boys in various state regiments and militia units depending on geography and the stage of the war, but generally speaking more boys entered the service as the war progressed. Most of these were over thirteen, but even younger boys were present. Some as young as nine or ten enlisted in the army, though at that age they were usually enlisting with officer fathers, uncles, or family friends and served them as waiters. Cyrus Allen served at age eleven as waiter to his father, Captain Daniel Allen. Israel Trask enlisted as a waiter to his father, a lieutenant, and to other officers in his regiment at age ten. Bishop Tyler had arrived at the advanced age of thirteen when he enlisted as a waiter to a Connecticut friend and neighbor.[17]

If that had been their only connection to the army, none of these boys would have been considered real soldiers or would have qualified for a pension. After all, a number of officers brought servants or slaves from home to wait on them without them actually enlisting. Cyrus Allen, though, was able to prove that he had been a regular soldier. Another veteran who had served with him was able to confirm that even though Cyrus had been "but a youth of about twelve years," he not only had been a waiter but had occasionally stood "as a sentinel": that is, he had performed at least some of the duties of regular soldiers. The most important evidence that supported Cyrus's application was a receipt he had showing that his father had been "credited £24. 9s. 4 [twenty-four pounds, nine shillings, and four pence] for his sons wages." So Cyrus, at eleven or twelve, had done a soldier's duty, and his father had collected his pay. Israel Trask also qualified for a pension because he had been responsible for "care of the baggage" and had done guard duty. Israel was sure his father had received his rations and his wages, since Israel "never received either." Bishop Tyler was able to prove that he had been "engaged in actual military service" and had been involved in "many skirmishes with the enemy" to qualify for his pension.[18]

Not all families agreed on the appropriate age for joining the service. Even in families where support for the revolutionary cause was energetic there could be dissent. The mother of James Ayers strongly objected to her son going off at about age fourteen. The family lived in the Carolina backcountry, and James's father, Daniel, was "a good whig and much in the service." Daniel Ayers was anxious for his son to be active also and "enlisted him" for an eighteen-month term in the North Carolina troops, serving on the frontier. A family friend remembered the enlistment because "Mrs. Ayres, mother of the said James was in great distress blaming her husband for Enlisting and taking her son a lad or boy not over fourteen years of age . . . as he was quite small about a good size to send to mole"—that is, very small. Not only, then, was there no generally understood societal understanding of what age was appropriate for service, but there was not even one within families. James himself seems to have had no say in the matter. Cyrus Allen, who also went off with his patriot father, did appear to have had a choice about enlisting. His brother-in-law, David Carpenter, eleven years Cyrus's senior, testifying in support of Cyrus's pension application, noted that he had counseled Cyrus before his enlistment about "going into the service so young." Frustratingly, he did not say how he had counseled him.[19]

Many families seemed to share Mrs. Ayers's concern about physical readiness while they decided whether to let their sons go. Boys also saw that as a critical element in the decision. Cyrus Allen made a point of telling the pension commissioners that he had been "a stout boy" for eleven. Bishop Tyler said that he had been "stout & strong," and Samuel Branch, who enlisted at fourteen, said that he had told a recruiter he was sixteen and had gotten away with the lie because he was "big for his age." Twelve-year-old John Jenks knew his small stature was the reason he had initially not been accepted into the Continental army. He had run away from his guardian to enlist but was soon sent home, dismissed "in consequence of my Infancy & size (my very short Stature)."[20]

The experience of some boys confirms that the period between twelve and fourteen was key to a change in status. Adults respected, and the boys themselves felt entitled to claim, a more adult role. Meshack Burchfield was quite clear that he did not go off to war when some of his friends did when he was between thirteen and fourteen because he was then "only a boy" but that a year later he did go—presumably no longer a boy. Bishop Tyler had been desperate to enlist when he was twelve "if his father's consent could be obtained," but his father had refused. The boy nagged his father for permission to go (Bishop's words were that he "continually importuned" him). His father only relented a year later when he arranged for Bishop to go as waiter to his friend Captain Miles. Mr. Tyler was surely being protective, but that strategy backfired when Miles and some soldiers from the company were taken prisoner by the British while they were out on an "exploring excursion."[21]

Decades later, when these men were applying for veterans' benefits, pension authorities appear to have had the same rough age range in mind as appropriate for service when assessing an applicant's veracity. Jacob Gundy, who had been thirteen when he enlisted, had his application challenged by the pension commissioner. Gundy quickly realized the source of the problem. On some of his paperwork his date of birth was noted incorrectly, and the commissioner thought that he had been eleven when he enlisted. Gundy was quickly able to prove that he had in fact been thirteen, and thus the matter was resolved and the pension approved. Similarly Nathaniel Warner, who had served two and a half years in a Connecticut regiment of the Continental army, had written his date of birth down incorrectly on one of the many letters connected to his application. The pension commissioner thus suspected Warner's claim because he also appeared to have been only eleven years old when he enlisted in 1781. Warner was able to correct the misunderstanding and show that he had, in fact, been thirteen; that information satisfied all involved.[22]

Some enlistment stories shed light on the halting journey to adulthood and independence. Many of these veterans indicated that at the time of enlistment they had been dependent sons, emphasizing that before and after their service they had lived with their parents or guardians. A number of them noted that they had gone off to serve for repeated periods and had lived at home between service periods. Stephen Hammond served multiple terms in the Rhode Island militia from the time he was thirteen onwards and interspersed these with longer service in the marines. He "resided with his parents" when he first enlisted, returned home between his militia and marine service, and after his last service as a marine "returned to the residence of his parents."[23]

Steven Hammond did not say whether he kept his pay for himself. Many youth, especially those over sixteen, would have been able to do so. Thus the option of repeated short military service greatly expanded working opportunities that allowed young men to escape their fathers' authority and accelerate their transitions to semidependence and even independence. It offered poor or unskilled youth a chance for steadier pay than day labor and had the additional inducement of the bounty, a signing bonus at the time of enlistment, or a payment for being a substitute for another man. Even for youth from more prosperous circumstances whose families did not need their earnings, these inducements were attractive and could be a significant step toward their ultimate ability to live independently of their parents. In the pension records and memoirs, most of those who were over sixteen when they enlisted present themselves as independent actors, masters of their own fate.[24]

Most younger boys, such as Ebenezer Atwood, were clearly dependents. In June 1780, fourteen-year-old Atwood was living in Thompson, Connecticut, with John Younglove, "who was his guardian both of his parents being dead." That month, with his guardian's consent, he enlisted in the Continental army for six months. When Ebenezer returned home that December, he duly turned his discharge papers over to Younglove. Three months later, he enlisted again with his guardian's consent, this time for one year. When that term of service was completed in March 1782, he again returned to Younglove, and his guardian "received his wages for the years [sic] service."[25]

The issues of pay and dependence throw boys' service and lack of citizenship rights into relief. They were old enough to earn money and perform military labor, cook their own food, repair their own clothes, and live away from the supervision of parents and guardians. Yet they were not old enough to join the militia in their own right, and no matter which branch of the service they were in, they returned from it still under the legal control of parents or guardians. It is not surprising that Atwood remembered the details of what he had done with his pay fifty years later or that there were tensions between boys' desire for autonomy and parental authority even if these were not openly expressed.

The stories of boy soldiers illustrate a great diversity of experience rather than supporting any narrow generalizations. Decisions to enlist ran the gamut from compulsion, to negotiation, to independent action. Many were combinations of these, capturing the vague status of semidependence and the tenuous connection to the rights of citizenship. Ebenezer Atwood appears to have made his decision to enlist independently of his guardian, yet he requested permission to do so and then handed his pay and papers over to him at the end of his service. For Cyrus Allen, the suggestion of serving appears to have come from his father, although he seems to have had a choice whether to go or not. He also did not receive any pay himself. Simeon Hewitt, who had substituted for his father at age fourteen, was, at fifteen, eager to go away again to join the state troops for a one-year term. He later remembered that his father had resisted this and that his longer enlistment "at a young age was a subject of conversation" but that his father had finally relented. He did not say whether he had kept his pay.[26]

A few other boy soldiers were independent actors making their own decisions and able to keep their hard-earned money. These boys operated with almost complete agency over their lives and offer a glimpse of how war gave opportunities to young boys who were restless or unhappy. The sixteen-year-old Thomas Painter enlisted because he had a desire "for a roving life." After being orphaned at aged eleven, he had been apprenticed to an uncle who was a shoemaker. Thomas found that work complete drudgery and the army an attractive option. Ebenezer Fox of Roxbury, Massachusetts, was fifteen when he served in the militia as a substitute, but he had already lived away from home intermittently for years. He had been seven when his poor father, struggling to support "a large family," had placed him with a neighboring farmer with whom Ebenezer lived for five years, "performing such tasks as were adapted to my age and strength." He was twelve when war broke out, and he ran away to sea, but returned home shortly thereafter with little to show for that experience. At age thirteen he still did not want to stay at home "and be a burden" on his father, so he went to work for a barber and wigmaker until he entered the militia as a substitute for his master when he was fifteen, glad to go to get away from the "monotonous" and "irksome" duties of the shop.[27]

Some boys were so desperate to get away from bad situations that they would sign up for longer terms in the army. Fourteen-year old George Hofstalar was miserable when he was sent to live with relatives in North Carolina after his father died. So, "induced by the bounty," he joined the army for a nine-month term. He did not indicate that he had sought permission, and he almost certainly kept his pay. John Jenks was about twelve when he joined the Continental army and couldn't wait to get away from his guardian. In 1775, when Jenks had been about seven or eight, his father had died leaving the family impoverished. Jenks reported, "My Eldest sister Sabrina & younger Brother Obadiah were Bound out . . . and myself, to Samuel Whipple . . . who was a distant relative." Twice Jenks ran away and joined the Connecticut Continentals, but on each occasion he was apprehended and returned to his hated guardian. Then his luck changed. Mr. Whipple himself was drafted and "managed the affair as to get me enlisted and mustered among the same recruits from whom a short time before I had been mustered out!!!" Thus the arrangement suited guardian and ward. Mr. Whipple found someone at no cost to meet his military obligation, and Jenks got to leave him, even though it cost him three years of service.[28]

For Jenks, service was an escape from a bad situation, and there was no hint of regret in his application. Not so for Obadiah Benge. Benge was fifteen or sixteen when he became a private soldier and served a nine-month term in the North Carolina troops. However, he had not entered the service willingly. He had been living in Surry County in the Carolina backcountry when he was "forced" into the service "by his step-father, John Fielder, as a substitute for one James Green, [and] his said stepfather received from said James Green a horse, bridle and saddle for the same." Bartered away by his stepfather, Obadiah at least had the comfort of serving in the same regiment, although not in the same company, as his older brother. The boys tried to take control of their situation and asked to be put together. Their respective captains were sympathetic, and as the troops marched to what would be the Battle at Kings Mountain Obadiah was transferred to his brother's company. However, the comfort of sibling companionship was short-lived. His brother was killed in the battle and Obadiah was badly wounded. Fortunately, he had a relative living nearby with whom he stayed for about three months, but he never rejoined the service and was permanently crippled by a musket ball.[29]

Not surprisingly, the tone of Obadiah Benge's pension application was bitter. He was unembarrassed about letting the pension commissioner know that his service in Revolutionary War had been coerced and that he was the victim of his father's mercenary actions. James Ayers, the boy "a good size to send to mole," also made sure the pension commissioner knew that for his initial period of service his father had "enlisted him." He made the distinction that he had volunteered for his later service, even though he knew there was no distinction in calculating his pension. All boys were subject to the authority of their fathers or guardians, so their state of mind at the time was irrelevant to the success or failure of their applications. But it is telling that decades after the fact these boys wanted someone to know about the perceived injustice, and the resentment they felt percolates out of the sources and over the centuries.

The factors that drew these soldiers into the service indicate the great diversity of experience in boyhood in revolutionary America. In the glimpses we have of them and their families at the moment of enlistment, we see that some enjoyed the care and protection of their parents while others suffered at the hands of mercenary ones. Some went to war against their parents' inclinations while others were thrust into it over their own objections. A few boys thought that the army would be a more hospitable place than the places they lived or that it would be an escape from jobs that were tedious and frustrating. For many more, military service was an issue around which they could negotiate with their fathers when they wanted opportunities that could take them away from home. Some saw a real opportunity to contribute to the financial well-being of their families. They could do this either directly by turning over their pay or bounty money or indirectly by substituting for an older family member, allowing the more needed laborer to stay home, or by relieving their families of the need to support and feed them. A few, such as Josiah Brandon, were drawn by the cause itself to set their own course.

Their service, especially as substitutes, shows the complex nature of late eighteenth-century citizenship as Americans moved from being subjects of a king to being citizens in a republic. Property owners and patriarchs felt that their military responsibilities to the new government could be met by anyone it was convenient to send, even if that person was a dependent youth. Whatever the circumstances of enlistment, the spectrum of family relations reflected the tensions in the new nation as boys, particularly those in their early teens, attempted to assert their own inclinations and become masters of their own fate.

NOTES

1. Josiah Brandon, W335, Revolutionary War Pension Applications (RWPA), Record Group (RG) 15, National Archives Building (NAB).

2. Josiah Brandon, W335, RWPA, RG 15, NAB.

3. Holly Brewer, *By Birth or Consent: Children, Law, and the Anglo-American Revolution in Authority* (Chapel Hill: University of North Carolina Press, 2005).

4. Constance B. Schulz, "Children and Childhood in the Eighteenth Century," in *American Childhood: A Research Guide and Historical Handbook*, ed. Joseph M. Hawes and N. Ray Hines (Westport, CT: Greenwood Press, 1985), 58.

5. RWPA, RG 15, NAB; Caroline Cox, *A Proper Sense of Honor: Service and Sacrifice in George Washington's Army* (Chapel Hill: University of North Carolina Press, 2004), xiii–xiv.

6. Samuel Aspenwall, W20634, RWPA, RG 15, NAB.

7. Howard Henry Peckham, ed., *The Toll of Independence: Engagements and Battle Casualties of the American Revolution* (Chicago: University of Chicago Press, 1974), 131–33; Cox, *Proper Sense of Honor*, 134–35.

8. Brewer, *By Birth or Consent*, 140–45, 64–70, 130–40; William Lambarde, *Eirenarcha; or, Of the Office of the Justices of the Peace* (London, 1581), 378; quote from 137.

9. Brewer, *By Birth or Consent*, 137, 139.

10. Joseph F. Kett, *Rites of Passage: Adolescence in America, 1790 to the Present* (New York: Basic Books, 1977), 11–13.

11. "Size Rolls," George Washington Papers, Library of Congress, Microfilm, Series 4; "The Muster Rolls of New York Provincial Troops, 1755–1764," New York Historical Society, *Collections* 24 (1891).

12. Cox, *Proper Sense of Honor*, 2–3.

13. Joseph Plumb Martin, *Ordinary Courage: The Revolutionary War Adventures*

of Joseph Plumb Martin, ed. James Kirby Martin (St. James, NY: Brandywine Press, 1993), 38; Barnabas Hailey, S30477, RWPA, RG 15, NAB.

14. Simeon Hewitt, W25766, RWPA, RG 15, NAB.

15. Bennett Cuthbertson, *A System for the Compleat Interior Management and Oeconomy of a Battalion of Infantry* (Dublin, 1768), 12–13, quoted in John Rees, "The Music of the Army: An Abbreviated Study of the Ages of Musicians in the Continental Army," 1993, www.revwar75.com/library/rees/musician1.htm.

16. General Edward Hand, letters, May 21, 1781, and July 16, 1782, quoted in Holly A. Mayer, *Belonging to the Army: Camp Followers and Community during the American Revolution* (Columbia: University of South Carolina Press, 1996), 58.

17. Cyrus Allen, W8094, and Bishop Tyler, S30377, RWPA, RG 15, NAB; Israel Trask's deposition for his pension application is transcribed in John Dann, ed., *The Revolution Remembered: Eyewitness Accounts of the War for Independence* (Chicago: University of Chicago Press, 1980), 406–7.

18. Cyrus Allen, W8094, and Bishop Tyler, S30377, RWPA, RG 15, NAB; Israel Trask quoted in Dann, *Revolution Remembered*, 406.

19. James Ayers, R334, Cyrus Allen, W8094, and David Carpenter, W16892, RWPA, RG 15, NAB.

20. Cyrus Allen, W8094, Bishop Tyler, S30377, Samuel Branch, W8717, and John Jenks, S39775, RWPA, RG 15, NAB.

21. Meshack Burchfield, S16668, and Bishop Tyler, S30377, RWPA, RG 15, NAB.

22. Jacob Gundy, S32284, and Nathaniel Warner, S23990, RWPA, RG 15, NAB.

23. Stephen Hammond, S10800, RWPA, RG 15, NAB.

24. Fred Anderson, *A People's Army: Massachusetts Soldiers and Society in the Seven Years' War* (Chapel Hill: University of North Carolina Press, 1984), 39.

25. Ebenezer Atwood, W23469, RWPA, RG 15, NAB.

26. Cyrus Allen, W8094, and Simeon Hewitt, W25766, RWPA, RG 15, NAB.

27. Thomas Painter, *Autobiography of Thomas Painter Relating His Experiences during the War of the Revolution* (Privately printed, 1910); Ebenezer Fox, "The Revolutionary Adventures of Ebenezer Fox," in *Narratives of the American Revolution*, ed. Hugh Rankin (Chicago: R. R. Donnelley and Sons, 1976), 9–10, 20, 29–33.

28. George Hofstalar, S15176, and John Jenks, S39775, RWPA, RG 15, NAB.

29. Obadiah Benge, R743, RWPA, RG 15, NAB.

||||||||||||||||||||||||||||||||||||||||||||||||||||||

2

Martha Jefferson and the American Revolution in Virginia

Cynthia A. Kierner

Children's experiences in revolutionary America ranged from the prosaic to the profoundly unsettling. Those who lived far from the battlefields and army encampments and whose parents avoided military or political service could enjoy a secure and stable family life, perhaps blissfully unaware of the war and its attendant hardships. Others, by contrast, experienced wartime violence in communities under siege, or as camp followers or underage soldiers; many more lost a father or another close relation in the unexpectedly long war that claimed more than twenty-five thousand American lives.[1]

Martha Jefferson's first decade—which coincided with the rise, progress, and ultimate triumph of the American Revolution—fell between these two extremes. "Patsy" Jefferson was the oldest of six children of Martha Wayles Skelton and Thomas Jefferson, who drafted the Declaration of Independence in 1776, presided over the revolutionary revision of Virginia's laws, and served for two years as the commonwealth's wartime governor. Although war brought military prisoners and eventually armed conflict to their Albemarle County neighborhood, the adult Jeffersons' efforts to isolate their household from the ill effects of war were surprisingly successful, especially in the war's early phases. Years later, when Patsy wrote a memoir of her childhood, personal tragedy and political controversy overshadowed war-related experiences in her brief account.[2] Nevertheless, the Revolution was a formative experience for Martha Jefferson, who came to see herself as a patriot whose family had sacrificed mightily for the revolutionary cause.

Born in 1772, Martha Jefferson spent most of her first decade at Monticello, her father's home outside Charlottesville, a town that consisted of "only of a Court-house, one tavern, and about a dozen houses" in the 1770s. The house at Monticello, whose first version was nearly completed by the war's end, sat atop a mountain that took half an hour to climb, despite the good road. Like many of his contemporaries, Thomas Jefferson idealized affectionate family life. Visitors' accounts routinely noted the serenity and comfort of the Jefferson family circle, conveying the impression that this ideal was attained at Monticello. But the Jeffersons' home was also a working plantation that employed approximately 185 slaves, including Betty Hemings and her children, at least some of whom were light-skinned progeny of Patsy's maternal grandfather, John Wayles.[3]

Love and death marked the years of Patsy's infancy and early childhood. In keeping with the gentry's increasingly sentimental domestic ideals, the adult Jeffersons expressed affection openly to each other and to their child. Patsy recalled that her father's "manners in his family were familiar and affectionate" and that "we always kissed him good night . . . unless strangers were present." At the same time, the pervasiveness of mortality made family ties both precious and precarious. During Patsy's first decade, she lost her two surviving grandparents, an aunt, a favorite uncle, and finally her mother. Of her five younger siblings, only one lived beyond the age of three.[4]

Patsy's upbringing and early education at Monticello were largely conventional for the times. Like most Virginia fathers, Jefferson oversaw his child's intellectual development. Like them, he believed that education should train girls to please men and tend children, but he also shared the popular contemporary notion that the influence of literate and sensitive women improved men by promoting virtue and civility, which, in turn, benefited all society. Jefferson urged his daughter to become "good and accomplished" by reading widely, writing well, studying her French, and practicing music (at which, like her parents, she excelled) and drawing (at which she did not). Patsy later recalled that her father had "bestowed much time & attention" on her lessons. Although little is known about the precise nature of her earliest education at Monticello during the war, it is clear that by 1783 she could read serious books and letters and that she knew some music and French.[5]

Thomas Jefferson could be a demanding taskmaster who used emotional manipulation to elicit achievement, but for Patsy time spent reading and learning to play the harpsichord at Monticello was cherished time with a man she loved. Patsy consistently strove to please a father who, even as he played a leading role in the creation of an independent American republic, claimed that his own happiness depended chiefly on his daughter's moral and intellectual excellence. "No distress which this world could now bring on me could equal that of your disappointing my hopes," he informed eleven-year-old Patsy in 1783. "If you love me then, strive to be good under every situation . . . and to acquire those accomplishments which I have put in your power" to obtain.[6]

Patsy's relations with her mother appear to have been more distant. She described Martha Wayles Skelton Jefferson as "having a vivacity of temper that sometimes bordered on tartness" toward her children, though not toward her husband, whom she deeply loved. As an adult, Patsy told a story about her mother that cast Martha Jefferson in a comparatively negative light. On one occasion, she later recalled, her mother had punished her "for some fault, not harshly nor unjustly, but in a way to make an impression." Some time later, when Martha was displeased with her daughter "for some trifle," she "reminded her in a slightly taunting way of this painful past." Some forty years after this incident, Patsy still remembered feeling "deeply mortified" and tearful until her father rose to her defense. "My dear, a fault in so young a child once punished should be forgotten," he gently observed. Patsy "could never forget the warm gush of gratitude that filled her childish heart at these words, probably not intended for her ear."[7]

As a child, Patsy probably could not appreciate the toll that illness, frequent pregnancies, and grief exacted from a woman already burdened by the onerous domestic responsibilities of a plantation mistress, which Martha Jefferson by all accounts performed well. Although she recalled that her mother's virtues included "neatness, order, good housewifery and womanly accomplishment," Martha Jefferson apparently did not impart her domestic skills to Patsy, who years later told her own daughter that when she herself had married she had been "well grounded in all the solid branches of a woman's education, save only the arts of housewifery, which she afterwards attained with pain & difficulty, by untiring perseverance."[8]

The fact that Patsy's memories of her childhood at Monticello focused overwhelmingly on her relations with her parents suggests that they largely succeeded in protecting her from the ill effects of war. In late 1775, when Virginia's royal governor, Lord Dunmore, bombarded the coastal towns of Hampton and Norfolk and promised freedom to slaves who joined the king's forces, civilians experienced violence firsthand, often in their own houses. For instance, Mary Webley of Norfolk was "suckling her child" in her home in Norfolk when her leg was broken by an exploding British cannonball. Webley and her "little Children" survived, but their house was "destroyed in the Flames of Norfolk." By contrast, Thomas Jefferson clearly believed that his family would be safe in Albemarle, which was far removed from the early fighting and had few Tory inhabitants to harass the county's patriot majority. As Jefferson explained to his uncle in 1776, "Our interior situation is to me the most agreeable as withdrawing me in a great measure from the noise and bustle of the world. . . . Our idea is that every place is secure [from enemy attack] except those which lie immediately on the water edge."[9]

Jefferson was often away from Albemarle in 1775–76, as Congress and Virginia inched toward independence, but his political service in some respects merely extended the commitment he had made to public life as early as 1769, when he first entered Virginia's colonial House of Burgesses. During the Revolution, when he journeyed to Williamsburg or Philadelphia on public business, Jefferson corresponded with his wife and with friends and family near home, as he had done since his marriage in 1772. When he came home, he arrived bearing gifts—chocolate, lace, shoes, a doll for Patsy—which must have conveyed a sense of well-being to his family, despite the troubled times.[10]

When public business took Thomas away from home, he and Martha relied on kin or friends for protection and companionship and to maintain a semblance of normal domestic life. In particular, they turned to Francis Eppes and his wife Elizabeth Wayles Eppes (Martha's half-sister), who lived at The Forest in Charles City County, in Virginia's Tidewater region. During Dunmore's raids, Jefferson urged Eppes and his family "to keep yourselves at a distance from the alarms" by moving further inland to Albemarle, where they would be welcome additions to the Monticello household while he attended Congress. In July and August 1776, Patsy and her mother stayed at The Forest, where Elizabeth saw Martha through a seemingly dangerous illness and four-year-old Patsy enjoyed the company of her three-year-old cousin.[11]

These domestic arrangements would not have seemed extraordinary to Patsy, who was only two in 1774, when her father made his first trip north to Philadelphia to attend Congress, nor would they have seemed entirely strange to her mother, the product of an elite Virginian culture in which long-term visits to close kin were common. In colonial Virginia, where most gentlefolk lived on widely dispersed plantations, visiting provided opportunities for socialization and sociability. Women, who often were lonely and isolated at home, especially valued time spent with distant mothers, sisters, and other female relatives.[12]

At the same time, like other revolutionary wives, Martha Jefferson regretted and possibly even resented her husband's frequent absences. Perhaps for that reason, Thomas turned down a judicial appointment that would have required his continual attendance at court and cited domestic concerns when he declined Congress's offer of a diplomatic post in September 1776. Alluding to his wife's recent illness, yet another pregnancy in its early stages, and perhaps also thinking of his four-year-old daughter's need to begin her studies, he explained that "circumstances very peculiar in the situation of my family, such as neither permit me to leave nor to carry it, compel me to ask leave to decline a service so honorable & at the same time so important to the American cause."[13]

Jefferson's decision to turn his attention to state politics after 1776 allowed Patsy, for the first time, to live in a conventionally patriarchal two-parent household for an extended period. Between 1777 and 1779, Jefferson's membership in the House of Delegates, Virginia's state assembly, necessitated his being in Williamsburg for weeks or even months at a time, but he still spent less time away from home than he had in previous years, and on at least one occasion Martha (and possibly Patsy) went with him to the capital. During these years, Jefferson focused primarily on revising Virginia's legal code to make it more compatible with the political values of a now-independent commonwealth. This project allowed his family to enjoy a relatively stable domestic life while he worked in his library at Monticello.[14]

For nearly three years, from her fourth birthday in September 1776 until her father became Virginia's governor in June 1779, Patsy's life was relatively predictable, harmonious, and even fun. Jefferson resumed construction at Monticello, planted fruit trees in his orchards, returned to his scientific activities and research, and attended to his daughter's education. The Jeffersons hoped to add to their family, and Martha became pregnant roughly every two years, despite her husband's absences. Although this interval between pregnancies was typical for elite Virginia women of the era, the mortality rate of Martha's offspring far exceeded contemporary averages. The family mourned an infant, an unnamed boy, who was born in late May 1777 and died three weeks later. In August 1778, however, they rejoiced in the birth of Mary—known as "Polly"—the only Jefferson child, besides Patsy, who lived to adulthood.[15]

At Monticello, the main discernible impact of the war between 1777 and 1779 probably came in the form of shortages. The disruption or stoppage of trade in wartime meant that goods that Virginians normally imported became either extremely expensive or unavailable. Plantation mistresses and their enslaved workers began sewing and spinning to make or mend clothing and other necessary items. In western Virginia, Sarah Nourse and her daughters spent these years patching old clothes, awaiting a parcel of goods from Europe that arrived only after the war was over. Another Virginia woman lamented a shortage of ink that prevented her from writing longer letters to her husband. In Albemarle, the army's demand for food, especially meat, diminished supplies for the civilian population.[16]

Another perceptible consequence of the war was the arrival of thousands of military prisoners in Patsy's neighborhood, which vastly improved social life at Jefferson's Monticello. In October 1777, American troops defeated a combined force of British regulars, Germans, and Tories in a pivotal battle at Saratoga, New York. Congress later interned prisoners from Saratoga in and around Charlottesville. Although some Albemarle residents resented the prisoners' presence, Jefferson extended his hospitality to captured gentlemen-officers. "It is for the benefit of mankind to mitigate the horrors of war as much as possible," he wrote to Governor Patrick Henry in 1779. "The practice . . . of treating captive enemies with politeness and generosity is not only delight in contemplation, but really interesting to the world—friends, foes, and neutrals."[17]

Although the Jeffersons undoubtedly did not socialize with common soldiers interned in Albemarle, the presence of officers—who were educated and presumably honorable members of the European social elite—afforded Patsy her first exposure to genteel cosmopolitan society. A family dinner at nearby Blenheim plantation, hosted by a captive British major general, included an invitation for seven-year-old "Miss Jefferson" and her parents, along with Baron von Riedesel and his wife and three daughters, who had accompanied the Hessian officer on his tour of duty in America. The Monticello family especially enjoyed the "agreeable society" of the accomplished, English-speaking Riedesels, whose eldest daughter, Augusta, was a year older than Patsy.[18]

Martha Jefferson, whom Baron von Riedesel praised as an "amiable" hostess, became young Patsy's exemplar of genteel feminine sociability. The Jeffersons had welcomed European guests to their home as early as 1773, when Thomas persuaded the Florentine Philip Mazzei to settle at nearby Colle plantation. Impressed by the taste and hospitality of his hosts, Mazzei reported to a friend in Italy, "If you knew Mr. Jefferson and his worthy spouse I am certain you would not seek any benefit other than that of living with them." Patsy herself remembered her mother as "a very attractive person . . . with considerable powers of conversation, some skill in music, all the habits of good society, and the art of welcoming her husband's friends to perfection"—all attributes that Thomas Jefferson clearly valued. Subsequent visitors described the mistress of Monticello as "gentle and amiable," "very agreeable, sensible, and accomplished," and a skilled performer on both the harpsichord and pianoforte. Decades later, others praised Patsy's performance as a hostess in similar terms, suggesting that she had learned the rites of genteel sociability in childhood from her mother.[19]

The fact that Patsy did not recall any discussion of the war during these mostly happy years suggests that, from her perspective as a young child, Monticello was a bucolic refuge from the mixture of good and bad news about a revolution whose failure would result in the ruin (and perhaps the execution) of its leaders. Jefferson corresponded regularly with prominent officials and military commanders, so he (and possibly Martha) knew that the war, having been fought to a stalemate in the Middle States, had moved decisively southward with the British capture of Savannah and then all of Georgia beginning in December 1778. Patsy's youth and residence more than a hundred miles away from the Williamsburg presses that at that time produced Virginia's only newspapers made it somewhat easier to shield her from war-related issues and anxieties. By contrast, Betsey Ambler, who was seven years older than Patsy and lived in York, a coastal town near Williamsburg, had strong recollections of the war from its beginning and acute awareness of the movement of troops in its later stages.[20]

Nevertheless, Patsy must have become increasingly conscious of the war and its costs after June 1779, when the Virginia legislature chose her father to be governor. Thomas Jefferson's assumption of the governorship changed his family's circumstances in at least two respects. First, because his new office necessitated his presence in the capital, Martha Jefferson and her daughters, like many political and military families, left home, joining Thomas in Williamsburg, where they took up residence in the Governor's Palace in the old colonial capital. Second, because Jefferson was now responsible for overseeing the state's war effort, his house became a central clearinghouse for military and political information. Not long after Patsy arrived in Williamsburg, her father issued a proclamation, pursuant to a recommendation from the Continental Congress, that set aside a day of "public and solemn thanksgiving and prayer" to commemorate recent military successes and seek "the continuance of [God's] favour and protection to these United States." The governor encouraged "all the good people of this commonwealth," including presumably his own family, to pray and attend church services to support the war effort—activities that presupposed at least a vague understanding of current events.[21]

Despite her growing awareness of the war raging in Georgia and later South Carolina, Patsy may have enjoyed her first year as the governor's daughter. No major military engagements occurred in Virginia. In Williamsburg, she had her first taste of town life, which included regular lessons at Sarah Hallam's dancing school for young ladies. The installation of some Monticello slaves as a necessary workforce in the Governor's Palace also must have fostered an atmosphere reminiscent of the Jeffersons' normal domestic life. The family's domestic servants accompanied them to Richmond when the state capital moved there in 1780. Unlike Williamsburg, Richmond was a rustic village that offered few opportunities for sociability. Betsey Ambler, who was fifteen when her family moved there from Williamsburg, complained that "this famous Metropolis . . . will scarcely afford one comfort in life."[22]

Jefferson's second one-year term as governor was significantly more turbulent, as enemy forces converged on Virginia from both north and south. Beginning with a British attack on Richmond and the surrounding area in January 1781, war-related violence affected large numbers of Virginia civilians for the first time since 1776. Some families fled their homes in anticipation of enemy raids, while others braved the onslaught in hope of preserving their families' property. Widow Mary Willing Byrd, who lived with her eight children on her James River plantation, was poorly treated by soldiers on both sides. In February, Americans, who suspected Byrd of aiding the British, made her entire family prisoners in their home and, she later claimed, inflicted "*savage* treatment" on them. A few months later, the British commandeered Byrd's house as temporary quarters. When they left, forty-nine slaves and several horses departed with them.[23]

The year 1781, which culminated in the decisive American victory at Yorktown, brought hardship and dishonor to Patsy and her family. In January, rumors that the enemy planned to attack Richmond led Jefferson to send Martha and the children to Tuckahoe, the nearby home of his friend Thomas Mann Randolph (whose eldest son Patsy would later marry). The next day, the family moved to Fine Creek, a Goochland County property that Thomas had inherited from his father. While the governor took rumors of an impending attack on Richmond seriously enough to ensure the safety of his family, he delayed calling out the militia until it was too late to mount an effective defense of the capital. With the Continental army occupied elsewhere, the town's citizens fled, leaving Richmond undefended when British forces commanded by the traitor Benedict Arnold arrived there on January 5. "In ten minutes, not a white man was to be seen in Richmond," recalled Isaac Jefferson, a young slave who remained at the governor's residence. The British searched the Jeffersons' rented house, plundered its wine cellar, and confiscated meat and grain, aggravating any food shortages the family had experienced during their stay in the new capital. They also burned public buildings and warehouses, destroyed records, and looted ships docked on the James River as they made their way back toward the coast.[24]

When the British withdrew from Richmond, ten of the Jeffersons' slaves left with them: Jupiter (Thomas's personal attendant since his college days), Sukey (the cook), Ursula (the family's housekeeper, who had nursed Patsy in infancy), George (Ursula's husband), Mary (a seamstress), and five children, including Isaac (Ursula's son). Slave owners liked to think that their bondpeople were "carried off" forcibly by the British, but thousands left of their own accord in hopes of obtaining freedom. Though none of the Jeffersons commented on the loss of these enslaved workers, with whom they had been on familiar or even intimate terms, they must have keenly missed both their company and their labor. Like most white Virginians, the adult Jeffersons also must have harbored a profound fear of wartime slave insurrections, which had led to more rigorous policing of slave activities as early as 1775. Governor Jefferson certainly pondered the possibility of race war. In 1781, all ten of his escaped slaves went to Yorktown, where, according to Isaac Jefferson, the British "treated them mighty well," though American forces recaptured them after the battle and returned them to Monticello.[25]

By spring, Virginia was the war's main theater, as British forces under Arnold and General William Phillips again moved toward Richmond and General Charles Cornwallis marched northward from North Carolina to join them. As Governor Jefferson awaited the arrival of Continental forces in Richmond, Patsy and her parents mourned the death of the infant Lucy Elizabeth, the family's youngest member. Two weeks later, on April 29, the Marquis de Lafayette arrived with a force of some 1,200 men to save

Richmond and its military stores from falling into enemy hands. On May 1, however, the state's legislators decided to flee westward and reconvene in Charlottesville.[26]

The ensuing months must have been exciting (and frightening) times for Patsy and her family. In roughly five weeks, the family lived in at least six different places—Richmond, Tuckahoe, Monticello, Blenheim and Enniscorthy (both plantations in Albemarle), and Poplar Forest (roughly sixty miles from Monticello in Bedford County)—sometimes with and sometimes without their putative head. The family of Betsey Ambler, whose father chaired Virginia's Board of Trade, undertook a similar wartime odyssey from Richmond to Louisa County to Charlottesville and then back to Louisa, and she found the situation both horrifying and inspiring. "What an alarming crisis is this," Betsey wrote to a friend from Louisa in 1781. "War in itself, however distant is indeed terrible, but when it is brought to our very doors—when those we love are personally engaged in it, when our friends and neighbors are exposed to its ravages, when we know assuredly that without sacrificing many dear to us as our own lives, our country must remain subject to British tyranny, the reflection is overwhelming."[27]

When the state assembly met in Charlottesville on May 28, Patsy was with her family at Monticello, where her father still attempted to preserve calm in the face of impending peril. After a messenger arrived on the morning of June 4 bearing news that Lieutenant Colonel Banastre Tarleton was marching toward Albemarle in hopes of capturing the state's government, Patsy and her family persevered and "breakfasted at leisure with our guests," who included the speakers of both legislative houses. One visitor described their host as "perfectly tranquil and undisturbed," but the legislators resolved to reconvene in Staunton, thirty-three miles to the west, and to postpone choosing Jefferson's successor as governor, though his term had expired on June 2. Jefferson, whose official status was at that point ambiguous, moved his family several times before settling at Poplar Forest in Bedford, where they remained for six weeks while the former governor, who had fallen from his horse, recovered from a broken arm.[28]

The 1781 campaigns hurt Jefferson and his family both personally and politically. Besides the material losses they sustained at their Richmond residence, Jefferson later reported that, though Tarleton and his men had "behaved very genteelly," doing no real damage at Monticello, Cornwallis had destroyed crops, barns, and livestock—and "carried off also about 30 slaves," of whom three may have attained permanent freedom—from Elk

Hill, his James River plantation. But far more painful in 1781 was the damage Jefferson's reputation suffered as a result of his alleged misconduct as Virginia's war governor. After reconvening and choosing Jefferson's successor on June 7, 1781, the House of Delegates formally resolved that "an inquiry be made into the conduct of the Executive of this State for the last twelve months." Jefferson's political enemies spearheaded this effort to—in his words—"stab a reputation by general suggestion under a bare expectation that facts might be afterwards hunted up to bolster it." In particular, they hoped to censure him officially for his failure to summon the militia to defend Richmond. Although these efforts ultimately failed, the accusations, Jefferson confided, "inflicted a wound on my spirit which will only be cured by the all-healing grave."[29]

After the decisive battle at Yorktown in October 1781 virtually ensured an American triumph, the pain of public dishonor, coupled with the fact that Martha was again pregnant and in poor health, led Jefferson to retire from public life and return to Monticello. Again he refused a diplomatic post, concluding that the "independence of private life under the protection of republican laws will . . . yield me that happiness from whi[ch] no slave is so remote as the minister of a Commonwealth." Jefferson invited friends to visit, pursued his scientific interests, and began writing the only book he ever published, *Notes on the State of Virginia*. But more than anything, retirement meant family time and the resumption of lessons for nine-year-old Patsy, three-year-old Polly, and their fatherless cousins, Peter and Samuel Carr, who had joined the Jefferson household. The birth of a baby girl in May 1782 may have signaled a return to the normal rhythms of domestic life as the war drew to a close. Any sense of peace and well-being, however, abruptly ended with the death of Martha Jefferson in September due to complications arising from the birth of Lucy Elizabeth (who was named for her deceased sister and who was herself destined to die in 1785).[30]

Although Patsy Jefferson lived through some of the most dramatic episodes in the republic's early history, her brief memoir indicates that personal tragedies—specifically her mother's death and its consequences—were the pivotal events in her life as a child in revolutionary America. As an adult, though she wrote little about the great public events of the Revolution, even to the extent that they affected her and her family directly, she produced a comparatively detailed account of her mother's death and her father's reaction to it. "As a nurse no female ever had more tenderness or anxiety" than her father, she reported, who "nursed my poor Mother in turn with Aunt Carr and her own sister [Elizabeth Eppes] setting up with her and adminstring her medicines and drink to the last. For the four months that she lingered he was never out of calling." Other sources corroborate Jefferson's deep devotion to his wife and his profound grief on her demise. Patsy's emphasis on her father's sensibility and tenderness was a bittersweet memory of her own happy childhood—which effectively ended when her mother died—and also a tacit reproach to her own husband, who was emotionally unstable and often absent by the time she wrote her memoir in the 1820s.[31]

The death of Martha Jefferson was a turning point in the life of ten-year-old Patsy, who purposefully became her father's sole companion while her aunts cared for Polly and the infant Lucy and attended to domestic matters at Monticello. Jefferson tried to distance his daughters from both their mother's suffering and his own intense grief after the "closing scene," when, Patsy later recalled, he "fainted and remained so long insensible that they feared he never would revive." His daughter, however, remembered that she had "almost by stealth . . . entered his room," where she had found him emotionally prostrate. The distraught widower remained in his room for three weeks, during which the youngster, by her own account, "was not a moment from his side," though he "walked almost incessantly night and day only lying down occasionally." By early October, Jefferson had left his room, but he was constantly on horseback. Patsy was "in those melancholy rambles . . . his constant companion, a solitary witness to many a violent burst of grief," which she remembered vividly decades later. She rode with him "5 or 6 miles a day," forging bonds of mutual devotion that would last their entire lives.[32]

Patsy's childhood ended in the ensuing months, as she prepared to leave her home and family. In October, as he emerged from "that stupor of mind which had rendered me as dead as she who occasioned it," Jefferson took his three "sacred charges" to Ampthill, the home of a friend in the Chesterfield County, to be inoculated against smallpox, and he nursed them through the aftermath of their inoculation. Although he professed that "the care and instruction of our children indeed affords some temporary abstractions from wretchedness," the two younger girls soon departed to live with their aunt Elizabeth. Patsy and her father prepared to move to Paris, where Jefferson now agreed to serve as one of the American negotiators of the treaty that would officially end the war with Britain. After residing for several months with family friends in Philadelphia, where she continued her studies, Patsy rejoined her father and they sailed together for Europe. She completed her education in a convent boarding school, then returned to Virginia in 1789 and married Thomas Mann Randolph of Tuckahoe.[33]

As Mrs. Randolph, Patsy enjoyed reminiscing about her Paris school days, and young people appreciated her ability to "bring back past events and portray the characters connected with them," but she had little to say about the public events of the revolutionary era, which had occurred during her childhood.[34] Her extreme youth at the war's beginning—she was, after all, only four when Congress declared independence in 1776—partly explains her reticence, as do her parents' efforts to protect her from wartime concerns and problems. Patsy was nine years old, however, when the British invaded Virginia, forcing her family first to flee Richmond and later to evacuate Monticello. The family's efforts to evade capture by enemy forces would have made compelling stories to share with youngsters in the postrevolutionary era, but there is no evidence that Martha Jefferson Randolph ever told her children, nieces, or nephews about this aspect of her childhood.

Her silence about these dramatic episodes, which she must have remembered, arguably arose from a profound desire, on the part of both Jefferson and his daughter, to downplay his still-controversial service as Virginia's wartime governor. Jefferson himself deemed these old allegations of cowardice and incompetence more painful (and more damaging) even than those concerning his long-term liaison with Sally Hemings, the Monticello slave woman who was also Patsy's aunt, the half-sister of his late wife. Jefferson defended his record as governor mainly by urging his friends and supporters to write histories of the era that would portray his leadership in a positive, patriotic light. Patsy, who, according to one sympathetic observer, "took the Dusky Sally stories much to heart," also internalized her father's sensitivity about his tenure as governor.[35]

When Martha Jefferson Randolph reminisced about her family's role in the American Revolution, she focused primarily on its financial costs, which had contributed to an escalating spiral of debt that ultimately resulted in the sale of Monticello. She told her own children that her father, as governor, had been allotted a nominal salary in depreciated paper currency, most of which he had never received. During the war, moreover, she believed, "he lost more than the others, in as much as being Governor his expenses were necessarily greater." In 1828, two years after her father's death, when the loss of Monticello was imminent, she described her family's "honorable poverty" as "the fruit, and the price we have paid, for a long and useful life devoted to the service of this country." Yet Randolph insisted that she had "never regretted the sacrifice he made, [for] his country had a right to his services." She also averred her own patriotism, staunchly asserting that "if a few must suffer for the advantages of the many it is a melancholy necessity, but I see no help for it."[36]

This last observation suggests that Patsy Jefferson's revolutionary childhood, though in many respects both family centered and unremarkable, had a discernible political impact on her adult life. Although scholars have argued that revolutionary Americans saw girls as prospective republican wives and mothers who should be educated to inspire patriotism in their husbands and children, there is no evidence that Patsy Jefferson ever received such a purposefully civic-minded education. Yet she may have observed the quiet patriotism of her mother, whose household produced homespun cloth during the revolutionary crisis and who wrote letters urging Virginia gentlewomen to support the efforts of the Philadelphia-based Ladies Association to raise money to benefit poorly supplied Continental soldiers in 1780. "I under take with chearfulness," Martha Jefferson averred, "the duty of furnishing to my country women an opportunity of proving that they also participate of those virtuous feelings" of patriotism.[37]

Perhaps this same spirit animated the efforts of Martha Jefferson Randolph, who years later oversaw the manufacture of more than 150 yards of homespun cloth at her husband's Albemarle County plantation. In 1807, Congress outlawed trade in an ill-fated attempt to stop warring European powers from violating Americans' neutral rights; patriotic women like Randolph responded by increasing domestic production (of cloth especially), as their mothers had done in the revolutionary era.[38]

Patsy Jefferson's revolutionary childhood may have made her a patriot, but it did not significantly alter the status of females, even in her own family. The revolutionary experience afforded girls no new rights when they attained womanhood, nor did it change appreciably the structure or gender expectations of Virginia's gentry families. Patsy's pregnancies—twelve in twenty-seven years—though ultimately more successful than her mother's, were just as frequent; her daughters' education was no better than hers, nor did it reflect a significant reconsideration of women's status and roles. Like others of her generation, however, the grown-up Martha Randolph perpetuated the legacy of her revolutionary childhood. She acknowledged and accepted the costs of war and independence, identifying with the American nation in the postrevolutionary era.

NOTES

1. Howard H. Peckham, *The Toll of Independence: Engagements and Battle Casualties of the American Revolution* (Chicago: University of Chicago Press, 1974), 130; Holly A. Mayer, *Belonging to the Army: Camp Followers and Community during the American Revolution* (Columbia: University of South Carolina Press, 1996), 126, 129, 132, 133, 138; Mary Beth Norton, *Liberty's Daughters: The Revolutionary Experience of American Women, 1750–1800* (Boston: Little, Brown, 1980), 196–224; see also chapter 1 of this volume.

2. The memoir is "Reminiscences of Th. J. by MR, copied by Mary and Caryanne," [ca. 1826], Edgehill–Randolph Papers (1397), Albert Shirley Small Special Collections Library, University of Virginia (hereafter ViU). See also Sarah N. Randolph, *The Domestic Life of Thomas Jefferson* (New York: Harper, 1871), 62–63.

3. Thomas Anburey, *Travels through the Interior Parts of America*, 2 vols. (London: William Lane, 1789), 2:184; Howard C. Rice, ed., *Travels in North America in the Years 1780, 1781 and 1782 by the Marquis de Chastellux*, 2 vols. (Chapel Hill: University of North Carolina Press, 1963), 2:390–91; Merrill D. Peterson, ed., *Visitors to Monticello* (Charlottesville: University Press of Virginia, 1989), 2, 9, 45–54; Dumas Malone, *Jefferson, the Virginian* (Boston: Little, Brown, 1948), 143–52; Lucia Stanton, *Free Some Day: The African American Families of Monticello* (Charlottesville, VA: Thomas Jefferson Foundation, 2000), 17–18, 33, 103.

4. "Reminiscences of Th. J. by MR"; Malone, *Jefferson*, 160–65, 434; Andrew Burstein, *The Inner Jefferson: Portrait of a Grieving Optimist* (Charlottesville: University Press of Virginia, 1995), 28–31, 56–57; Jacqueline S. Reinier, *From Virtue to Character: American Childhood, 1775–1840* (New York: Twayne, 1996), 1–19; Daniel Blake Smith, *Inside the Great House: Planter Family Life in Eighteenth-Century Chesapeake Society* (Ithaca: Cornell University Press, 1980), 31–33, 40–45.

5. Cynthia A. Kierner, *Beyond the Household: Women's Place in the Early South, 1700–1835* (Ithaca: Cornell University Press, 1998), 28, 40–41, 51, 60–61; Smith, Inside the Great House, 63–65; "Reminiscences of Th. J. by MR"; Jefferson to Martha Jefferson, November 28, 1783, December 11, 1783, January 15, 1784, February 18, 1784, March 19, 1784, March 28, 1787, in *The Family Letters of Thomas Jefferson*, ed. Edwin Morris Betts and James Adam Bear Jr. (Columbia: University of Missouri Press, 1966), 19–21, 23–24, 35; Jacob Rubsamen to Jefferson, Dec. 1, 1780, in *The Papers of Thomas Jefferson*, ed. Julian P. Boyd et al. (Princeton: Princeton University Press, 1954–), 4:174; Ellen Wayles Randolph Coolidge to Henry S. Randall, March 31, 1856, Ellen Wayles Randolph Coolidge Correspondence, ViU; Jane Blair Cary Smith, "The Carysbrook Memoir," 24–25, ViU.

6. Jefferson to Martha Jefferson, November 28, 1783, in Betts and Bear, *Family Letters*, 20.

7. Randolph, *Domestic Life*, 343–44; Ellen Wayles Randolph Coolidge to Henry S. Randall, March 31, 1856, Coolidge Correspondence.

8. Ellen Wayles Randolph Coolidge Diaries, 5:60, Massachusetts Historical Society; Ellen Wayles Randolph Coolidge to Henry S. Randall, March 31, 1856, Coolidge Correspondence.

9. John E. Selby, *The Revolution in Virginia, 1775–1783* (Charlottesville: University Press of Virginia, 1988), ch. 4; John Hammond Moore, *Albemarle: Jefferson's County, 1727–1976* (Charlottesville: University Press of Virginia, 1976), 56–57; Petition of Mary Webley, 1776, Legislative Petitions, Norfolk City, Library of Virginia; Jefferson to William Randolph, [ca. June 1776], in Boyd et al., *Papers,* 1:409.

10. James A. Bear Jr., and Lucia Stanton, eds., *Jefferson's Memorandum Books: Accounts, with Legal Records and Miscellany,* 2 vols. (Princeton: Princeton University Press, 1997), 1:403, 423, 426, 459.

11. Jefferson to Francis Eppes, November 12, 1775, July 16, 1776, August 9, 1776, in Boyd et al., *Papers,* 1:86, 458, 508; Jefferson to John Page, July 30, 1776, in Boyd et al., *Papers,* 1:483; Edmund Pendleton to Jefferson, August 26, 1776, in Boyd et al., *Papers,* 1:508.

12. Joan R. Gundersen, "Kith and Kin: Women's Networks in Colonial Virginia," in *The Devil's Lane: Sex and Race in the Early South,* ed. Catherine Clinton and Michele Gillespie (New York: Oxford University Press, 1997), 90–102; D. Smith, *Inside the Great House,* 197–230.

13. Edmund Pendleton to Jefferson, August 10, 1776, in Boyd et al., *Papers,* 1:489; Jefferson to John Hancock, October 11, 1776, in Boyd et al., *Papers,* 1:524; Burstein, *Inner Jefferson,* 63; Patricia Brady, *Martha Washington: An American Life* (New York: Viking Penguin, 2005), 97; Norton, *Liberty's Daughters,* 216–18, 222; Berkin, *Revolutionary Mothers,* 29–31.

14. "Itinerary and Chronology of Thomas Jefferson, 1771–1779," in *The Writings of Thomas Jefferson,* 10 vols., ed. Paul Leicester Ford (New York: G. P. Putnam's Sons, 1892–99), 2:xvii–xxiii; Malone, *Jefferson,* 287.

15. Malone, *Jefferson,* 287–90; D. Smith, *Inside the Great House,* 26–31, 176–77; Jane Turner Censer, *North Carolina Planters and Their Children, 1800–1860* (Baton Rouge: Louisiana State University Press, 1984), 24–25.

16. Moore, *Albemarle,* 56–57; Selby, *Revolution in Virginia,* 177–83; Nicholas Cresswell, *The Journal of Nicholas Cresswell* (Port Washington, NY: Kennikat Press, 1968), 192; Anburey, *Travels,* 2:246–47, 429; Carole Shammas, "Black Women's Work and the Evolution of Plantation Society in Virginia," *Labor History* 26 (1985): 24; Cynthia A. Kierner, *Southern Women in Revolution: Personal and Political Narratives, 1776–1800* (Columbia: University of South Carolina Press, 1998), 9–10; Frances Bland Randolph to St. George Tucker, [July 1777], Tucker-Coleman Papers, Swem Library, College of William and Mary.

17. William M. Dabney, "Jefferson's Albemarle: History of Albemarle County, Virginia, 1727–1829" (PhD diss., University of Virginia, 1951), 47–56; Moore, *Albemarle,* 57–64; Randolph, *Domestic Life,* 50–51; Jefferson to Henry, March 27, 1779, in Boyd et al., *Papers,* 2:242.

18. Marvin L. Brown, ed., *Baroness von Riedesel and the American Revolution: Journal and Correspondence of a Tour of Duty, 1776–1783* (Chapel Hill: University of North Carolina Press, 1965), xxvii, xxix, xxxiii–xxxiv; William Phillips to Jefferson, April 11, 1779, in Boyd et al., *Papers*, 2:252; Jefferson to Riedesel, July 4, 1779, in Boyd et al., *Papers*, 3:24.

19. Riedesel to Jefferson, December 4, 1779, in Boyd et al., *Papers*, 3:212; Jacob Rubsamen to Jefferson, December 1, 1780, in Boyd et al., *Papers*, 4:174; Mazzei to Giovanni Fabbroni, January 30, 1775, in *Philip Mazzei: Selected Writings and Correspondence*, 2 vols., ed. Margherita Marchione et al. (Prato: Edizioni del Palazzo, 1983), 1:77; Rice, *Travels*, 2:391; Ellen Wayles Randolph Coolidge to Henry S. Randall, March 31, 1856, Coolidge Correspondence; Peterson, *Visitors to Monticello*, 46, 48; "Horace Holley letter," September 6, 1824, University of Virginia Alumni Bulletin, 3rd ser., no. 2 [copy], Jefferson Library, Monticello; "Autobiography of Mrs. William Cabell Rives," 58, Rives Family Papers, ViU.

20. Elizabeth Ambler to Mildred Smith, [1780], and Elizabeth Ambler to Ann Ambler Fisher, 1809, both in Elizabeth Ambler Papers, Colonial Williamsburg.

21. "Itinerary and Chronology," 2:xxiii; Malone, *Jefferson*, 301–2; Virginia Gazette (Dixon and Hunter), November 20, 1779.

22. Selby, *Revolution in Virginia*, 235–36; "Memoirs of a Monticello Slave," in *Jefferson at Monticello*, ed. James A. Bear (Charlottesville: University Press of Virginia, 1967), 4–5; Bear and Stanton, *Jefferson's Memorandum Books*, 1:487, 490, 495. Betsey Ambler is quoted in Marie Tyler-McGraw, *At the Falls: Richmond, Virginia, and Its People* (Chapel Hill: University of North Carolina Press, 1994), 64–65.

23. Selby, *Revolution in Virginia*, chs. 13–14; "The Affair of Westover," in Boyd et al., *Papers*, 5:671–705.

24. Selby, *Revolution in Virginia*, 223–24; Malone, *Jefferson*, 336–41; "Memoirs of a Monticello Slave," 7–8; "Diary of Arnold's Invasion . . . ," [1796?], in Boyd et al., *Papers*, 4:259.

25. "Memoirs of a Monticello Slave," 10–11; Stanton, *Free Some Day*, 33; Sylvia R. Frey, *Water from the Rock: Black Resistance in a Revolutionary Age* (Princeton: Princeton University Press, 1991), 155–68; Frey, "Between Slavery and Freedom: Virginia Blacks in the American Revolution," *Journal of Southern History* 49 (1983): 381–86; Thomas Jefferson, *Notes on the State of Virginia* (1787), 264, http://etext.virginia.edu/etcbin/toccer-new2?id=JefVirg.sgm&images=images/modeng&data=/texts/english/modeng/parsed&tag=public&part=14&division=div1.

26. Malone, *Jefferson*, 349–50; Selby, *Revolution in Virginia*, 273–77.

27. Malone, *Jefferson*, 358; Elizabeth Ambler to Mildred Smith, 1781, Elizabeth Ambler Papers, Colonial Williamsburg.

28. Malone, *Jefferson*, 350, 355–58; Selby, *Revolution in Virginia*, 281–83; Moore, *Albemarle*, 64–65; "Diary of Arnold's Invasion," 4:261; "The 1816 Version of the

Diary and Notes of 1781," in Boyd et al., *Papers*, 4:265; Deposition of Christopher Hudson, July 26, 1781, in Boyd et al., *Papers*, 4:277.

29. Jefferson to George Nicholas, July 28, 1781, in Boyd et al., *Papers*, 6:14-5; Jefferson to James Monroe, May 20, 1782, in Boyd et al., *Papers*, 6:185; Jefferson to William Gordon, July 16, 1788, in Boyd et al., *Papers*, 13:363-64; Stanton, *Free Some Day*, 53-55.

30. Randolph, *Domestic Life*, 57-58; Malone, *Jefferson*, 393; Jefferson to Lafayette, August 4, 1781, in Boyd et al., *Papers*, 6:112; Jefferson to Gates, December 14, 1781, in Boyd et al., *Papers*, 6:138; Jefferson to George Rogers Clark, December 19, 1781, and Jefferson to Wythe, December 31, 1781, in Boyd et al., *Papers*, 6:144-45; "Reminiscences of Th. J. by MR."

31. "Reminiscences of Th. J. by MR"; Edmund Randolph to James Madison, September 20, 1782, in Boyd et al., *Papers*, 6:199 n.; Malone, Jefferson, 393-96; Burstein, *Inner Jefferson*, 60-64; William H. Gaines, *Thomas Mann Randolph: Jefferson's Son-in-Law* (Baton Rouge: Louisiana State University Press, 1966), ch. 11.

32. "Reminiscences of Th. J. by MR"; Jefferson to Elizabeth Wayles Eppes, [Oct. 3?, 1782], in Boyd et al., Papers, 6:198-99.

33. "Reminiscences of Th. J. by MR"; Jefferson to Elizabeth Wayles Eppes, [Oct. 3?, 1782], in Boyd et al., *Papers*, 6:198-99; Jefferson to Chastellux, Nov. 26, 1782, in Boyd et al., *Papers*, 6:203; Malone, *Jefferson*, 397-400.

34. "Reminiscences of Th. J. by MR"; J. Smith, "Carysbrook Memoir," 53; Ellen Wayles Randolph Coolidge Diaries, 2:63.

35. Andrew Burstein, *Jefferson's Secrets: Death and Desire at Monticello* (New York: Basic Books, 2005), ch. 8; Annette Gordon-Reed, *Thomas Jefferson and Sally Hemings: An American Controversy* (Charlottesville: University Press of Virginia, 1997), 210-23; Henry Randall to James Parton, June 1, 1868, in Gordon-Reed, *Thomas Jefferson*, 254-55; Joshua D. Rothman, *Notorious in the Neighborhood: Sex and Families across the Color Line on Virginia, 1787-1861* (Chapel Hill: University of North Carolina Press, 2003), 40-41.

36. Martha Jefferson Randolph to Ellen Wayles Randolph Coolidge, [1826?], Virginia Historical Society; Ellen Wayles Randolph Coolidge to Nicholas Trist, September 27, 1826, Coolidge Correspondence; Martha Jefferson Randolph to Margaret Bayard Smith, November 10, 1828, Henley Smith Papers, Library of Congress, box 2; Marc Leepson, *Saving Monticello: The Levy Family's Epic Quest to Rescue the House That Jefferson Built* (New York: Free Press, 2001), 10-27.

37. Bear and Stanton, *Jefferson's Memorandum Books*, 1:391 n.; Martha Wayles Skelton Jefferson to Eleanor Conway Madison, August 8, 1780, in Boyd et al., *Papers*, 3:532-33; Norton, *Liberty's Daughters*, 177-88, 256-94; Linda K. Kerber, *Women of the Republic: Ideology and Intellect in Revolutionary America* (Chapel Hill: University of North Carolina Press, 1980), chs. 7 and 9; Jan Lewis, "The Re-

publican Wife: Virtue and Seduction in the Early Republic," *William and Mary Quarterly*, 3rd ser., 44 (1987): 689–721.

38. Anne Cary Randolph to Jefferson, March 18, 1808, in Betts and Bear, *Family Letters*, 334; J. Smith, "Carysbrook Memoir," 83. On women's cloth making in the era of the War of 1812, see Kierner, *Beyond the Household*, 134–36.

||||||||||||||||||||||||||||||||||||||||||||||||

3

In Franklin's Footsteps

News Carriers and Postboys in the Revolution and Early Republic

Vincent DiGirolamo

American historians have long paid homage to the communication networks that spread the revolutionary fervor necessary to create a new nation. But they usually refer to the process in vague, impersonal terms. Newspapers and pamphlets "circulated in the colonies" or "found their way into the countryside," they say, understating the precarious human exchange it really was. One way to explore this process is to track some of the carriers and postboys who perambulated the city streets and country roads of New England, New York, and Pennsylvania in the late eighteenth and early nineteenth centuries. These forgotten middlemen of journalism left few records, but their lives and labors can be glimpsed in poems, pamphlets, memoirs, local histories, and carriers' addresses—topical verses printed up by newspapers for distribution on New Year's Day. These sources show that carriers and post riders of all ages—including very young boys—played an indispensable role in that world-shaking explosion of letters, literacy, and democracy known as the "print revolution." As both producers and products of this revolution, they helped generate the political tumult that transformed British subjects into American citizens.[1]

The term *newsboy,* made famous on the streets of American cities in the late nineteenth and early twentieth centuries, had a related but much broader meaning a century earlier. There were no more than forty newspapers on the continent before the War for Independence. Most were four-page weeklies and none appeared more frequently than triweekly. Their average circulation was six hundred, the minimum an editor needed to survive. Most newspapers were sent through the mails or picked up at print shops. Others were delivered to the homes and offices of their sub-scribers by young apprentices known as printer's devils. Apprenticeship was by no means the only system of labor utilized in the distribution of newspapers. News carrying was also casual paid employment, as indicated by an advertisement in the *New York Mercury* in 1761 for a "nice boy" to deliver papers to city patrons two hours every Monday morning. Such side-work was commonly performed by servants who hired themselves out with their masters' permission.[2]

Although most carriers' addresses refer to their bearers as boys—carrier boys, postboys, printer's boys, and newsboys—the word *boy* did not necessarily signify a youth but could refer to an unmarried male in his twenties or a servant of any age. Nevertheless, many addresses spe-cifically identify carriers as "lads," "shavers," or "striplings" and describe them as "small," "bashful," or "callow." One address issued in 1805 begins, "Though in my teens, unskill'd in learned lore"—a rare early reference to the teen years as a distinct stage of life. Other addresses, by contrast, were expressly written for "news-men" and allude to their "sage experience." It is difficult to speculate about the average age of news carriers, but half the population was under sixteen, and the presence of children and adults in the same trade was not uncommon. As in most agrarian societies, chil-dren took on adult responsibilities early. They were expected to contrib-ute to the family livelihood by seven, enter college at thirteen, and begin military training at sixteen. Youth was defined more by one's social and economic dependence than by years lived.[3]

Yet clearly many were boys or young men in spirit, if not age. Benjamin Franklin, who had delivered newspapers as a printer's devil in the 1720s, wrote a carriers' address nearly twenty years later, when he was editor of the *Pennsylvania Gazette*, that did not praise his carriers' dedication, as was customary, but suggested they were preoccupied with youthful di-versions such as games, gossip, and girls. He called his carriers "*stripling Tatlers*," who between

> Their Sports on Pavements, & those on the Green,
> Pick up a Thousand Tidings by the way . . .
> Next them, and scarce a single Step behind
> Are *Betty, Molly, Susy*, unconfin'd.[4]

Franklin placed his carriers among a cheeky "Errand-Class" whose la-bor blended easily into leisure. Indeed, the life of a printer's devil was not

all ink and toil. Isaiah Thomas, who became a printer's helper and occasional peddler of ribald ballads as a six-year-old in Boston in 1755, nevertheless found time to play at the shore, hunt wild fowl, and later raise a
ruckus with other youths at the annual Gunpowder Plot celebration. The
bill of indenture his mother had signed forbade him from playing cards
or dice, frequenting taverns or alehouses, or committing fornication, but
such behavior obviously was common enough to require proscription.[5]

While it is tempting to distinguish carriers from post riders, the two are
not easy to tell apart. Carriers generally distributed newspapers on foot
in the towns where they were printed, while post riders delivered them
farther afield, often traveling by horse, wagon, or stage. Some post riders dealt exclusively in newspapers, while others also carried mail, which
consisted mainly of papers. They might work for postmasters, for printers,
or directly for subscribers. Carriers might contract with subscribers, but
they were usually hired by—or apprenticed to—master printers. If their
routes took them into rural areas and required a mount, they too might
be called post riders. But delivering papers would be just one of the many
duties spelled out in their bonds of indenture. One apprentice's contract
listed his responsibilities as "riding post, sawing wood, feeding pigs, and
learning to print." The latter task involved everything from sweeping the
floor and tending the fire to washing forms and wielding ink balls.[6]

In addition to newspapers, colonial printers issued a barrage of fiery
tracts, hard-hitting pamphlets, and anonymous broadsides as they felt
increasingly aggrieved by imperial powers. In this context the youngest
newsboys and post carriers participated in the swelling outcry against the
English government, perhaps because youths' peddling of seditious material might not incur the full wrath of the crown. If questioned about the
source of their stock, carriers typically replied that it had "dropped from
the moon."[7]

Although he was already an adult in the 1750s, Lawrence Sweeney of
New York City helped newsboys of all ages win reputations for wit and
radicalism. Sweeney delivered the mail and newspapers, specifically the
New York Gazette and Weekly Mercury. He earned the nickname "Bloody
Sweeney" from his habit of calling out the sanguinary details of the
French and Indian War. Sweeney also composed and distributed satiric
pamphlets and addresses. At the height of the Stamp Act crisis in 1765, he
hawked the *Constitutional Courant*, a pamphlet containing several "spirited essays against the obnoxious stamp act."[8]

The Stamp Act imposed a tax on all paper goods, everything from calendars and playing cards to diplomas and marriage licenses. Printers stood to lose much, for they would have to pay duty on the paper they used (one shilling per page) and the advertisements they sold (two shillings), as well as for drawing up articles of apprenticeship, post riders' oaths, and other contracts. Virtually all American newspaper editors opposed the law, and so did their carriers. They felt it would ruin them financially but also objected to the presumption that Parliament could levy taxes on colonists not represented there, a blatant violation of their constitutional rights as Englishmen. Though pragmatic printers took steps to comply with the law, others resisted it. The pamphlet Sweeney distributed in 1765 featured Franklin's "Join or Die" motto and his logo of a snake cut in eight parts representing the colonies. Sweeney was summarily hauled before the New York Council and asked "where that incendiary paper was printed." As instructed, he replied, "At Peter Hassenclever's Iron Works, please your honor." Hassenclever was an entirely innocent iron manufacturer in New Jersey.[9]

Sweeney did not lie low after this brush with the law but issued a "New Year's Ode for the Year 1766, Being actually dictated by Lawrence Swinney, Carrier of News, Enemy to Stamps, a Friend to the Constitution, and an Englishman every Inch." "I am against the Stamp Act," he declared in the first line. "If it takes Place, I'm ruined for ever."[10] Sweeney's declaration reminds us that economic and political rights were indistinguishable to most patriots and that carriers no less than editors weighed in on the issues of the day.

Most carriers came out against the tax in poetry rather than in person. An address issued on behalf of "The News-Boy Who carries the Boston Evening-Post," for instance, bore the title "Vox Populi. Liberty, Property, and No Stamps" (figure 2). The newsboy, embodying the voice of the people, ridicules King George for imposing the Act:

> Say Monarch! Why thy furrow'd brow
> Frown from thy Chariot on us now?

The boy reminds his majesty of the existence of a higher power: "He over King and Senate rules; Oppressors, sometimes, are his Tools." Parliament repealed the act four-and-a-half months after it had gone into effect. Carriers took as much pride in their victory as anyone else in the colonies. In fact, Sweeney achieved a kind of celebrity as a "Vehicle General of News, and Grand Spouter *of* Politics."[11]

The newspaper and pamphlet war erupted into a shooting war in April 1775 when American militia clashed with British soldiers in Massachusetts at Lexington and Concord. But the war of words continued. Newspaper publishers divided into patriot or loyalist camps; there was no middle ground. Many other printers entered the fray and used their presses to inform and persuade their countrymen. Some seventy-five new newspapers appeared and disappeared during the period. All were plagued by paper shortages, unreliable sources, and erratic distribution. Some newspapers introduced midweek supplements called "extraordinaries" to provide late-arriving news and advertisements. Loyalist editors risked mob violence but also enjoyed the benefits of official patronage. James Rivington, for example, supplied four hundred copies of each edition of the *New York Gazetteer* to Massachusetts Governor Thomas Gage for distribution to military personnel and Tory civilians in Boston.[12]

The outbreak of war hastened the development of independent methods of distributing newspapers in the colonies. Up to the war, most subscribers received copies via the Royal Post, which was expensive and liable to ban any publication critical of colonial authorities. The *Boston Gazette* expressed widespread fears when it said, "Our News-Papers, those necessary and important Alarms in Time of public Danger, may be rendered of little Consequence for want of Circulation." Chafing under such "oppressive dictation," the Continental Congress instituted a Constitutional Post—a free mail not intended to generate tax revenues—in 1775 and appointed Benjamin Franklin postmaster general. The British system disintegrated in the face of this competition, and its post riders were discharged for lack of funds. In their stead galloped patriotic American postboys, whose work was deemed so vital that in 1777 the Continental Congress exempted them from military service. Unfortunately, Postmaster General Richard Bache, Franklin's son-in-law and successor, failed to establish an effective postal network during the war, which forced army commanders George Washington and Nathanael Greene to set up their own teams of post riders to keep communication lines open.[13]

As the war dragged on, some newspaper subscribers offset the unreliability of the post by forming "clubs," "companies," or "classes" and distributing their papers on a cooperative basis. Their children sometimes helped out. In 1780, Isaiah Thomas's brother in Lancaster, Massachusetts, secured fifty-two subscribers to the *Massachusetts Spy*, which they took

Mr. *Lawrence Sweeny*, Efq;
Vehicle General *of* News, and Grand Spouter *of* Politics, *to his humble Petitioners, this* New-Year's *Morning, One o'Clock*, P. M. 1769. Sheweth :

BY St. Patrick *!* with Bawling and Squalling along,
Poor Sweeny has filenc'd the Noife of his Tongue ;
But zounds tho' he *fpeak* not, he thinks, d'ye' hear
To *whifper* fome Trifles *aloud* in your Ear.
> Sing, *Balinamona ora, a fight of your Purfes for me.*

Arrah Joy ! you will pity poor me from your Soul,
If your Hearts are not *frozen* quite up to a *Coal*;
By my Shoul ! to the *Bone*, Sirs ! I've worn out my *Shoes*,
With *walking* on *Horfeback* to bring you the News.
> Sing, *Balinamona ora, the found of the* ready *for me.*

T'other *Morn*, as at *Supper* I merrily fate,
A *fcratching* my *Fingers*, and *biteing* my *Pate*,
Says my Landlady, " Sweeny ! I care not a Souce,
" When you're *out* wether ever you're *into* my Houfe."
> Sing, *Balin. &c. a dumb, dumb Woman for me.*

Honey deareft ! faid I,---tho' my Pocket this Minute
Is *empty*, you're welcome to *every Groat in it* ;
But I've Friends *dead* in *Dublin* who *live* in *this Pliafhe*
That *next New-Year* fhall make your *Heart leap* in your *Faifhe.*
> Sing, *Balin. &c. your Irifh Hearts for me.*

But perhaps my *fweet Folks !* you're fuch *four* Politicians,
You've no Humour to ponder on Sweeny's Petitions ;
---But hearken one Moment---you'll quarrel fo long,
That you'll *never* be *right*, till you find you are *wrong.*
> Sing, *Balin. &c. your good-natur'd Faces for me.*

Before I was *born* in the dear *Irifh Nation*,
I never faw *here* fuch a queer *Baderation*,
Such *Murder* of *Ink*, and fuch *Blood-fhed* of *Paper*,
It makes all the *Brains* in my *Belly* to caper.
> Sing, *Balin. &c.* no Fighting *nor* Biteing *for me.*

Figure 2 "Carriers' Address—Vox Populi," issued by Lawrence Sweeney, who styled himself "Vehicle General of News, and Grand Spouter of Politics." "Carrier's Address—Vox Populi. Liberty, Property, and No Stamps," Boston, 1765, American Antiquarian Society, BDSDS 1765. Credit: Courtesy of the American Antiquarian Society.

turns fetching in Worcester, sixteen miles away. When it was his turn he mounted his eight-year-old son Alexander on horseback and sent him off on the two-day journey.[14]

Newspapers were rarely hawked on the streets at this time. Down-on-their-luck printers occasionally peddled their wares, but they were roundly denounced for stooping so low. Reputable printers required the steady patronage of subscribers and did not expect random pedestrians to part with hard coin for papers they could read and discuss freely in taverns and coffeehouses. One exception occurred shortly after New York fell to the British in 1776. The artist Charles Willson Peale recalled hearing a boy known as "pegged-legged Jemmy M'Coy" stumping through the streets of Philadelphia shouting, "Here is your bloody news! Here is your fine, bloody news!" M'Coy may have been America's first disabled newsboy; a long line would follow in his crooked footsteps.[15]

The number and circulation of newspapers multiplied after the war, and so did their carriers. In 1786, the *Salem Gazette* hired boys to deliver the weekly paper to the homes of subscribers while other employees collected payment. This practice soon became widespread. In 1789, John Fenno, publisher of the *Gazette of the United States* in New York, claimed circulation in all twelve states of the Union, as well as in Canada, the West Indies, and Europe. "This intense circulation renders it a proper vehicle for Advertisements of a general, commercial and governmental import," he told readers.[16]

Postal acts passed in the 1790s fostered an expansion of the press by setting cheap postage rates for newspapers and allowing editors to exchange papers among themselves for free. In 1790, the year of Franklin's death, there were ninety-two papers—including eight dailies—in sixty-two towns, which accounted for about 70 percent of the mail by weight but for only 3 percent of the postage. Letter carriers were now hired on a small scale and worked mainly on commission. The carriers' address of the *New-York Weekly Museum* for 1790 features one of the first woodcuts of a newsboy. It depicts a flamboyantly capped carrier in a long coat handing a paper to a person leaning through the doorway of a house on a tidy street. The carrier is of indeterminate age, but the accompanying verse identifies him as the printer's devil.[17]

Women also carried papers in the early republic, as is evident in the carriers' address of the *American Telegraphe* in Newfield, Connecticut, in 1799:

> To you, generous patrons, see Polly appear,
> To congratulate you on the birth of the year.
> A song—a mixture of humor and folly,
> At a season like this, is expected from Polly.
> For carriers must sing, whether female or male,
> On New Year's Day, or their purses will fail.[18]

The fact that some addresses were "Humbly adress'd to the Gentle-men and Ladies" suggests that women were also readers of newspapers and potential tippers of carriers. The vast majority of white women in the colonies and early republic were literate, and, judging from the con-tent of newspapers—the letters, poems, and articles addressing domestic concerns—they probably perused the papers that came into their homes. Nevertheless, they and Polly were interlopers in the affairs of men. In pro-ducing, distributing, and even reading newspapers, women entered an implicitly masculine public sphere.[19]

By 1800 the number of newspapers in America had risen to 235, of which twenty-four were dailies. Ten years later the total topped 350, and by 1820 it had reached 512. This proliferation prompted observers to dub America "a nation of newspaper readers." The English traveler John Lam-bert marveled at the cheapness and availability of American newspapers, noting that "there is scarcely a poor owner of a miserable log hut, who lives on the border of the stage road, but has a newspaper left at his door." Lambert's visit in 1808 coincided with the expanded use of stagecoaches, yet he pointed out that readers who were on the stage line sometimes had to satisfy themselves with papers that agreed with the politics of their coachman. One of the drivers he encountered "happened to be a federal-ist" and refused to cater to the Democratic-Republicans on his route. "No sooner did he blow his horn than up scampered men, women, and chil-dren to the coach, eagerly begging for their favourite paper," said Lam-bert. "If they wanted a democratic one, they must either take a federalist, or go without. He had a few of the others with him, but he never would deliver them if he could avoid it."[20]

Few coachmen abused their power so blatantly as Lambert's driver, but his partisanship reminds us that the distribution of newspapers re-mained a highly political and idiosyncratic activity in the early republic. Under such conditions, most printers continued to rely upon their own apprentices to circulate their papers. And, given their low or nonexistent earnings, most apprentices still looked forward to the gratuities they received on New Year's Day. Among them was Joseph T. Buckingham, who carried the *Greenfield Gazette* in western Massachusetts as a seventeen-year-old in 1797. "Being the youngest apprentice," he wrote in his memoirs, "it was a part of my duty, on publication days, to distribute the Gazette to the subscribers living in the village, the number of which amounted to no more than thirty or thirty-five. According to time-indefinite custom, I had a New-Year's Address, with which to salute my customers. It was written by an acquaintance, about my own age, and a clerk in a store at Guilford, Vt. It consisted of five stanzas of six lines each; but, though short, it was rich in patriotic sentiment, and expressions of regard for the patrons of the Gazette."[21]

The poem apparently struck the right note. Buckingham was ecstatic over the proceeds: "SIX DOLLARS AND SEVENTY-FIVE CENTS,—all in quarters and eighths of a dollar. . . . Never before had I been the owner of so much money,—never before so rich."[22]

Buckingham's windfall presented him with a new dilemma—What to do with the money? "I was sadly puzzled," he admitted, "to decide how I should employ my cash; for my wants were so numerous that the amount, *large as it was*, was altogether inadequate to supply them." Buckingham knew poverty. His father—a shoemaker, tavern keeper, and revolutionary war veteran—had died when he was three years old, leaving ten children and considerable debt. The family broke up and his mother went on the public dole. Buckingham was placed with a farm family until the age of sixteen, when he began his apprenticeship with the publisher of the *Greenfield Gazette*. Buckingham was to receive $5 a year for shoes and "a certain fixed price for all the work done over the prescribed daily task." That extra work never materialized, however, and the only cash he and the two other apprentices earned was by printing up ballads and small pamphlets for peddlers, who he said were "tolerably good customers to country printers." Here we catch a glimpse of an indigenous shadow economy in ephemeral literature produced with or without the wink of the master. Even with this income, "before the first winter expired, my wardrobe was in a most degenerate condition," said Buckingham. His tips thus went toward a new hat, a pocket handkerchief, a cravat, and a pair of stockings, purchased partly on credit.[23]

Buckingham's attention to appearance was not just a symptom of his youth but a concern common to his trade, as indicated by the well-clad newsboy pictured on the carriers' address of the *New-York Weekly*

Museum. Post riders also enjoyed reputations as fancy dressers whose tastes defied traditional sumptuary standards. Some devised elaborate uniforms to convey the dignity of their positions. Mr. Martin, a post rider in New Jersey in the 1780s, for example, wore a military-like "blue coat with yellow buttons, a scarlet waistcoat, blue yard stockings, and a red wig topped by a cocked hat." He may have made some of his clothes himself, for he liked to knit as he rode horseback from office to office.[24]

Decent clothes required a decent income. Young Eber Howe's escalating stipend as an apprentice and post rider at the *Buffalo Gazette* beginning in 1816 rose from $40 to $80 per year. This was more money than he made as publisher of the *Cleveland Herald* in 1819. Howe distributed the *Herald* himself on horseback to three hundred subscribers, some of whom paid him in corn whiskey. Other post riders reported being paid in butter, cheese, and poultry. Many supplemented their incomes by running errands for their subscribers or holding other jobs or offices. Joseph Alward bore the double honor of constable of Willink, New York, and carrier of the *Erie County Gazette*. But he betrayed both trusts in 1811 when he absconded to Canada, taking two horses, a clutch of watches, and other property, for which the *Gazette* denounced him as "a delinquent and a villain." The post rider who was most adept at diversifying his income was William "Extra Billy" Smith, future governor of Virginia. He started out as a mail carrier in Culpepper County in the 1820s and soon acquired the route to Washington, D.C. His government contract allowed him to take on "extra" jobs, which became so numerous and remunerative they became the focus of an 1834 congressional inquiry.[25]

Post riders were generally allowed to keep half of the subscription price, which averaged $2 a year in the early 1800s. A route of one hundred subscribers, then, might generate an annual income of $100. Nonpaying subscribers were a real problem, however. Some post riders were authorized to collect subscription payments, but they were notoriously slow to turn over their receipts. Consequently, printers or their agents often accompanied post riders on their collection tours, especially those who were minors or otherwise untrustworthy.

African Americans served as pressmen and post riders in early America, but under more trying conditions than whites. Isaiah Thomas remembered meeting an "African" slave named Primus who had worked fifty years for his master in Boston and Portsmouth, New Hampshire, and a free black named Andrew Cain who was employed by a printer in Philadelphia. Thomas Fleet employed three African Americans in his print shop, including Black Peter, who delivered the *Boston Evening-Post* and earned enough during his lifetime to leave his son a "small property."[26]

Ironically, the immediate and gradual abolition of slavery in northern states at the start of the nineteenth century helped doom the practice of indentured servitude that had long frustrated apprentices and other bound workers. As slaveholders in the North tried to indenture their former bondservants rather than free them outright, state legislators and judges increasingly held that all forms of bonded labor were illegal, except in the case of immigrants and debtors. Minors, too, could be indentured as apprentices or servants in Massachusetts and New York. But free labor, defined in opposition to slavery and indentured servitude, gradually became the norm. Unlike their forerunners, newsboys in the early republic would enjoy the right to quit their jobs.[27]

The War of 1812 gave carriers and post riders a new opportunity to demonstrate that their courage matched that of their revolutionary forebears. Fought in part over British impressments of American sailors and seizure of American ships, this second war for independence reminded Americans that commerce was the source of enterprise, progress, and liberty. News carriers embodied these attributes, especially those who worked in the two theaters of war along the Great Lakes and Atlantic seaboard.

One such carrier was Paul Drinkwater, who delivered the *Buffalo Gazette* to American settlers in Upper Canada. The area lacked mail service until he fixed up a route from "a little village called Buffalo" to the head of Lake Ontario, a distance of some sixty miles, which he traveled once a week. Rumors of war had filtered back and forth across the border, but real news was in short supply until Drinkwater was spotted wading through snow almost to his knees. He stood "six feet four in his stockings" and was "slender out of all proportions," recalled Eber Howe, one of the settlers' sons. He said Drinkwater subsisted on hardtack and cider and offerings of metheglin, a Welsh liquor made from boiled honey and herbs. "His advent and passage through the country was an era of much moment to boys and girls," said Howe.[28]

No less stalwart was Charles O'Conor, who distributed his father's paper, the *Military Monitor*, as an eight-year-old in New York during the war. He walked the length of Manhattan to Harlem every Saturday and then rowed a skiff across the Hudson River to continue his route in Hoboken, New Jersey. O'Conor felt himself a true patriot carrying the anti-British weekly. "Sometimes the publication was delayed," he recalled, "and to get through my circuit of delivery would take all night; but I boldly went up door-steps, chucking papers under the doors; plunged into areas and down through alleyways, fearless of the police and every body, for my bundle of papers was a perfect safeguard, as good to me as the aegis and crested helmet to Hector." O'Conor's reference to the hero of the Trojan War speaks not only to his classical education but also to the persistent glorification of carriers during times of war.[29]

Although their role in delivering war news and the conditions created by the war added drama and a sense of urgency to the lives of the boys and men delivering newspapers, their work was not without challenges in peacetime. Like booksellers, they could be punished for any libels contained in the works they distributed. American law, drawing on English common law, explicitly stated that there were two modes of libel—*traditone,* setting it in type and handing it out, and *verbus aut cantilenis,* reading or singing it in the presence of others. A screed against peddlers and post riders published in Dover, Delaware, in 1817 put the case more boldly: "He that utters, that is to say, that circulates the devil's nods, winks, peeps, puns, whispers, letters, way-bills, shrugs, ughs, whews! and the whole circulating medium of his bank notes and joint funds of defamation, is an accessory in slander."[30]

There was no real publishing center in the United States in the early 1800s, although the urbanizing Northeast obviously enjoyed an advantage over the sprawling, rural South. Influential newspapers flourished in Worcester, Massachusetts, Hartford, Connecticut, and Portsmouth, New Hampshire, and they circulated far and wide because of the expansion of roads and canals. No region prospered more during this period than central New York. The building of the Erie Canal brought prosperity to this backwater. Commerce was the lifeblood of the region, and even the smallest villages boasted their own newspapers. Yet many subscribers still lived in remote hamlets or farmsteads. Post riders helped rescue them from their isolation. Nothing shattered the dull routine in rural communities like the blare of the postboy's horn (figure 3). The boys were required by law to announce their arrival in this way to ensure that they did not slip quietly into town and favor any one party with a preliminary peek inside the public pouch. The post rider's horn was thus an instrument of democracy, its blast the sound of egalitarian ideals.

Historians often observe that communication was slow in early America because news traveled only as fast as a person could walk, ride, or row. They point out that it took a post rider two days to travel from New York to Philadelphia, a week to go from New York to Boston, and a fortnight

Figure 3 Postboys were required by law to blow their horn upon entering a town. Woodcut from the banner of the *American Weekly Mercury* (Philadelphia), January 28–February 4, 1741–42. Credit: Courtesy of the American Antiquarian Society.

to reach the southern states—and even longer in winter when roads were bad. But speed is relative; Americans in the early republic were more often astonished that newspapers arrived at all than that they were slow in coming. John Greenleaf Whittier captured the sheer wonder of a world glimpsed through weeks-old newspapers in his poem "Snow Bound":

> At last the floundering carrier bore
> The village paper to our door
> . . . .
> In panoramic length unrolled
> We saw the marvels that it told
> . . . .
> We felt the stir of hall and street,
> The pulse of life that round us beat;
> The chill embargo of the snow
> Was melted in the genial glow;
> Wide swung again our ice-locked door,
> And all the world was ours once more![31]

Relatively few carriers wrote memoirs later in life, but their accounts reveal much about the perils and pleasures of the trade they pursued as youngsters during the early years of the United States. Consider the experiences of two of them: Orsamus Turner and Anson Spencer.

Turner, a young printer's apprentice, covered a backwoods route near Palmyra, New York. He hit the trail in 1818 when his master ordered him to clerk for a blind newspaper carrier. "It was a most unpromising region of log cabins, stinted improvements, of chills and fevers," he recalled. "The owls hooted from tops of the hemlock trees, wolves howled, and foxes barked in the dark forests; the saucy hawk would be perched upon trees in close proximity with solitary log cabins, ready to pounce upon truant chickens that strayed a few rods from the coop before the door." Turner returned thirty years later and marveled at the comfort, luxury, and abundance of the region. He confessed to one resident, "I used to pity you that were obliged to live here; now I almost pity those that cannot."[32]

In nearby Ithaca, Anson Spencer served the first two years of his apprenticeship in 1820 and 1821 as a newsboy and post rider. He carried newspapers, mail, and free little broadsides called "dodgers." He usually traveled in a one-horse wagon, but if the roads were bad he went on horseback. He, too, passed through remote villages that would be transformed by the opening of the Erie Canal in 1825. He recalled traveling "through Enfield to Burdette in Hector; thence down the lake to 'Peach Orchard' (North Hector); thence across 'Hector's Back Bone' to Reynold-slow (Trumansburgh); thence home on the turnpike, through 'Harlow's Corners' (Jacksonville)." These precisely remembered routes allow us to hear the pride these youths felt in living up to their responsibilities in the mixed-aged world of work. They also enable us to see not just the pace and price of progress in the area but what historian William Gilmore calls the "otherwise invisible web of market connections." The newspapers carried by men and boys were at once products of and stimulants to the growing market economy.[33]

However lonesome or arduous the work, most post riders looked back on it fondly, as it permitted much freedom from supervision and opportunity for social intercourse. Take as a final example the case of apprentice printer Franklin S. Mills of West Chester, Pennsylvania, who served his first two years of indenture from 1826 to 1828 distributing newspapers on horseback. He covered a route through Chester, Berks, and Lancaster counties, which took him three to five days every week. Mills recalled being greeted as a minor celebrity in small towns and villages. Blowing his horn always brought out the townsfolk and inspired this anonymous verse:

> Here comes the herald of a noisy world,
> With spattered boots, strapped waist and frozen locks;
> News from all nations lumbering at his back.[34]

Rural postboys, even more than city news carriers, were agents of the spoken word as well as the written word. Wherever the postboy stopped for lunch or stayed the night, neighbors would assemble to receive their letters and papers and to pepper him with questions about current events. Mills felt himself an honored guest at apple-paring, corn-husking, and sleighing parties. "It may be a weakness," he said, "but I still remember the pleasant glances of country lasses, who would go some distance to meet the post-boy around the ample social fire to chat with him about the town folks, and what they did and how they lived."[35]

Delivering papers, in addition to all else, was still a good way for boys to meet girls. Not much had changed in this regard since Franklin's "*stripling Tatlers*" had tarried with the errand girls of Philadelphia. But in other ways much had changed. America was no longer a colonial outpost but a sovereign nation, and not an "infant nation," to use a common phrase, but one in the full vigor of youth. The political order that pitted Federalists against Democratic-Republicans had crumbled following the Federalists' opposition to the War of 1812, but a new party system was on the horizon. Meanwhile, the agriculture-based mercantile economy of the early republic was giving way to a more dynamic and diversified boom-and-bust market economy, which led to the decline of apprenticeship as a viable labor system. Last but not least, newspapers were no longer exotic luxuries but common necessities.

Carriers and post riders from Lawrence Sweeney, Alexander Thomas, Jemmy M'Coy, Polly, Joseph Buckingham, and Eber Howe to "Extra Billy," Black Peter, Charles O'Conor, Orasmus Turner, Anson Spencer, and Franklin Mills helped bring about these changes by uniting a people who were separated geographically but also by age, culture, and class. America's first newsboys were indentured servants and independent tradesmen who blurred the lines between childhood and adulthood; they were inheritors of an oral tradition who physically ushered in a modern written one; and they were both agents and symbols of the shift from an old politics of deference to an emerging one of equality. Some also happened to be scoundrels, but they too helped define the evolving relationship between capitalism and democracy.

NOTES

I wish to thank the staff of the American Antiquarian Society (AAS) for their aid in researching this essay and Peter Benes, James Marten, April Masten, and John Murrin for their comments on earlier drafts.

1. Jeanne Boydston et al., *Making a Nation: The United States and Its People*, (Upper Saddle River, NJ: Prentice Hall, 2002), 1:325; Gary Nash et al., *The American People: Creating a Nation and a Society*, brief 4th ed. (New York: Longman, 2003), 120.

2. Alfred McClung Lee, *The Daily Newspaper in America: The Evolution of a Social Instrument* (New York: Macmillan, 1937), 25–26.

3. David Everett, *Farmer's Cabinet* (Amherst, NH, 1805), and "The news-man's address to his kind and generous benefactors, the subscribers to the New-York Mercury" (1765), Nos. 476 and 73 in *A Checklist of American Newspaper Carriers' Addresses, 1720–1820*, comp. Gerald T. McDonald, Stuart C. Sherman, and Mary T. Russo (Worcester, MA: American Antiquarian Society, 2000), 68, 10; "The Verses Of the News-Carrier, of the Daily Advertiser, To his Customers on the New Year, 1790," in *American Broadside Verse: From Imprints of the 17th and 18th Centuries*, ed. Elizabeth Winslow (New Haven: Yale University Press, 1930), 211.

4. David A. Copeland, *Colonial American Newspapers: Character and Content* (Cranbury, NJ: Associated University Presses, 1997), 154, 275; Clarence S. Brigham, *Journals and Journeymen: A Contribution to the History of Early American Newspapers* (Philadelphia: University of Pennsylvania Press, 1950), 20–21; Benjamin Franklin, "The Yearly Verses of the Printer's Lad," January 1, 1739, in Brigham, *Journals and Journeymen*, 93.

5. Clifford K. Shipton, *Isaiah Thomas: Printer, Patriot and Philanthropist, 1749–1831* (Rochester, NY: Printing House of Leo Hart, 1948), 3–5; W. J. Rorabaugh, *The Craft Apprentice: From Franklin to the Machine Age in America* (New York: Oxford University Press, 1986), 16–31.

6. Milton Hamilton, *The Country Printer* (New York: Columbia University Press, 1936), 31–32.

7. Isaiah Thomas, *The History of Printing in America* (1810; repr., New York: Weathervane Books, 1970), 524; Carl Bridenbaugh, *Cities in Revolt: Urban Life in America, 1743-1776* (New York: Knopf, 1955), 186.

8. Lawrence Sweeney, *New Year's Verses* (New York: William Weyman, 1762), Shipton & Mooney 41767; I. Thomas, *History of Printing*, 524.

9. Francis G. Walett, "The Impact of the Stamp Act on The Colonial Press," in

Newsletters to Newspapers: Eighteenth-Century Journalism, ed. Donovan H. Bond and W. Reynolds McLeod (Morgantown: School of Journalism, West Virginia University, 1977), 157–69; Edmund S. Morgan and Helen M. Morgan, *The Stamp Act Crisis* (Chapel Hill: University of North Carolina Press, 1953); I. Thomas, *History of Printing,* 524–25; Frederic Hudson, *Journalism in the United States, from 1690 to 1872* (New York: Harper and Brothers, 1873), 119. Hudson misidentifies him as Samuel Sweeney.

10. Lawrence Sweeney, "New Year's Ode for the Year 1766," New York, 1765, Shipton & Mooney 41663.

11. "Carrier's Address—Vox Populi. Liberty, Property, and No Stamps," Boston, 1765, AAS, BDSDS 1765; Lawrence Sweeney, "Mr. Lawrence Sweeny, Esq; Vehicle General of News, and Grand Spouter of Politics . . . ," New York, 1769, Shipton & Mooney 42008, American Antiquarian Society (AAS), BDSDS 1769.

12. Copeland, *Colonial American Newspapers,* 350 n. 11. On the origins of the term *extra,* see James B. McMillan, "Historical Notes on American Words," *American Speech* 21 (October 1946): 179; Arthur M. Schlesinger, *Prelude to Independence: The Newspaper War on Britain, 1764–1776* (New York: Knopf, 1958), 222.

13. *Boston Gazette,* May 2, 1774. In 1774, William Goddard, printer of the *Maryland Journal,* complained that the post office had charged him fifty-two pounds sterling to carry 350 papers 130 miles. "Our Post-Office," *New Englander and Yale Review* 6 (July 1848): 403; Lee, *Daily Newspaper in America,* 27; Schlesinger, *Prelude to Independence,* 190–95; U.S. Continental Congress, *In Congress,* May 12, 1777; Richard R. John, *Spreading the News: The American Postal System from Franklin to Morse* (Cambridge, MA: Harvard University Press, 1995), 27.

14. Hamilton, *Country Printer,* 222; E. S. Thomas, *Reminiscences of the Last Sixty-Five Years* (Hartford, CT: Case, Tiffany, and Burnham, 1840), 2:4–5.

15. *Pennsylvania Evening Post* editor Benjamin Towne, who became a Tory the minute redcoats occupied Philadelphia, exposed himself to further scorn in the 1780s when he took to printing and peddling occasional handbills entitled "All the News, for two coppers." Later, Richard Folwell, founder of the *Spirit of the Press* in Philadelphia, gained notoriety and a "scanty pittance" when he "hawked his paper about the streets himself." He died penniless and received a proper burial only after a collection was taken up at a local coffeehouse. See I. Thomas, *History of Printing,* 399–400; Clarence S. Brigham, ed., "William McCulloch's Additions to Thomas's History of Printing," *Proceedings of the American Antiquarian Society* 31 (April 1921): 103; and Charles Coleman Sellers, *Charles Willson Peale,* vol. 1, *Early Life, 1741–1790* (Philadelphia: American Philosophical Society, 1947), 136.

16. *Gazette of the United States,* December 2, 1789, n.p., cited in Willard Grosvenor Bleyer, *Main Currents in the History of American Journalism* (Boston: Houghton Mifflin, 1927), 107.

17. Lee, *Daily Newspaper in America,* 711; Jeffrey L. Pasley, *"The Tyranny of Printers": Newspaper Politics in the Early American Republic* (Charlottesville: University

Press of Virginia, 2001), 48–49; Richard Kielbowicz, *News in the Mail: The Press, Post Office, and Public Information, 1700–1860s* (Westport, CT: Greenwood Press, 1989), 102; "Verses from the year 1790," *New-York Weekly Museum*, AAS 1790, in McDonald, Sherman, and Russo, *Checklist*, No. 259, 35.

18. "Address of the carrier of the American Telegraphe to its patrons," January 1, 1799, in McDonald, Sherman, and Russo, *Checklist*, No. 369, 51, viii.

19. "The News-Boy's Verses at the Conclusion of the Year 1757," AAS BDSDS 1757.

20. Charles E. Clark, "Early American Journalism: News and Opinions in the Popular Press," in *A History of the Book in America*, vol. 1, *The Colonial Book in the Atlantic World*, ed. Hugh Amory and David D. Hall (New York: Cambridge University Press, 2000), 361; Lee, *Daily Newspaper in America*, 711; Carol Sue Humphrey, *The Press of the Young Republic, 1783–1833* (Westport, CT: Greenwood Press, 1994), 135; Edwin Emery, *The Press and America: An Interpretive History of the Mass Media*, 5th ed. (Englewood Cliffs, NJ: Prentice Hall, 1972), 135. One collector counts 582 newspapers in 1820 and says that between 1704 and 1820 1,634 newspapers "came to life and died," which suggests that news carriers were not such rare specimens. R. J. Brown, "Colonial American Newspapers," www.historybuff.com/library/refcolonial.html,accessed April 4, 2004; Robert A. Gross, "The Print Revolution," in *Encyclopedia of American Cultural and Intellectual History*, ed. Mary Kupiec Cayton and Peter W. Williams (New York: Scribners, 2001), 1:274; John Lambert, *Travels in Lower Canada, and the United States of North America, in the years 1806, 1807, & 1808*, 2nd ed. (London: C. Cradock and W. Joy, 1814), 2:498–99.

21. Joseph T. Buckingham, *Personal Memoirs and Recollections of Editorial Life* (Boston: Ticknor, Reed, and Fields, 1852), 1:26–27.

22. Ibid.

23. Ibid.

24. John, *Spreading the News*, 18.

25. Eber D. Howe, *Autobiography and Recollections of a Pioneer Printer* (Painesville, OH: Telegraph Steam Printing Press, 1878), reprinted in *Publications of the Buffalo Historical Society* 9 (1906): 3–19, 403; Brigham, *Journals and Journeymen*, 26; Crisfield Johnson, *Centennial History of Erie County, New York* (Buffalo, NY: House of Matthews and Warren, 1876), 199; John W. Bell, *Memoirs of Governor William Smith of Virginia, His Political, Military, and Personal History* (New York: Moss Engraving, 1891), 96–98, 103.

26. I. Thomas, *History of Printing*, 128; Charles E. Clark, *The Public Prints: The Newspaper in Anglo-American Culture, 1665–1740* (New York: Oxford University Press, 1994), 199, 201.

27. Robert J. Steinfeld, *The Invention of Free Labor: The Employment Relation in English and American Law and Culture, 1350–1870* (Chapel Hill: University of North Carolina Press, 1991), 137–38.

28. Howe, *Autobiography and Recollections,* 378.

29. *New York Herald,* October 1869, cited in Hudson, *Journalism,* xxxiv–xxxv.

30. Brigham, *Journals and Journeymen,* 57; Allan R. Pred, *Urban Growth and the Circulation of Information: The United States System of Cities, 1790–1840* (Cambridge, MA: Harvard University Press, 1973), 12–17; "The indictment, trial, and punishment of the Devil's pedlars, postriders, traders, and receivers of slander, by a lover of whole bones" (Dover, DE, 1817), 46, AAS.

31. John Greenleaf Whittier, *The Complete Poetical Works of John Greenleaf Whittier* (Boston: Houghton, Mifflin, 1894), 293.

32. Orasmus Turner, *History of the Pioneer Settlement of Phelps & Gorham's Purchase, and Morris' Reserve* (Rochester, NY: W. Alling, 1851), 400.

33. J. K. Selkreg, ed., *Landmarks of Tomkins County, New York* (Syracuse: D. Mason, 1894), 123; William J. Gilmore, *Reading Becomes a Necessity of Life: Material and Cultural Life in Rural New England, 1750–1835* (Knoxville: University of Tennessee Press, 1989), 85.

34. F. S. Mills, "The Post-Boy," Minutes of the 29th Annual Meeting of the Editorial Association of the State of New Jersey, Trenton, NJ, 1885, 16.

35. Ibid., 18.

Part II

Finding a Place to Belong
Raising Ideal Children

Much of Lucy Larcom's memoir deals with the lessons she learned as a child from teachers, ministers, parents, and other family members. The overwhelming feeling one gets is of a creative, interesting, and thoughtful little girl desperately trying to fit into her community, which was rapidly modernizing from its colonial past, and her family, who were hard-pressed for money and unfamiliar with the creative processes already bubbling up in their unusual daughter and sister.

Two passages describing two of Larcom's earliest memories reveal her own belief that she was not like the other children in her family, even as they show that children of the early nineteenth century—at least in the childlike puzzlements they express that so delight adults—were not so different from modern youngsters. "I did firmly believe that I came from some other country to this," Larcom recalled with amusement. She believed in her old age that as a girl she must have had a "vague notion that we were all here on a journey"—that this life was actually a stop along the way to the "place where we really belonged." Her family told her that even before she could speak clear sentences she would sing an eerie little song that went "My father and mother / Shall come unto the land." No one quite knew what it meant, but it was a famous story within her family. Larcom also recalled a time in her life in which she was unclear about whether she was a Gentile or a Jew. Her confusion stemmed from the Bible, in which the former "were not well spoken of." Adults' answers to her questions seemed not to help; at one point she decided that all children must be "heathens," since only adults could be "Christians."[1]

These amusing anecdotes seem superficial, yet they actually reflect those timeless efforts by children to become part of the societies into which they are born. Although some hints of children's points of view surface in the essays in this section, they really focus on the ways in which parents strove to help their children fit into early republican society. Martha Saxton shows how similar goals among the French and American residents of St. Louis led to quite different expectations for their daughters. She also reveals the dark reality that the assumption that elite girls would live specific kinds of lives was based on another assumption: that slave girls were a "necessary" part of those lives. An even more complicated set of child-rearing choices arose when Native Americans and Euro-Americans came together. Andrew Frank explores the culturally hybrid parenting of whites and Creek Indians who intermarried; they tried to honor both traditions without isolating their children from either. The interior relationships described by Saxton and Frank contrast with the very public debates over child rearing in which emerging religious denominations engaged. According to Todd Brenneman, the implementation of religious freedom in the new republic inspired radical sects to multiply, with important ramifications for the lives of the children in those new religions.

NOTE

1. Lucy Larcom, *A New England Girlhood: Outlined from Memory* (Boston: Houghton Mifflin, 1889), 47, 50.

French and American Childhoods
St. Louis in the Early Republic

Martha Saxton

The newly American city of St. Louis in the early years of the nineteenth century offers a unique view of a multicultural assortment of parents as they tried to do their best for their daughters in the young republic. Historians of childhood have described the new republic as a time of heightened and multifaceted anxiety for mothers and fathers raising children in whose hands the future well-being and reputation of the fledgling nation rested. St. Louis provides the opportunity to compare the child-rearing practices and convictions of old French families and of the Anglo-Americans pouring into the Louisiana Territory, who were bringing with them an increasingly unstable and unequal society. It also permits us to examine and try to identify the goals and values of slave parents whose girls served both.[1]

Americans, some with approval and others with distaste, noted that the French placed high value on leisure and pleasure and that their children reflected this. Anglo-Americans, on the other hand, displayed more worry than the French, as they brought with them a more volatile economic and political culture that demanded caution in assessing others and restraint over oneself. They believed that the new republic needed citizens capable of maintaining what the historian of childhood Bernard Wishy called the "distant ideals of 1776." Apart from their differences, however, both sets of parents worked to produce well-behaved, reasonably informed, and presentable daughters, trained to groom intimate relationships. And both found the labor of slave girls indispensable to achieve this end. For their part, slave parents, who were routinely denied control over their own children, tried to prepare their girls for the independence and self-reliance required to survive on their own while serving the many needs of white families.[2]

The cultural mix of early St. Louis highlights the tensions between the nation's ideals for its girls and parents' actual child-rearing practices. It also captures the lived experiences of some of these girls. Prosperous Americans, anxious to shape their girls into mothers embodying the morality of the republic, trained their daughters for emotional and economic dependence, chastity, and a sometimes-stifling self-restraint. French parents trained their girls to tend relationships and to cultivate the social enjoyment in giving and receiving pleasure in sanctioned human connections. Slave parents shared the French and American preoccupation with sustaining relationships but were working against the sometimes overwhelming odds of slavery. Unlike white Americans, they trained their girls for self-reliance. Slave parents found the ideals of 1776 very distant indeed.

Within the broad shared privileges of whiteness and prosperity, and sharing many ideas about what Jacqueline Reinier has called "enlightened child-rearing," Anglo-American and French cultures produced girls with different ideas about pleasure, expressivity, and sociability. Evangelical energy intensified the differences. French families seem to have communicated to their girls a comfortable acceptance of physicality and emotional expression, as well as an appreciation of pleasure for its own sake. Anglo-American girls were trained to more reserve, a distrust of pleasure, and a certain watchfulness in relationships. While the first generation of French and American girls to grow up together in St. Louis seem to have had quite different inner lives, they went to the same schools, learned each other's language, and received a similar education, both intellectual and behavioral. The school training they received in reading, writing, and social skills, particularly in paying careful attention to relationships, would identify them as women of the young country's emerging elite. By the late 1830s, Anglo-American evangelical nativists would condemn Catholicism and old French families would rue the growing Anglo-American numbers, but in the early decades the two groups tolerated and at times even enjoyed each other's differences.[3]

In 1764, French merchant fur traders had founded this multicultural city in which girls of French, American, and African descent would mingle. A few Creole families, dominated by the Chouteaus and the Gratiots, presided over the settlement. When the United States took possession of the city and the Louisiana Territory in 1804, Americans began arriving, a few at first, but soon larger and larger numbers. They found a town with a nucleus of about two hundred French families and a few hundred African American and Indian slaves. The Upper Louisiana Territory had a population of about 10,350, of whom 15 percent were slaves.[4]

The French elite, comfortable with their stable, slow-to-change societal hierarchy, worried about what the American takeover might mean. Indicating the kind of change they feared most of all, their first act as Americans was to enforce a new, tight code of discipline over those restive slaves dreaming that American rule might mean emancipation. After securing slave control, French merchants and land owners worked to firm up their land claims and acquire more land in anticipation of the heated speculation that would begin as settlers began arriving. This competition, however, was restrained by the many family ties of an interconnected, provincial aristocracy, by the tradition of centralized control of the economy, and by a belief in the organic, interdependent nature of hierarchical society. St Louis's unusually democratic, egalitarian social structure and the economic freedom and general prosperity it encouraged produced independent, peaceable colonists, unused to great stratification except for slavery. And since slavery was race based and the French had developed their own brand of racism, the radical subordination of slaves did not challenge white French settlers' security in their superiority.[5]

Slavery under the French and the Spanish was a somewhat more flexible and less absolute institution than it would be under American law. The French did not rely on slave labor for the bulk of their income. Under French rule, the Code Noir gave slave families some protection from the sale of members, and manumission was not uncommon, creating a free black and Native American community that became the nucleus of what would later be called St. Louis's colored aristocracy. With the American takeover, part of Missouri became increasingly dependent on slave labor for the production of tobacco, hemp, and cotton. Protections for keeping slave families intact dissipated (except in Perry County, where there was a strong Catholic presence), and manumission became less frequent, although slaves continued to use the courts to sue for freedom. Missouri made increasing efforts to prevent the growth of the free black community, culminating in the 1830s, when it required bond of $1,000 and a white person to vouch for any free black desiring residency. The growing numbers of slaves in the territory were accompanied by more pervasive racism, and the growing level of brutality required to maintain an increasing number of slaves challenged the customary peace of French St. Louis.

This is emphatically not to argue that the French were "better" slave masters than the Americans; rather, for cultural, demographic, and economic reasons, slavery became more monolithic under the Americans. French ideas about girlhood played out in the context of this small "society with slaves," to quote Ira Berlin.[6]

In the first years of the new republic, the city absorbed large numbers of Americans from the South, the mid-Atlantic, and the Northeast who mingled with the Creole inhabitants who had been there since the eighteenth century as well as a few newcomers escaping the revolutions in France or Haiti. Southern whites often brought slaves with them, and northerners sometimes acquired them there. Americans transformed St. Louis and its hinterland into what Berlin has described as a slave society, although Missouri was only a fully committed slave society in "little Dixie," or the fertile counties running east to west, bordering the Missouri River. Urban slaves, who historically had been as much sacrifices to white ideas of status as to systematic economic exploitation, increased numerically while declining as a percentage of St. Louis's expanding population.[7]

Not surprisingly, American ideas about girlhood diverged from those of their French neighbors. Americans—unlike the French—lived in a society in which competition and conflict were the rule. Arriving white Americans were striving to better themselves in Louisiana Territory through an eye for the main chance, an understanding and ability to manipulate the differences between French and American law, and, sometimes, violence or duplicity. By the 1830s, they had converted a peaceful town where, as one observer wrote, "neighbors pay and return visits: for visiting and talking are so indispensably necessary to a Frenchman . . . that . . . there is not one settler of that nation to be found, whose house is not within reach or within sight of another" into an urban center where economic and political competition routinely produced arguments, brawls, and duels.[8]

American men struggled with one another and with members of the old French elite for status, wealth, and power. Rufus Easton, a member of the St. Louis Land Commissioners, savagely clubbed another member at a meeting in 1806. By the end of his career, Judge John Smith, an emigrant from Tennessee, had killed fourteen men in duels. Democratic Senator Thomas Hart Benton was a dueler, and Thomas Biddle was killed in a duel over President Andrew Jackson's attack on the National Bank, run by his brother, Nicholas. The foremost historian of Saint Louis has written that "eye-gouging fights, cursing and shouting, political arguments, and generally churlish behavior became commonplace on the streets" when the Americans took over St. Louis. Philippine Duchesne, the founder and Mother Superior of the Sacred Heart Convent whose schools taught girls from both French and American families, remarked that the Americans "from a Christian point of view . . . go too far in their passion for knowledge, their personal ambition, and their desire for worldly success."[9]

While religion was a central element in the lives of both French and American girls, American religious experiences could be far more unsettling than those of French Catholics, who generally anticipated the afterlife as a predictable reward for how they lived this one. Evangelical Protestants, who grew in number in early nineteenth-century St. Louis, grasped at salvation in an emotionally charged crisis and thereafter had to pursue a Christian life sufficiently energetic and focused as to quench further flickers of sin or risk falling back into alienation from God and damnation. Watchful piety and attention to the moral condition of oneself and others helped keep fear at bay and salvation in sight. Evangelical ambition could match that of entrepreneurs in intensity and anxiety for success.[10]

However, another kind of change—death, particularly of children— was endemic to both French and American society in the early republic. French and American mothers shared ongoing anxiety over their children's health. As childhood came increasingly to be seen as unique and children as individually precious, mothers in particular appear to have suffered over the loss of their young with new intensity. As historians of childhood have showed, American parents, unlike their French counterparts, also saw physical and moral health as inseparable and charged mothers with the care of both. This added to the pressure mothers felt to infuse their sons and particularly daughters, as future mothers, with concern over their behavior and spiritual state.[11]

Exploring the literature and correspondence of French and American settlers gives us an intimate view into their thinking about their daughters. The evidence that follows derives from a blend of books, letters, and newspapers to suggest, as well as documents can, how French and American parents tried to educate their daughters for their future responsibilities. French settlers had extensive libraries that contained numerous volumes of moral fables, children's literature, and Enlightenment texts. Although we do not know who read them or what relation these texts had to lived experience, this literature reflects the more measured worldly ambitions of the French and their expectations for happiness and connection within a stable social hierarchy whose members placed high value on the pleasures of human connection, pleasures that both transcended

and validated class boundaries. For French Americans, who had not undergone a revolution, society had been stable, the status of families was
not likely to change dramatically over time, and ambition was tempered
by commitments to extended family, the Catholic Church, French culture,
and sociability itself.[12]

One of Arnaud Berquin's stories in his children's magazine, *L'Ami des
Enfants*, published in the very early nineteenth century, celebrates the
friendship between a rich and a poor girl after the wealthy mother first
tests this relationship to make sure that poor Madelon does not love rich
Clementine for her gifts of sweets and pretty clothes. When Madelon,
alone of Clementine's friends, continues to visit and nurse her during a
grave illness, Clementine's mother acknowledges that she is not a child-
adventuress and gratifies her daughter by resuming gifts to Madelon. In
similar stories, young aristocrats befriend and patronize cottagers, creating cross-class bonds of fealty in which the bounty and goodness of the
elite produce rapturous gratitude and loyalty in peasants. In the American colonial context, where differences in status and wealth among white
people had been relatively small and interdependence great, the message
of cross-class interconnectedness and reciprocal affection in these stories
carried a naive promise of pleasure in relationships. French moralists recommended empathy broadly as basic to virtue.[13]

American moralists, on the other hand, advocated a more limited empathy and promised different rewards to those who exercised it. As Lydia
Maria Child wrote in *The Mother's Book*, a classic child-rearing guide in
the early republic, "The poor are apt to be unreasonably suspicious of the
rich; they begin by being cold and proud to their wealthy acquaintance,
for fear the wealthy mean to be cold and proud to them." She also warned
mothers about the bad habits of servants who would corrupt young children's minds with sexual knowledge and other impure ideas. In a society
in which the status of all white people could fluctuate, it required acumen
to know how to treat others. Child advised readers to "measure out to the
rich man, as well as to the poor man, just as much of respect and regard
as their character deserve, and no more." Evangelical Christian language
blended moral appraisal with the calculations of a bank teller.[14]

Democratizing American politics also required that children learn to
distinguish among people and to calibrate their status and value accord-
ingly. William Lane, Democrat, doctor, and first mayor of St. Louis, wrote
to his young daughters who were away at school in Philadelphia a note introducing an acquaintance named Samuel Owens. He described Owens as

a "backwoods gentleman" whom they would "see at once where to place." He continued by saying that with all the "half-bred, & the vulgar" they should adopt a more carefully courteous attitude than with well-bred people or they might "fancy themselves to be overlooked, and are apt to be offended." In the early republic, democracy among white men was expanding along with political equality, but the social inequalities among white people made it urgent for well-to-do parents to train their girls in subtle discernment, if for no other reason than to marry within or above their own rank. At the same time, as Americans and members of a democracy, they also needed to know how to pretend to overlook those gradations and to fake cordiality, so essential to maneuvering tactfully among people of different classes in a society that prided itself on being without class.[15]

Along with the French prescriptive embrace of goodwill across classes came child-rearing advice and practices that emphasized a steady basis of unworried affection and pleasure as the reward for benevolence and virtue. Berquin's *L'Ami des Enfants* includes a story that teaches five-year-old Fanchette about breast-feeding. She hears her new baby brother crying and wants to give him something to eat. Her parents explain that he has no teeth but that God has put milk in their mother's breast to feed him. Fanchette wonders if she drank from her mother's breast as well, and her father tells her that for two years her mother fed her as much as she could, although the little girl often ate very little. While the story's focus is allaying sibling rivalry, it also suggests an ease with discussions of reproduction and the body. Jules de Mun, who came to St. Louis, after escaping not only the revolution in France but also the revolution in Sante Domingue, wrote his wife an imagined scene about his absent family. "I love to picture my pretty Julie on your lap toying with the breast and watching you with her pretty little smile: at your side the big Isabelle caressing her little sister and the mother admiring them both." De Mun's charming portrait of his wife, her body, their daughters, and the affection circulating among all three is notable not only for its comfortable expressiveness but also for its remarkable contrast to the more anxious writings of Americans.[16]

Lydia Maria Child's only mention of breast feeding was a warning that children had expired of convulsions when nursing from mothers who were experiencing "violent passion or emotion." "Who can tell," she asked, "what moral evil may be traced to the states of mind indulged by a mother, while tending to the precious little being who receives everything from her?" *The Mother's Book*, written to impress upon mothers their crucial role in raising moral children to be virtuous citizens in the new United States, also impresses the reader with the terror with which evangelicals imagined the consequences for the nation of thoughtless or impulsive child rearing.[17]

Child advised parents not to indulge flaws like forgetfulness, lest their child develop lifelong bad habits. "If a little girl cannot find her gloves or her bonnet, when you are about to take a walk, oblige her to stay at home. Let no tears or entreaties induce you to excuse it. . . . For your child's sake have resolution enough to do it." If a child who was normally stingy displayed generosity, the parent was to praise him or her "even more than you would think safe under any other circumstances." In the background of this instruction is the notion that praise could be dangerous and should be doled out in cautious quantities, of indeterminate but crucial size, because the good character of one's child would depend on it.[18]

In contrast, Jules de Mun unworriedly wrote his wife about the inevitability of their daughter's taking on "bad little mannerisms." He advised her to be attentive to the problem but warned, "Do not reprove her except with the greatest sweetness and above all never lose your calmness, and . . . she will learn to obey and will love you even more, and if you are obliged to punish her, she will see that it is not from capriciousness or anger, but only that the fault makes you do it." Absent is the urgency that Child communicates, which gives small matters of discipline frightening significance. Instead, de Mun stays focused on sustaining the love between mother and daughter and does not magnify the childish misdeed or view it as potentially derailing the moral and emotional development of the child.[19]

The letters of educated French girls in the early nineteenth century to their friends and family expressed strong bonds of affection, a comfort in expressing a range of emotions, and the girls' enjoyment in describing varieties of pleasure. The common French closing "*Je t'embrasse*" invokes the kiss as a routine expression of affection and confirms its basis in physical warmth. William Lane's daughters ended their letters home with expressions including "I remain your very affectionate child," "Give my love to everybody that you think me worthy asking after," and, most provocatively, "I won't trouble you with any more letters soon, Adieu, my Dear Mother." The Lane girls had an unhappy mother, but even an unambivalently affectionate closing in English did not transform language into bodily warmth as the French did as a matter of course.[20]

Clara Berthold, wrote a friend in 1836, in her piquant English, "What satisfaction it is for me to tell you that I love you, and that you are always present in my mind." The rewards of relationship for Clara were the pleasures of affection. Declaring affection was itself happiness. Clara went on to write about the arrival of her beloved brother. "You cannot conceive the joy I felt in seeing him. I was most crazy. . . . I assure you that we are not lonesome with him, everything is different since that day." Finally she wrote about her pleasure in visiting friends. "We had such fine rides on horse back and eat as many fruits as we desired." Clara's adolescence seems to have been marked by joyous relationships and the satisfaction of many innocent pleasures. These delights bore repeating to others who, she knew, would enjoy them as well, and they had value in themselves simply as pleasures. Emilie de Mun similarly wrote her sister about the very special affection she felt for her to whom she believed she could say anything. She closed, "Goodbye dearest one . . . and believe me your ever devoted & attached."[21]

While insisting that their daughters remain chaste, French parents seem to have permitted them to enjoy more freely the company of the opposite sex than their American counterparts did. The eighteenth-century moralist Jean Marmontel found women's efforts to please men a mark of moral excellence. And the *St. Louis Beacon* published in 1829 the remarks of the Abbe Francois Fenelon, eighteenth-century moralist and writer, endorsing dancing. In St. Louis, the French seemed to have enjoyed openly the pleasures of dance, dress, and flirtation that these writers affirmed. Mme Duchesne, head of the Sacred Heart school and convent, was perhaps the only exception. She wrote with disgust about the ribbons and decorations stitched into the glamorous underclothes of her wealthier students. Emilie de Mun, one of Jules and Isabelle de Mun's daughters, wrote a cousin in 1842 that she had been "very much abused" by St. Louis gossip, although she admitted to having been "wild." She announced that she had changed, although her next sentence makes the reader wonder how much. She asked her cousin to tell their mutual friend, Mr. March, that "she hopes often again to be able to drink eight glasses of champagne with him and try to walk a line on the rug without swaying from side to side." If Emilie de Mun expressed this hope after reforming from wildness, it is exciting to try to imagine what the unreformed Emilie would have hoped for. In any case, she clearly enjoyed many pleasures and intended to go on doing so.[22]

American moralists like Child and Abigail Mott advised adolescent girls to reprimand young men engaged in improper behavior—not to challenge them to drinking contests. As Mott explained, "females" should

"maintain their proper dignity." If they would "discountenance that familiarity which gives confidence to the other sex . . . it would contribute very
much to the improvement of society." American writers charged girls and
women with a special responsibility for wielding reserve and withdrawal,
a particularly burdensome responsibility in a fast-moving, mobile society. These writers lingered on the purity of motives, not the pleasures of
benevolence. As Mott expressed it, "The exercise is the reward [for doing
good], the . . . work is the wages." In other words, the reward for behaving
correctly is the satisfaction of behaving correctly. American moralists did
not take up the possibility of mutual satisfactions.[23]

Indeed, letters from Anglo-American parents suggest that their affection was often tempered by ever-present behavioral and moral anxieties.
William Lane, who appears to have been an affectionate and attentive
father, nevertheless wrote his daughter in 1830 that he desired her to be
"obedient & attentive & defferential to your Ma, kind to your sisters . . .
that you will become as well-bred as my favorite, Miss Von Phul, to whom
I send a kiss." He did not send a kiss to his own child, just the news of his
preference for another girl. Lewis F. Linn (senator from Missouri from
1818 to 1838) wrote one of his daughters, "Father is very anxious to do
well for his children and to see them good, virtuous, religious and happy,
so that gray hairs may not be brought with sorrow to the grave by their
wicked conduct. This I hope you will never forget, when you want to
[do] anything as sinful or bad." Linn's letter was, in the end, about Linn's
anxieties and wishes: his desire to succeed, his desire for his children to
succeed within his moral vision, and his worry that their future conduct
might turn his hair gray and eventually kill him.[24]

The combination of learning to employ restraint as a social duty and
often receiving affection flavored with moral advice seems to have produced sufficient reserve in Anglo-American women as to noticeably in-
hibit some. The behavior of middle-class girls and women seems to have
corresponded to the advice of the moralists. One adolescent girl recorded
her fear of the ease with which some misreported or misunderstood in-
discretion could destroy a woman socially. Her own strategy was to with-
hold sentimental information, to behave prudently, to be vigilant. In her
journal she remarked on "how very careful ought ladies to be—The least
word or look is remembered—there is always someone to catch at any
thing and when least thought of it is remembered." Eliza Ott complained
of living with "too much reserve" between herself and her future sister-in-
law. Mary Sibley, educator and evangelical, wrote that after her husband's

longed-for conversion she went into her room to celebrate—by herself. The *St. Louis Enquirer* published a story entitled "The Evils of Reserve in Marriage" about a husband who dies after a long marriage in which his wife's uncommunicativeness has alienated him. And Sarah Ward, a devout Episcopalian, wrote to a friend, "I think I have written you a full return in quantity for your two letters and can only transcribe myself truly your friend." Ward's accountant-like concern for equivalences appears to restrict the flow of affection.[25]

French and American girls grew up in different emotional climates with somewhat different parental expectations, but they mingled in school in the first decades of American rule. In the early years of the territory, both Anglo-American and Franco-American girls went to the convent schools that Philippine Duchesne founded before St. Louis provided non-Catholic schools other than a few short-lived academies run by Protestants. Not until 1833 did Mary Sibley found Linden Wood, a school for girls ("the first," its nativist Presbyterian founder wrote pugnaciously, "that lifted up the standard of opposition to convent Education in the West . . . of sufficient importance in the eyes of the Arch enemy, to make the Jesuits its traducers"). At Philippine Duchesne's schools, girls learned French and English and acquired an ornamental education that resembled the training of elite eighteenth-century girls more than the utilitarian education for being a helpmeet that Benjamin Rush advocated for republican mothers. Students learned to read and write, do needlework, acquire good penmanship, be orderly and well behaved, and cultivate relationships with one another, the nuns, and absent families.[26]

These first generations of St. Louis girls to be sent to boarding schools were learning to be members of the city's new multicultural elite. The Anglo-American parents of girls were aware of the responsibilities that attended the creation of a uniquely moral nation, and it was in that spirit that Mary Sibley would found Linden Wood. In the meantime, the boarding school experience itself identified girls as virtuous not only by the kinds of knowledge they acquired and the kinds of activities in which they became proficient but also by emotional characteristics: enhanced dependency along with a highly developed attention to relationships. An anxious focus on separation deriving from being away from home shaped these girls' understanding of being female, endowing one of the supposedly natural female priorities with special force.

Among the late eighteenth-century gentry in Great Britain, France, and the United States, the intensity of the experience of relationship, empathy, and feeling for others had come to mark refinement and sensibility. Exhibiting these feelings was one sign of membership in the gentry. In educational institutions girls both learned and experienced a preoccupation with relatedness that would come to be identified with widespread nineteenth-century middle-class attributes like a tender heart, a melting disposition, sweetness, and dependence on the presence and approval of others. As we have seen, parents and moralists also explicitly tutored daughters in the appropriate degrees of confidence with which to cultivate different kinds of intimates.[27]

Girls quickly learned to see the significance of their letters in maintaining relationships and performing properly within them. Their letters reveal mild involvement with or curiosity about their studies. (Sarah Lane, in a letter to their father, wrote that she would "tri to appli my salf to my book.") But the nearly ubiquitous apology for a letter's appearance and excuse for its brevity or poor writing betrays girls' anxiety about letter writing.[28]

Prosperous girls' training in early St. Louis included the ability to display facility in both English and French. Julia de Mun wrote painstakingly that she had not written her father for a long time but that she hoped her "letter . . . will please you . . . because it is in English and I assure you that no person did correct it." Penmanship was also an essential part of the performance in letters. The philanthropist Brian Mullanphy wrote a young relative that "it looks very pretty in a little girl to write a neat & clean hand." He then recounted the story of a young girl living in a small village in France who wrote asking a favor of a wealthy man. "That person was so delighted with the neatness of her letters, that he sent for the young woman and granted her request. In addition to this, he presented her with a handsome portion and gave her away in marriage to a distinguished officer in the army." The importance of a girl's penmanship could not be overestimated.[29]

While girls ritually blamed themselves for being faulty correspondents, behind the excuses was their desire to stay in touch with all those people who constituted and secured their worlds. Distance from home intensified parents' already substantial worries about the health of their children, and children could not have avoided some of those fears themselves. Over and over, the letters reflect their writers' desire for and effort to sustain relatedness. Jane Chambers wrote about hearing from her "dear mother," about her sister Anne's illness, about baby Meziere learning to walk, about hoping her aunts would visit, about a schoolmate who would be visiting

St. Louis, about writing to her sister Ellen, about sending a greeting to a different aunt, and about her intentions to write still another aunt.[30]

Jules de Mun wrote his daughter Louise, complaining that her sisters had not written him. He then expressed the fear that absence always raised. "I hope that you, dear child, will not forget me and that you will write me quite often." Exchanges of phrases of remembrance, so commonplace as to be unnoticed, could suddenly make visible the underlying fragility of relationships when a girl was sent from home. Most people in St. Louis had just arrived and had left people behind. Health along the river was often poor, and lives were often cut short. Absence could mean many things or nothing, but being forgotten or forgetting was a grievous breach.[31]

In their letters, both French and American parents urged girls to nurture an intimate circle of relationships. While French girls seem to have expected more pleasure from those relationships and to have been more at home expressing their emotions than Anglo-American girls, both would grow up trained to create what would become mid-nineteenth-century sentimental culture. This culture confined white middle-class women in a small domestic landscape, ideally one of warm feelings, coziness, and sensitivity, while it excluded most from its trust and intimacies. As one critic has written, sentimental culture encourages "depersonalization of those outside its complex specifications . . . [while] it elaborately personalizes, magnifies, and flatters those who can accommodate its image."[32]

Elite women in the new republic were trained to be artists of relationship and were not to exist outside them. To educate their daughters to take a leading role in this emerging culture of family life, families had to replace their girls' labor with that of a slave or servant. Unable by virtue of their color to "accommodate [the] image" of sentimental culture, slave children worked to make it possible for others. Household help granted white mothers the free time to shape family life around religion, morality, and sensitivity to intimate relationships. This entailed disruption for slave families and confronted slave parents and children with desperate choices about how to stay connected. Nor was this the only bitter irony of the growth of the cult of domesticity in St. Louis. White society exalted in its daughters the very same qualities it systematically denied to black girls: dependence, refined sensibility, modesty and chastity.[33]

American rule had increased segregation of the races in Missouri. While the French dominated St. Louis, Africans were often included in Catholic practice (although the French increasingly discouraged slave marriages to evade the family protections under the Code Noir). Church records document the baptisms and marriages of slaves and free blacks. When the United States took over, evangelical congregations came to include some slaves, but most owners objected even to a Sunday school for slaves. After the United States took over, Catholic officials deferred in their institutional practices to what they described somewhat self-servingly as the rabid race prejudice of Americans. Philippine Duchesne began offering separate, one-day-a-week education to African American girls; otherwise, she wrote, "we should not hold the white children in school." She also wrote that a "Mulatto" desired to enter the convent but that "we may not accept her as a religious." She dreamed of setting up a separate institution for women of color, but she failed to achieve that, and women of color could not achieve the status of sisters, only serve the nuns as domestics.[34]

The market for slave women and children in St Louis prospered in the antebellum period because white elite families considered owning "a girl" crucial to their maintenance and to the education of their daughters. A girl was a female servant, owned or hired, anywhere from age four to sixteen who would do any kind of work, inside or outside the house. If a slave, "a girl" would cost from $350 to $400 and was a particular bargain because male slaves would not do housework.[35]

Because of the high demand for slaves in the deep South, all slaves in the Upper South had a 30 percent chance of being sold away during their lifetime—the highest possibility being when they were between the ages of twelve and twenty-five. In Boone County, Missouri, 30 percent of children under fifteen were sold off. In Callaway County, little girls were sold away from their mothers frequently when they were as young as seven. Mary Bell was hired out by the year to take care of three children starting when she was seven. John Mullanphy noted that he had a four-year-old mulatto girl living with him whom he willed to the Sisters of Charity in the event of his death. George Morton sold to his daughter Ellen "a certain Mulatto girl a slave about fourteen years of age named Sally." The market in children had unique atrocities. A St. Louis trader took a crying baby from its mother, both on their way to be sold, and made a gift of it to a white woman standing nearby because its noise was bothering him. In 1834 in Marion County, north of St. Louis, a slave trader bought three small children from an owner, but the children's mother killed them all and herself rather than let them be taken away.[36]

While the only acceptable context for white girls was in sanctioned relationships to others, the slaveholding world customarily described slaves outside relationships. Jules de Mun wrote that he had been a little extravagant while shopping for slaves in Cuba, picking up both a woman and a *"jolie"* little boy. He never commented on whether or not they were related. In Anglo-American writing about slaves, the adjective *likely* was more common and usually reserved for advertisements selling people, but the silence on relationships was routine for both French and Americans. The family was the only appropriate moral and social context for white girls, and it was by definition isolated from—and morally uncontaminated by—the market.[37]

An advertisement for two runaway slaves in the *St. Louis Enquirer* described Louisa, twelve, and Clara, thirteen, only through unflattering remarks about their appearance. One was "small for her age," and the other was "middle size, African face, heavy built." Clara had "toes somewhat turned inwards and scattering," while Louisa had "slender feet for a negro" and worse, a "bad face and bad expression." Their owner, on the other hand, was described in terms of her present and former relationships. Mrs. Henrietta Jacobs was a "helpless widow" with "three little children." Deft word choice evoked Mrs. Henrietta Jacobs as virtuous, fragile, and needing protection from these delinquent girls connected to no one.[38]

The abbreviated narrative style of advertisements for runaway slaves almost always deprived them of human qualities unless these were useful as markers of identity. The editors situated Clara and Louisa outside the moral world of females—that is, the world of relationships. Their behavior, therefore, was without emotional and ethical logic. The girls may well have been sisters. As the most common cause for girls' running away was to be with their mother, they had probably just been separated from theirs or mistreated by their owner. Whites never referred to slaves as orphans, reserving that word so evocative of sadness for white children, who qualified even if they had lost only a father. Outside the context of relationships, Clara and Louisa emerged from the newspaper page not as unhappy girls trying to escape their misery but as malicious predators victimizing a vulnerable woman and her sweet babes.

A similarly decontextualized newspaper notice turned a raped little girl into a sexual miscreant. A one-line item in the *St. Louis Beacon* about a "coloured girl" of eleven years and two months who "gave birth to a healthy female child" expressed, by omission, the white community's view of this abused and exploited child. Family details would have transformed the stories of female slaves into tragedies about little girls sold from their families, raped, and abused, not demonstrations of the criminal unreliability and abnormal fecundity of African Americans.[39]

Antebellum African Americans did not leave a prescriptive literature from which we can infer their values, nor did parents and children leave many letters giving us suggestions about their hopes. But we have some memoirs and other evidence that testifies to the centrality of connections in their imaginations and in motivating their deeds. We also know that in West Africa identity hinged on being part of a set of kin and community relationships and that the social meaning of West African women's lives developed in the context of their relationships with their mothers, with women's social groups, and with their children's husbands and extended kin. Ties of blood were more valued than conjugal ties, and responsibilities were divided along gender lines. Slavery's relentless attack on the nuclear family and on fathers' authority reinforced the strength of ties between mothers and their children in this country. Parents and children separated by sales and hiring out knew what researchers now tell us about how to heal psychic trauma, that "recovery [can] take place only within the context of relationships. It [can]not occur in isolation."[40]

In St. Louis and its environs, slave mothers and daughters worked vigorously to keep relationships together, whether in slavery or freedom. Scholars have noted that slave women ran away much less frequently than men because they usually had the care of children. This seems to contain a criticism of slave women as insufficiently freedom loving. But as Jacqueline Jones has pointed out, trying to keep the family together was a revolutionary act in the face of the rules that governed slavery. In a similar vein, Peggy Davis has identified black abolitionists' mission as "a moral quest for affiliation." If freely choosing and maintaining relationships was central to slave parents, particularly mothers, it explains Harriet and Dred Scott's decision about when to sue for freedom. Although they presumably might have left their owner, with his blessing, many times before his death, they waited till after his death to initiate the case. Their new owner no longer shielded them as a family as their old one had, and their daughters had become ripe for sale as "girls" to the infamous New Orleans market. Freedom acquired crucial significance when it could protect families and particularly children.[41]

St. Louis provides a number of instances of mothers and daughters working to achieve freedom together. A free black woman named Jenny sued for her freedom and that of her daughter in 1825. From 1805 through 1834, three Scypion women, Catiche, Celeste, and their mother Marie, sued for freedom in a concerted effort to find liberty together.[42]

Polly Wash had been separated from her own mother by the time she was fourteen, when she was sent from Kentucky to Illinois. After her husband was sold away, she managed to walk from St. Louis to freedom in Chicago but returned, fearing that her escape might jeopardize the safety of her enslaved daughter, Lucy. Meanwhile, Polly's other daughter, Nancy, escaped to Canada during her owner's visit to Niagara. Polly then sued for her freedom in 1839, winning it in 1843 on the grounds that she had been held illegally in the free state of Illinois. In 1844 she sued for the freedom of her remaining daughter, Lucy, on the grounds that she was free and that a child's condition followed that of her mother. In 1844 Polly and both her daughters were free.[43]

Mattie Jackson and her mother were separated from Mattie's father by twenty miles. Jackson eventually escaped to Chicago. Two years after his escape, his wife and daughter ran away to Illinois, hoping to reach Chicago. But they were caught and returned to their owner. (Although Illinois was a free state, there were slave owners and sympathizers with slavery in southern Illinois, and escaped slaves were unsafe until they had gone a good distance north.)[44]

If African American girls grew up learning to make every effort to sustain relationships, they also grew up with a kind of independence without its benefits thrust on them very young. Lucy Delaney was taking care of an infant and doing a family's laundry at twelve years old. One wash required an average of fifty gallons of water, weighing about four hundred pounds, and was a two-day process involving boiling the clothes, rinsing them in the muddy water of the Mississippi, and drying them. Her first clumsy effort got her whipped.[45]

As children, slave girls were trained to self-reliance and the mastery of a variety of practical skills. In addition to tending children and doing laundry, slave girls also learned ironing and field work, cooking and serving food, tending the kitchen fire, housecleaning, making homespun, and sewing. Mary Bell's owner began hiring her out to take care of three children when she was seven. Elizabeth Keckley, later dressmaker to Mary Todd Lincoln, took care of children as a child of four.[46]

Unlike white mothers in the early republic, who had books, doctors, ministers, and relatives to consult, slave mothers did not have much guidance in raising their children. Fil Hancock, a former slave from Missouri, remembered that his mother had beaten him often and hard with a strap and that he probably deserved more. A slave mother was caught in the middle of circulating violence that victimized her and, as she well knew, would victimize her children. If she disciplined her children fiercely, she may have hoped to arm them with a shell of obedience that would protect them from their owners. One way or another, slave girls were likely to experience violence young and often. One of Mattie Jackson's earliest memories was learning that her new owner had beaten a "little slave girl she previously owned nearly every night . . . [so that she would] wake early to wait on her children." A sixty-year-old man bought fourteen-year-old Celia to cook and serve his sexual needs; her first lesson was to be raped the day he bought her. Some years, three children, and countless rapes later, Celia killed her owner. She was trying to preserve a relationship she had established with a fellow slave and to preserve her health and her unborn baby, as she was pregnant again. At her trial she learned that unlike a free woman she was not legally permitted to defend herself against rape.[47]

In very different ways, both elite and slave girls focused their attention on preserving relationships. White girls learned to perform their attentiveness in refined ways. Slave girls often had to conceal their most important attachments and reserve public affection for the children of their owners. The tough and often violent road that slave girls in St. Louis force-marched to adulthood made it possible for white girls from prosperous families to participate in fashioning and performing the refined, sentimental culture of the nineteenth century. The demands of white domesticity meant that many slave girls had to labor long and hard to enjoy moments of loving intimacy or to try to recover sundered relationships.

In St. Louis, child rearing in the new republic took many forms depending on where parents were situated with respect to the "ideals of 1776." White girls learned that chastity and tending family relations would constitute their oblique contribution to the young nation. Slave girls, who were at an even greater remove from those ideals, were to contribute their labor to a republic that might well deny them even the chastity and family relations required of its white daughters.

NOTES

1. Bernard Wishy, *The Child and the Republic: The Dawn of American Child Nurture* (Philadelphia: University of Pennsylvania Press, 1968); Jacqueline S.

Reinier, *From Virtue to Character: American Childhood, 1775–1840* (New York: Twayne, 1996).

2. Wishy, *Child and the Republic*, 5.

3. Reinier, *From Virtue to Character*, xi–xii.

4. Jay Gitlin, "'Avec Bien du Regret': The Americanization of Creole St. Louis," *Gateway Heritage* 9 (1989): 2–11.

5. Martha Saxton, *Being Good: Women's Moral Values in Early America* (New York: Hill and Wang, 2004), 173–74, 344 n. 1; Lorenzo Greene, Gary Kremer, and Antonio Holland, *Missouri's Black Heritage*, rev. ed. (Columbia: University of Missouri Press, 1993), 20–21; William Foley, *A History of Missouri* (Columbia: University of Missouri Press, 1986), 1:50, 77; Charles van Ravenswaay, *Saint Louis: An Informal History of the City and Its People, 1764–1865* (St. Louis: Missouri Historical Society Press, 1991), 120–21.

6. William B. Cohen, *The French Encounter with Africans: White Response to Blacks, 1530–1880* (Bloomington: Indiana University Press, 1980), 62–70; Sue Peabody, *"There Are No Slaves in France": The Political Culture of Race and Slavery in the Ancien Regime* (New York: Oxford University Press, 1996); Alfred Hunt, *Haiti's Influence on Antebellum America: Slumbering Volcano in the Caribbean* (Baton Rouge: Louisiana State University Press, 1988); Lloyd Hunter, "Slavery in St. Louis, 1804–1860," *Bulletin of the Missouri Historical Society* 30 (July 1974): 233–65; James Neal Primm, *The Lion in the Valley* (St. Louis: Pruett, 1981); Foley, *History of Missouri*, 73–77; Ira Berlin, *Generations of Captivity: A History of African-American Slaves* (Cambridge, MA: Harvard University Press, 2003), 8.

7. Richard Wade, *The Urban Frontier: Pioneer Life in Early Pittsburgh, Cincinnati, Lexington, Louisville, and St. Louis* (Chicago: University of Chicago Press, 1964), 88–90; Greene, Kremer, and Holland, *Missouri's Black Heritage*, 9–15, 71; Stafford Poole and Douglas Slawson, *Church and Slave in Perry County, Mo., 1818–1850* (Lewiston, NY: Edwin Mellen Press, 1986); Hunter, "Slavery in St. Louis," 233–65, 248, 253; Primm, *Lion in the Valley*, 75–85; Gitlin, "Avec Bien du Regret," 2–11; Foley, *History of Missouri*, 174–76.

8. Carl J. Eckberg, *Colonial Ste. Genevieve: An Adventure on the Mississippi Frontier* (Tucson, AZ: Patrice Press, 1996), 217–18; Charles Peterson, *Colonial St. Louis: Building a Creole Capital* (Tucson, AZ: Patrice Press, 1993), 12–23; Winstanley Briggs, "Le Pays de Illinois," *William and Mary Quarterly*, 3rd ser., 47 (1990): 30–56; Primm, *Lion in the Valley*, 12–15.

9. Van Ravenswaay, *St. Louis*, 195–201, 261–64; *Missouri Argus*, July 10, 1835; Primm, *Lion in the Valley*, 85, 141; Joanne Freeman, *Affairs of Honor: National Politics in the New Republic* (New Haven: Yale University Press, 2001); Joyce Appleby, *Inheriting the Revolution: The First Generation of Americans* (Cambridge, MA: Belknap Press, 2000), 40–45; Louise Callan, R.S.C.J., *Philippine Duchesne, Frontier Missionary of the Sacred Heart, 1765–1852* (Westminster, MD: Newman Press, 1957), 391.

10. Arnaud Berquin, *L'Ami des Enfants par Berquin* (Paris: Didier, 1845), 543–48.

11. Reinier, *From Virtue to Character*, 15–16; Saxton, *Being Good*, 289–98.

12. Wishy, *Child and the Republic*, 35; Reinier, *From Virtue to Character*, 46–71.

13. Berquin, *L'Ami des Enfants*, 90–101,110–19, 153–54, 507–20. I used a later collection of the tales, as I did not find the originals in St. Louis or Paris. For a catalog of the libraries of several French families, see John Francis McDermott, *Private Libraries in Creole St. Louis* (Baltimore, 1938). Prescriptive literature included Madame de Genlis, *Nouveaux contes moraux et nouvelle historiques* (Paris, 1804); Jean Francois Marmontel, *Marmontel's Moral Tales*, trans. George Saintsbury (London: G. Allen, 1895); Mme. Sophie Cottin, *Elizabeth, or Exiles of Siberia* (London, 1822); Jean-Jacques Rousseau, *La nouvelle Heloise*, trans. Allan Bloom (New York: Basic Books, 1979).

14. Lydia Maria Child, *The Mother's Book* (Boston, 1831), 131, 151–53. See also Wishy, *Child and the Republic*, 16.

15. William Lane to Ann and Sarah Lane, March 26, 1836, Carr-Lane Papers, Missouri Historical Society, St. Louis, MO; C. Dallett Hemphill, *Bowing to Necessities: A History of Manners in America, 1620–1860* (New York: Oxford University Press, 1999), 142, 156–59.

16. Berquin, *L'Ami des Enfants*, 2–3; Jules de Mun to Isabelle Gratiot de Mun, February 1, 1815, and Jules de Mun to Isabelle Gratiot de Mun, July 16, both in De Mun Papers, Missouri Historical Society.

17. Child, *Mother's Book*, 4.

18. Ibid., 42.

19. Jules de Mun to Isabelle Gratiot de Mun, July 21, 1816, De Mun Papers.

20. Anne Lane to her parents, September 9, 1829, Anne Lane to Mary Ewing Lane, January 24, 1831, and Anne Lane to Mary Ewing Lane, July 15, 1828, all in Carr-Lane Papers, Missouri Historical Society; Jane Chambers to her aunt, May 15, 1834, Mullanphy Papers, Missouri Historical Society; Julie Chenie de Mun (?) to Jules de Mun, Ap[ril] 25, 1836, and Isabelle de Mun to her mother, August 7, 1832, both in De Mun Papers.

21. Clara Berthold to Louise de Mun, September 22, 1836, and Emilie de Mun to Louise, April 22, 1842, both in De Mun Papers.

22. Marmontel, *Marmontel's Moral Tales*, 170, 30–38; *St. Louis Beacon*, March 24, 1829; Callan, *Philippine Duchesne*, 15–53; Emilie de Mun to Louise de Mun, April 22, 1842, De Mun Papers.

23. Abigail Mott, *Observations on the Importance of Female Education and Maternal Instruction with Their Beneficial Influence on Society* (New York, 1827), 10.

24. William Lane to Anna Lane, December 25, 1830, Carr-Lane Papers; Lewis F. Linn to his children, May 14, 1834, Linn Papers, Missouri Historical Society.

25. Fragment of Journal, 1845, Potosi, Mullanphy Papers; Eliza Ott to Alton Easton, May, 1848, Lindenwood College Collection, Missouri Historical Society; Mary Easton Sibley, Journal, Lindenwood College Collection; Sarah Ward to

Maria von Phul, July 21, 1823, Von Phul Papers, Missouri Historical Society; *St. Louis Enquirer*, August 25, 1819.

26. Mary Easton Sibley, Journal; see also Saxton, *Being Good*, 154–64.

27. G. J. Barker-Benfield, *The Culture of Sensibility: Sex and Society in Eighteenth-Century Britain* (Chicago: University of Chicago Press, 1992), 27–28; Julie Ellison, *Cato's Tears and the Making of Anglo-American Emotion* (Chicago: University of Chicago Press, 1999), 1–22.

28. Marilyn Ferris Motz, *True Sisterhood: Michigan Women and Their Kin, 1820–1920* (Albany: State University of New York Press, 1983), 5–6; Sarah Lane to William Lane, 1829, Carr-Lane Papers; Jane Chambers to her grandmother, 1835, Mullanphy Papers.

29. Julia de Mun to Jules de Mun, January 27, 1832, De Mun Papers; Brian Mullanphy to Margaret Chambers, December 4, 1830, Mullanphy Papers; Richard Bushman, *The Refinement of America: Persons, Houses, Cities* (New York: Vintage, 1993), 90–95.

30. Ann Chambers to her grandmother, April 28, 1835; Eliza Chambers to her aunt, November 15, 1838, both in Mullanphy Papers; Ann Lane to Mary Lane, January 24, 1831, Carr-Lane Papers; Isabelle de Mun to her mother, August 7, 1832, De Mun Papers.

31. Jules de Mun to Louise de Mun, October 16, 1831, De Mun Papers.

32. .Shirley Samuels, ed., *The Culture of Sentiment: Race, Gender and Sentimentality in Nineteenth-Century America* (New York: Oxford University Press, 1992) 17.

33. Ibid.

34. St. Charles Borromeo Church Records, 1792–1846, vol. 1, Missouri Historical Society; Cohen, *French Encounter*, 97; Mary Easton Sibley, Journal; Callan, *Philippine Duchesne*, 277, 519; Louise Callan, R.S.C.J., *The Society of the Sacred Heart in North America* (New York, 1937), 80.

35. William Lane to Mary Lane, April 17, 1819, Carr–Lane Papers; Anita Mallinckrodt, *From Knights to Pioneers: One German Family in Westphalia and Missouri* (Carbondale: Southern Illinois University Press, 1994), 247; Adolf Schroeder and Carla Schulz-Geisberg, eds., *Hold Dear as Always, Jette: A German Immigrant in Life and Letters* (Columbia: University of Missouri Press, 1988), 130.

36. See Saxton, *Being Good*, 348 n. 4; Brenda Stevenson, *Life in Black and White: Family and Community in the Slave South* (New York: Oxford University Press, 1996), 206–25.

37. Jules de Mun to Isabelle de Mun, 1832, De Mun Papers.

38. *St. Louis Enquirer*, December 20, 1823.

39. *St. Louis Beacon*, May 24, 1832.

40. Niara Sudarkasa, "Roots of the Black Family" and "African and African American Family Structure," in *The Strength of Our Mothers: African and African American Women and Families: Essays and Speeches* (Trenton, NJ: Africa World

Press, 1996), 77–87 and 89–102 respectively; Joyce Ladner, "Racism and Tradition: Black Womanhood in Historical Perspective," in *Black Women Cross-Culturally*, ed. Filomina Chioma Steady (Cambridge, MA: Schenkman, 1981), 269–88; Judith Herman, *Trauma and Recovery: The Aftermath of Violence from Domestic Abuse to Political Terror* (New York: Basic Books, 1992), 133.

41. Jacqueline Jones, "Race, Sex, and Self-Evident Truths: The Status of Slave Women during the Era of the American Revolution," in *Women in the Age of the American Revolution*, ed. Ronald Hoffman and Peter J. Albert (Charlottesville: University Press of Virginia, 1989), 293–337; Peggy Davis, *Neglected Stories: The Constitution and Family Values* (New York: Hill and Wang, 1997), 38; Lee Vandervelde and Sandya Subramanian, "Mrs. Dred Scott," *Yale Law Journal* 106 (1997): 1033–1122.

42. "Petition of Jenny, A Free Woman of Color," St. Louis Circuit Court Documents, Folders 21–22, May 9, 1825; "Jenny v. Ephriam Musick and others," St. Louis Circuit Court Documents, Folders 21–23, June 1825; "Marguerite v. Pierre Chouteau, Sieur," St. Louis Circuit Court, November 30, 1836, all in Missouri Historical Society; Katherine Corbett, *In Her Place: A Guide to St. Louis Women's History* (St. Louis: Missouri Historical Society Press, 1999), 27–28.

43. Lucy Delaney, *From the Darkness Cometh Light, or Struggles for Freedom* (St. Louis: J. T. Smith, 1891); Corbett, *In Her Place*, 56–58.

44. William Andrews, *Six Slave Narratives* (New York: Oxford University Press, 1988), 2–9.

45. Andrews, *Six Slave Narratives*, 2–9; Susan Strasser, *Never Done: A History of American Housework* (New York: Pantheon Books, 1982), 104–5.

46. Andrews, *Six Slave Narratives*, 2–9; Elizabeth Keckley Brown, *Behind the Scenes, or Thirty Years a Slave, and Four Years at the White House* (1868; repr., New York: Arno Press, 1968), 38, 44–45, 49–50.

47. Marie Jenkins Schwartz, *Born in Bondage: Growing Up Enslaved in the Antebellum South* (Cambridge, MA: Harvard University Press, 2000), 107, 109, 111, 113; Jacqueline Jones, *Labor of Love, Labor of Sorrow: Black Women, Work, and the Family from Slavery to the Present* (New York: Basic Books, 1985), 120–21; Deborah Gray White, *Ar'n't I a Woman? Female Slaves in the Plantation South* (New York: Norton, 1985), 9; Andrews, *Six Slave Narratives*, 24–25; James McGettigan Jr., "Boone County Slave: Sales, Estate Divisions and Families, 1820–1865," *Missouri Historical Review* 72 (1978): 176–96, 287–89. On Celia, see Melton A. McLaurin, *Celia, a Slave: A True Story* (Athens: University of Georgia Press, 1991), 24; Andrews, *Six Slave Narratives*, 2–9.

5

||||||||||||||||||||||||||||||||||||||||||||||||||||||

Growing up on the Middle Ground

Bicultural Creeks on the Early American Frontier

Andrew K. Frank

In the decades that preceded the 1830s forced removal of the Creek Indians out of Georgia, Florida, and Alabama, several hundred white men married or cohabited with Native women, with whom they bore and raised children. Creeks and southern colonists had married one another in earlier decades, but in the aftermath of the American Revolution these marriages became more frequent and the families they formed played a prominent place in Creek society and the United States' early Indian policy. Creeks used the marriages to regulate the trade with outsiders, an important concern especially as the Spanish and English presence in the region diminished. Americans, especially those committed to Thomas Jefferson's "plan of civilization," saw these marriages as a means to transform and pacify Indians. As a result, many Creeks and Americans freely engaged in marriages, and in the early republic they produced a generation of mixed-race children. Many of these children of intermarriages grew up in a peculiar position, one in which they garnered the attention of two parents with both competing and overlapping ambitions for their children. On a daily basis white and Native American parents struggled to find compromises and common ground in the socialization of their children. As a result, many of these mixed-race children received what can be called bicultural upbringings.[1] They learned western and Native manners, dress, customs, languages (usually Muskogee and English), cosmologies, and social norms. Whether through formal or ritualized lessons or through the natural mimicking of parents, the children of Creek-American relationships also learned how to be comfortable and act appropriately in both of their parents' societies. This socialization process was hardly a balanced one, with Creeks tightly controlling and regulating the actions of nearly all white fathers. As a result most Creek children of intermarriages never became fully bicultural. Instead, they lived in Creek villages and with their Creek kin, where they were more comfortable and more culturally fluent.[2]

In February 1797, Mrs. Barnard, a Creek woman, offered her daughter's hand in marriage to U.S. Indian Agent Benjamin Hawkins. The offer, initiated by a woman of the prominent Wind clan, adhered to many of the social norms and ambitions in the matrilineal Creek society. Marriages with outsiders were occurring with some regularity, and this proposed relationship would have provided Barnard and her matrilineal relations with access to the most powerful American in Creek society. Hawkins, who was charged with pursuing a "plan of civilization" among the Creeks, routinely provided gifts of cloth, looms, livestock, and other material goods needed to transform Indians into southern-style, yeoman farming families. Although Creeks tended to reject many of the elements of "civilization," especially those that required Creeks to relinquish authority and self-governance, the decline of the deer population and the increased pressures on their lands led some Creeks to see parts of the civilization plan as tools for survival and even prosperity.[3] As a result, even before Hawkins became the Indian agent in 1796, some Creeks embodied what historian Claudio Saunt has called "the new order of things."[4] Among other recent innovations, some Creeks owned slaves, wove cloth, herded cattle, read and wrote English, held private property, and engaged in the early American marketplace. If the marriage between Hawkins and her daughter took place, Mrs. Barnard and her Wind clan relatives would obtain a reciprocal social connection with Hawkins that would inevitably provide an even greater ability to engage in and control these innovations.

A concern for children immediately shaped how Hawkins interpreted Barnard's offer of marriage. Although he was relatively new to Creek Indian society, Hawkins understood that southeastern Indians raised their children and managed their households in ways that conflicted with white American norms. "The woman and most of these Creek women," he explained, are "in the habit of assuming and exercising absolute rule, such as it was over their children, and not attending to the advice of their white husbands." Hawkins would not accept this marginalization, even with the children that his potential wife already had, and he expressed his concerns to Mrs. Barnard. "The white men govern their families and provide clothing and food for them. The red men take little care of theirs, and the mothers have the sole direction of the children." He could, therefore, only agree to "take one of my red women for a bedfellow" if she could adhere to his own parenting norms. If "she has a child, I shall expect it will be mine, that I may clothe it and bring it up as I please," he explained. If he had any children from the relationship, "I shall look upon them as my own children." Mrs. Barnard responded to Hawkins by withdrawing the offer of marriage. She apparently could not submit to this agreement, as it violated the cultural norms of her community.[5]

Ethnohistorians and anthropologists have since repeated what Hawkins observed about parenting in Creek Indian society and expressed in a letter to Thomas Jefferson. A Creek "husband," he explained, "is a tenant [in] the *premises* of the women." In 1939, anthropologist J. N. B. Hewitt elaborated on Hawkins's observation when he wrote that a Creek father "had no more to do with the discipline and education of his children than an alien." In many ways, Hawkins and Hewitt astutely recognized that in matrilineal societies maternal uncles rather than biological fathers served as male role models for Creek children. Maternal uncles taught young boys to hunt, punished them for transgressions against Creek customs, explained the obligations of kinship or clan, helped orchestrate marriages, controlled scratching and tattooing rituals, and performed most of the parenting roles Americans associated with biological fathers. A Creek biological father belonged to a different clan and sometimes to a different village than his wife and children, and his "parental" obligations were to their clan and most specifically to his sister's children. Because they had multiple obligations and expectations elsewhere, Creek fathers had no cultural imperatives to raise or socialize their biological children. Biological fathers, if they had any relationship with their children, were informal advisors without authority, almost the opposite of the patriarchal norm in the American South.[6]

Hawkins's hesitancy to marry an Indian woman may have been based in southeastern Indian norms, but he misunderstood the place of white fathers in Creek society and the decisions in Creek villages that led to the proliferation of intermarriages in the early republic. A Creek mother and the members of her matrilineal clan may have controlled the socialization of Creek children, but Creeks could not and often did not want to prevent white fathers from interacting with their biological children.[7] Shielding children from their fathers' influence would contradict a major reason that some Creeks encouraged or allowed white men to marry Indian women.[8] Europeans and white Americans frequently recognized that intermarried men entered Creek villages out of a desire to pursue a career in the lucrative Indian trade, but they frequently failed to recognize that traders could have not remained in villages without the sanction of an Indian wife and clan. Marriages with these white newcomers, which occurred frequently, served as a means to regulate the new traders and to promote the interests of a family, or the matrilineal clan of the wife. If Creek mothers shut white fathers out of the household and out of their children's lives, they would lose some of their access to guns, ammunition, food, liquor, clothing, food, language skills, Western education, and a firsthand education of American social norms. Even more importantly, they would lose out on the potential advantages of having Creek children (identified as such by virtue of their matrilineal clan identity and village residence) who were able to interpret and negotiate treaties and trade without the need for an outsider. As a result, when white fathers sought to be active parents, they often discovered that their interests coincided with the desires of Creek mothers and clans. As long as children remained loyal to the clan and residents of the village, the children of intermarriages could learn and incorporate new ideas, customs, and materials into their Creek lives. Creek clans remained guarded, carefully regulating the actions and teachings of fathers, yet at the same time they encouraged white fathers to be more than the "tenants" that Hawkins feared they were.[9]

Traditionally, Creek Indians, as clan members teaching social and cultural norms in a daily and often ritualized manner, made little distinction between socialization and education. Boys learned to hunt with their maternal uncles, girls followed the women of a clan into the fields, and everyone observed and learned about the daily and seasonal rituals that structured Creek life. This informality and constant oversight by clan members frustrated many white fathers, who found it difficult to find a time or place for teaching of their own. Yet many of the children of intermarriages observed their white fathers in much the same way that they observed their Native uncles. They watched and often worked alongside their fathers as they engaged in the marketplace, and they listened to the English language as it was spoken between their father and other traders or merchants. At other times, fathers arranged for their children to attend formal schools. White fathers hired tutors and enrolled their children in nearby schools, employed their children in their trading enterprises, bequeathed property to them through wills and gifts, and took them as travel companions when they visited American settlements. As a result, the children of intermarriages were informally schooled and socialized by their Creek mothers, their clansmen, and their white fathers.[10]

Although most children of intermarriages did not receive formal Western educations, a few left Creek villages to attend school. These schooled Creeks often entered the historical record on account of the linguistic skills that they received. By becoming bilingual and comfortably negotiating the cultural differences between Indians and Americans, educated Creeks frequently became interpreters, traders, merchants, soldiers, and innkeepers. They also became employees of Hawkins, who hired Creeks to help spread "civilization" in Indian villages. Alexander McGillivray, perhaps the most prominent bicultural Creek, attended school in Charleston. His father, an intermarried Indian trader, arranged for his Scottish and Presbyterian cousin Farquer McGillivray to tutor the young Alexander and guide him otherwise to live according to white American standards. When the tutoring ended, Alexander's father arranged for him to work for a Savannah mercantile firm. Through these actions, Alexander became "well versed in [the] Language and customs" of early American society, became "acquainted with all the most useful European sciences," and obtained a reputation for outstanding oratory.[11] When McGillivray returned to Creek society and the world of his Wind clan mother, his education provided him with an understanding of Western notions of diplomacy, which he used to arrange personal and diplomatic relationships with all of the competing imperial powers. He pursued his personal interests as well as those of the Creeks through treaties with Spain like the 1784 Treaty of Pensacola and with the United States in the 1790 Treaty of New York. His comprehension of European diplomacy was augmented by his understanding (although not necessarily acceptance) of American conceptions of justice, the ideology of republicanism, the southern meaning of honor, and American standards of authority.[12] McGillivray's education, as well as his conscious self-fashioning, led Abigail Adams, wife of U.S. President John Adams, to write that McGillivray "dresses in our own fashion, speaks English like a native . . . is not very dark, [and is] much of a gentleman."[13]

Other intermarried white men took similar steps to educate their children. When Spain regained control of Florida in 1783, after two decades of British rule, it established a series of special schools to assist in the transition. The Spaniards made the religious and cultural rationale for this educational policy clear. They established and funded schools "in order that the children may learn in them to read, write, and speak Spanish, the use of their native tongue being prohibited; designating for the purpose teachers in whom are united the Christianity, competence, and good conduct, which are necessary for so useful and delicate a ministry." These schools would allow Florida's Natives to become immersed in Spanish norms and customs and otherwise become part of the Spanish Empire. Several dozen Creeks learned very rudimentary Spanish at these schools, and "mestizos" formed the bulk of the clientele. The Spanish schools, however, did not last long, as the Spanish hold in Florida was tenuous and Creeks resisted rules that declared that "no language except . . . Spanish be spoken." Spain did not hold a monopoly on the desire to educate Creeks. In the early nineteenth century, U.S. Indian Agent David Mitchell, an intermarried white man himself, proudly proclaimed that "several of the principal half breeds" educated "their Sons and daughters at School in Georgia and elsewhere." Several other intermarried white fathers enrolled their Creek children in the Alabama school of John Pierce. Although Pierce's Alabama school was close to many Creek villages—allowing for the oversight of mothers and uncles—Pierce and others recognized that Creek children rarely stayed in the schools for more than a few months.[14]

A few Creeks obtained formal educations at the Choctaw Academy and other schools out of Creek country. Rather than becoming acculturated into an American norm and being forced to abandon their cultural and social roots, many Creek students returned to their Native families with skills that their community desired. Thirteen Creeks, mostly of mixed ancestry, attended the Choctaw Academy in 1827. All of them would return to their Creek homes at least partially literate, with greater oratory skills, and with mathematical abilities.[15] Similarly, another intermarried father, Sam Moniac, enrolled his son, David, at the U.S. Military Academy at West Point in 1817. Already a proven warrior, as evidenced by his successes in the Red Stick War (1813–14), David graduated and returned to Creek society as a U.S. officer who was attached to the Indian agency.[16] Another Creek boy, David Tate, obtained schooling in Scotland and Philadelphia before returning to his Creek village, building a homestead on the Alabama River, and then working as an interpreter for the Creeks and the United States. His education also provided him with the ability to maneuver in the American court system. In 1810, when Joseph Cook sued to have Tate turn over stolen property that had been bequeathed to him, Tate successfully used his ties to Creek society to demonstrate that the law did not extend into his homestead. In the process, Tate used his Western education to provide an early defense of Native sovereignty. In this as well as in many other instances, Creeks used the skills of "civilization" to resist rather than embrace American interests.[17]

Just as Creek families challenged the teaching of Spanish and the banning of Muskogee in Spanish schools, Natives constantly regulated the educations of children outside their villages. Captain William McIntosh Sr., for example, discovered the limits of his parenting and the oversight of his children's clan in the late 1780s. McIntosh, a Scottish loyalist and Revolutionary War refugee, wanted to bring his two Creek sons to Scotland for schooling. McIntosh's wife and her brothers refused this request, but Captain McIntosh stubbornly went ahead with his plans. Without permission, he secreted his children to Savannah, where they boarded a Scotland-bound boat. Before the boat could leave the port, a small group of maternal uncles snuck onto the boat and brought the children back under the control of their matrilineal kin. Creek fathers like McIntosh could socialize their children, but they could do so only to the extent allowed or desired by their Native families.[18]

Because of resistance to taking children out of Indian villages, white fathers had their greatest influence within Creek villages. In a few instances, southeastern chiefs invited missionaries and others to build schools into their villages. This allowed village and clan leaders to introduce desired skills and crafts into their communities in a regulated setting. By placing the schools inside Creek villages, families obtained more oversight of their children's formal and traditional education. Children who attended village schools spent most of their time out of the classroom and surrounded by family members who taught Creek children more traditional values and skills. As an offshoot of the United States' "plan of civilization," Methodist and Baptist missionaries ran federally funded schools at the Asbury, Withington, and other short-lived missions on the margins of Creek villages. Most Creeks refused to let their children attend these schools, as they required children to leave their villages. As a result, enrollments at the Methodist school rarely topped twenty-five children, and most of them were the children of intermarriages.

To the chagrin of teachers and many American fathers, Creek women carefully watched and frequently intervened in the educations of their children. Religious teaching was almost forbidden—with one missionary regretting in 1822 that "the Big Warrior positively refused to allow us to preach." This resistance to Christian preaching resulted, not in the eviction of missionary schools, but in "a special understanding between the Indians & myself not to allow of preaching in the Nation." Interventions by mothers and clan members frequently took place on cultural grounds. In 1826, for example, Baptist Reverend Lee Compere complained that "another of our girls has been taken home under the pretense of visiting a sick sister." Compere thought he knew better: the "pretense" provided an excuse to take a child out of a school when the lessons betrayed Creek interests. Compere, however, misunderstood the reasons for stopping the education, insisting, "She has a mother so entirely opposed to civilized habits, that we fear it is only a trick to persuade her own child from school, who till now has been governed by her own inclinations." The child's mother and her clan, however, had originally encouraged her to attend the school, so a particular aspect of the teaching may have come under scrutiny rather than the teaching itself. Compere, who had translated hymns and biblical verses into the Muskogee language, may have been teaching unwanted lessons. Compere, who had between forty and seventy students at his Tuckabatchee school, lost all of his students after six years of teaching when he baptized one of the students. When skills such as literacy and geography were seen as useful, Creek families sanctioned them; when teachings were seen as violations, they intervened.[19]

Resistance by Creek families often resulted from violations of gender norms. Creek men often resisted attempts to teach young boys "agriculture and mechanics," preferring instead to have their male kinsmen continue to adhere to notions of masculinity that emphasized hunting abilities and considered farming the domain of women. In addition, Creek families frequently removed boys from the schools in time for the annual hunts. These were more than just a means to obtain meat and hides: Creek men used the time spent together to impart their knowledge to the children of their clan. Similarly, women usually resisted when the schools taught young girls foreign notions of cleanliness. Creeks had a complex set of rules and rituals that deal with pollution, and interference on this front threatened the very core of Native society. Resistance to missionary educations also occurred when schools encouraged women to leave the fields and learn how to spin and weave on a loom instead. These acts of resistance, though, demonstrate more than the continuing importance of clans. They also reveal that mothers and clans frequently consented to the American educations of their children, albeit within defined limits.[20]

When American fathers could not provide formal schooling for their children, they frequently socialized their children inside Native villages. Proximity to mothers and clan members, paradoxically, allowed fathers to teach their children a wide range of lessons. Because Creek women often married American men in order to control and attract the influx of material resources, some mothers urged their children to assist their biological fathers in their trading enterprises and diplomatic affairs. Creek children apprenticed with their fathers, shadowing and assisting them in their day-to-day affairs. Creek children learned American customs, basic bookkeeping, language skills, and the cultural and economic necessities of slavery, cotton planting, and herding. Many Creek children interacted with their fathers who established plantations, built Western-style homes, used slave labor, and fenced their property. These lessons were tempered by their daily experiences with Creek norms, leading many bicultural children to understand and reject some American norms.[21]

In many instances, white fathers educated their children through their positions in the deerskin trade and diplomatic affairs. Creek families often encouraged their children to participate in their father's affairs, as this would establish the child's place in intercultural affairs as well as restrain or regulate the behavior of the traders. If an intermarried trader stopped distributing resources to his family or became abusive, the Creeks could evict the trader and have his bicultural children take his place. As a result, many white fathers used their children as if they were apprentices. Timothy Barnard, for example, introduced his children to the deerskin trade and the Creek agency, relying on his children to perform many of the tasks required in economic and diplomatic exchange. When health prevented the elder Barnard from traveling, his Creek children Timpochee, Homanhidge, and Tuccohoppe brought "talks" and information into American society. Timpochee's biculturalism would later allow him to obtain the lucrative and influential position as an interpreter for the United States and a major in the U.S. Army.[22]

Intermarried American fathers also trained their children by employing them at various ferries, toll roads, and inns throughout Creek territory. These enterprises, much like the homesteads that the fathers often built, were typically located outside the female-controlled villages and on lands at least once considered hunting grounds and under male control. As a result, Creek mothers could not completely oversee them. Nevertheless, Creek families may have at least implicitly sanctioned them, for they went largely unmolested by Creek warriors, and Creek children assisted in the endeavors for many years. As a result, Sam Moniac helped his father run a tavern on the federal road that stretched from Fort Wilkinson near Millidgeville, Georgia to Fort Stoddert near Mobile, Alabama; Adam Hollinger help run a ferry across the Tombigbee River; and Jesse Wall used several Indian children to help run his tavern. Employing Creek children in these ventures served several functions that were quite analogous to the functions played by Creek wives and children in the Indian trade. Children served as laborers and interpreters, and they provided the sanction of Creek clans. Finally, and perhaps inadvertently, employing the children of intermarriages in frontier enterprises helped teach some American customs.[23]

Intermarried fathers also tried to find ways to provide financial resources to their children. Although Creeks typically passed property through the female line, intermarried white men lived in a peculiar position, as they had no female kin and thus owned property independently. As a result, they could occasionally give their children African slaves, horses, cattle, as well as other valuable goods. They also tried to bequeath their homes, inns, ferries, taverns, and trading stores. George Galphin, for example, used a will to pass cattle, slaves, buildings, and lands for "use during natural life" to several of his Indian children. With no matrilineal heirs within Creek society to make claims on the property, Galphin could pass their property as he wished.[24] Personal property, however, neither frequently nor easily passed from father to child. Some Creek customs made it difficult for children to inherit their father's property. As was common in the Native Southeast, Creeks buried many personal goods with the deceased. Creek warriors were buried with their "warlike appendages," and Alabama Creeks buried men with a knife in their hands to guard them from an eagle that "beset the spirit trail." When village chiefs or priests died, Creeks occasionally would put the deceased body and his personal possessions in his house and then set it all on fire. When Creeks did not burn their homes or destroy all of their possessions, custom required that property follow matrilineal lines. In these instances, which were the norm, household goods were distributed among clan members.[25]

By the early nineteenth century, the Creek national council, recognizing that intermarried white men could elude Creek property regulations because they were rarely members of clans, officially determined what to do with their property if they died or left the Creek nation when they had "gotten their hands full." Too often, the council explained in 1818, intermarried white men "have got tired of the Country and left their wife & Children to Suffer, which we think very unjust, and have therefore passed this law." In short, the law declared, "If a white man takes an Indian woman, and have children by her, and he goes out of the Nation, he shall leave all his property with his Children for their support." The writers of the law made it clear that this supported rather than defied Creek inter-est. Rather than consolidate the property into the hands of men, as some scholars have suggested, this law kept property within the controls of the matrilineage. The phrase "his Children" clearly deviated from the Creek conception of kinship, but in doing so it ensured that the property would remain within the community and in the hands, albeit not necessarily the right hands, of the wife's clan.[26]

Perhaps the most common, and encouraged, way Americans influ-enced their Creek children was through the teaching of English and Span-ish. Creek families had deep-rooted reasons for encouraging the spread of literacy. One Yazoo Creek Indian explained that learning English or Span-ish, rather than contradicting the traditional oral culture of the Creek majority, followed a universal custom in native society: "In all the Indian nations there is always someone who knows how to speak the language of the neighboring nation."[27] Villages that did not have members that could speak the language of their neighbors were in the unenviable position of having to rely on strangers to be their interpreters. When necessary, southeastern Indians used the Muskogean-based lingua franca of Mobil-ian. Yet it appears that whenever possible the Creek villages tried to use Muskogee or the language of their neighbors.[28]

Literacy could also allow for the defense of traditions and Creek needs. Many bicultural Creeks became interpreters for their villages, and while some proved to be what Stephen Aron called "cultural breakers," others served to protect and define Creek ambitions.[29] As long as political and social obligations remained village oriented, literacy and other cultural behaviors did not necessarily come under any suspicion. Misunderstand-ings about so-called "half-breed" interpreters led many Americans to con-clude that literate "white" men were making decisions for the Indian ma-jority. Such was the case for William Gilmore Simms, who claimed that the "writings [of the Creeks] were prepared by the white men, squatters in the nation." This resulted because "the savages . . . choose white men to be their chiefs and counselors. . . . In this way, a few white men of half breeds, possessed the most unqualified sway over the Indians."[30]

The process of middle-ground parenting also resulted in naming pat-terns that adhered to Creek norms as well as the desires of intermarried white fathers. Creeks traditionally received new names throughout their lives as indicators of status and personal experiences. In addition to their birth names, Creeks used titles of authority, village appellations, nick-names, and family names. In adherence to this tradition and their own sensibilities, some intermarried fathers also used English or Spanish names for their Creek children. These names often used a father's surname and a Spanish- or English-sounding first name. They augmented rather than replaced the children's Muskogee language names, in much the same way as nicknames coincided with birth names. In this way, Tustunuggee Hutkee was William McIntosh; Hillis Haujo was Josiah Francis; Lamochatee was known as William Weatherford and Red Eagle; and Efau Tustunnuggee was also called Davy Cornels or the Dog Warrior.[31] Other children of intermarriages received "Creek names" that "passed" for English names. Timpochee Barnard, for example, also went by Timothy Barnard. Several Creeks—like Siah Gray—used the first name of Josiah and a surname when operating within American society. Similarly, several Creeks went by Malee or Barbaree among the Creeks and Milly or Barbara in American society.[32]

Incorporating English and Spanish names into Creek naming patterns served the interests of Creeks and Americans alike. Once again, the benefits of having an English or Spanish surname occurred primarily in economic and diplomatic affairs. These names, usually in the language of one's customers, helped forge bonds of trust and subtly provided a way for some Creeks to make their fathers' identity known to strangers. In this way, Creeks could appear to be Americans. English and Spanish names also had very practical benefits, as they took some linguistic differences out of frontier exchanges. The Creek language of Muskogee, like all southeastern Indian languages, contains many phonemes that were foreign to most Americans. Muskogee, for example, contains a "thl" consonant combination that frequently appears in names and titles like "Thlucco," and as evidenced by the written record, Americans struggled to spell or pronounce these words. By using an English name, Creek traders and diplomats could cross part of this linguistic frontier.

American fathers, at least those who remained in Creek villages long enough to see their offspring mature, also helped arrange marriages for their children. Although according to Creek custom the women of a clan oversaw courtship and marriages, intermarried white men and even bicultural Creek men found common ground with their wives' families and helped arrange marriages with them. As a result, many bicultural Creeks married their father's business associates. For example, Creek chief William McIntosh arranged for his daughter to marry Indian agent David Mitchell. This relationship helped McIntosh expand his authority in Creek society and otherwise allowed McIntosh to provide resources for his clan and neighbors far beyond Creek norms.[33] Similarly, Timothy Barnard married his Uchee son Billy to Peggy Sullivan, the daughter of a trading associate; one of George Cornells' daughters married Billy McGirth, the son of a former loyalist and trader; and George Colvert married his "mestizo son" with the sister of a fellow trader. These marriages likely reflected the desires of Creek families, but the particulars of the arrangements show the active participation of white fathers.[34]

After the Revolution, American society and culture expanded into what was then called the frontier, incorporating Indian villages and families into trading and diplomatic relationships and increasingly bringing Indians into positions of dependency. With an increased need and desire to engage and control the marketplace, southeastern Indians increasingly encouraged marriages with Anglo-American men. In this context, Creek Indian women and their white husbands bore and jointly raised a generation of bicultural Creek children in Georgia, Alabama, and Florida. This process of middle-ground parenting defied and adhered to many of the norms that structured southeastern Indian society, but it almost always reflected the interests of Native society. Most fathers had the ability to influence the upbringing of their Creek children only when it suited their Indian mothers and families. Creek women and their matrilineal kin maintained the upper hand in this process, carefully regulating the actions of intermarried white men. When their interests coincided, however, white fathers played important fatherly roles. They provided formal and informal educations about American culture and mores. When combined with the Native upbringings, the socializing efforts of white fathers created bicultural Creeks, or at least Creeks who were comfortable moving in and out of the two societies. They had kin connections on both sides of the American frontier, spoke multiple languages, and understood both cultures.

NOTES

1. Richard White, *The Middle Ground: Indians, Empires, and Republics in the Great Lakes Region, 1650–1815* (New York: Cambridge University Press, 1991). Biculturalism had limits and was hardly the norm in Creek society. See Andrew K. Frank, *Creeks and Southerners: Biculturalism on the Early American Frontier* (Lincoln: University of Nebraska Press, 2005); Claudio Saunt, *A New Order of Things: Property, Power, and the Transformation of the Creek Indians, 1733–1816*

(Cambridge: Cambridge University Press, 1999); Stephen Aron, "Pigs and Hunters: 'Rights in the Woods' on the Trans-Appalachian Frontier," in *Contact Points: American Frontiers from the Mohawk Valley to the Mississippi, 1750–1830,* ed. Andrew R. L. Cayton and Fredrika J. Teute (Chapel Hill: University of North Carolina Press, 1998), 175–204. An earlier version of this exploration of bicultural children in Creek society appeared in Frank, *Creeks and Southerners.*

2. This experience contrasts sharply with the typical experience at the boarding schools of the late nineteenth and early twentieth centuries. In these instances, Natives had fewer choices and less ability to regulate the teaching. See Brenda Child, *Boarding School Seasons: American Indian Families, 1900–1940* (Lincoln: University of Nebraska Press, 1998), and David Wallace Adams, *Education for Extinction: American Indians and the Boarding School Experience, 1875–1928* (Lawrence: University Press of Kansas, 1995). It adheres more closely to the schools that Indians themselves established. See Devon A. Mihesuah, *Cultivating the Rosebuds: The Education of Women at the Cherokee Female Seminary, 1851–1909* (Urbana: University of Illinois Press, 1993).

3. This was the case throughout the Southeast, where some Natives were more innovative or cosmopolitan than others. See James Taylor Carson, *Searching for the Bright Path: The Mississippi Choctaws from Prehistory to Removal* (Lincoln: University of Nebraska Press, 1999).

4. Saunt, *New Order of Things.*

5. Benjamin Hawkins's Journal, February 16, 1797, in *Letters, Journals and Writings of Benjamin Hawkins,* 2 vols., ed. C. L. Grant (Savannah, GA: Beehive Press, 1980), 1:47 (hereafter cited as *LBH*).

6. Hawkins to Jefferson, July 11, 1803, in *LBH,* 2:455; J. N. B. Hewitt, "Notes on the Creek Indians," *Bureau of American Ethnology Bulletin* no. 123 (1939): 145; see also John R. Swanton, *Early History of the Creek Indians and Their Neighbors* (Washington, DC: Government Printing Office, 1922), 373; Bertram Wyatt-Brown, *Southern Honor: Ethics and Behavior in the Old South* (New York: Oxford University Press, 1982), 117–48.

7. In fact, Creeks often complained about white men abandoning their children. This grievance would not have been levied against Creek men, as fathers owed their children no obligations. See Creek Agency Records, McIntosh Papers, Laws of the Creek Nation, June 12, 1818, David B. Mitchell Papers, Newberry Library, Chicago.

8. Intermarriage, in many ways, resulted from and helped magnify cultural and economic differences within Native American societies. Among the Creeks, the Wind clan seemed more inclined that other clans to marry white outsiders, and by the early nineteenth century many of the wealthiest Creeks were of this clan. See Claudio Saunt, "Taking Account of Property: Social Stratification among the Creek Indians in the Early Nineteenth Century," *William and Mary Quarterly,* 3rd ser., 24 (2000): 733–60.

9. Many fathers abandoned their children or played little or no role on their upbringing. Similarly, many Creeks obtained literacy or herded cattle without having a white father. See Creek Chiefs to David B. Mitchell, November 22, 1819, David B. Mitchell Papers.

10. James Stuart, *Three Years in North America* (Edinburgh: Robert Cadell, 1833), 159. Many scholars have demonstrated how Creeks with white fathers disproportionately embraced what Americans called "civilization." See Saunt, *New Order of Things*, 2.

11. *Gentleman's Magazine*, August 1, 1793; George White, *Historical Collections of Georgia Containing the Most Interesting Facts, Traditions, Biographical Sketches, Anecdotes, Etc., Relating to Its History and Antiquities from Its First Settlement to the Present Time; Compiled from Original Records and Official Documents* (New York: Pudney and Russell, 1855), 154; John Walton Caughey, *McGillivray of the Creeks* (Norman: University of Oklahoma Press, 1938), 15.

12. John Stuart to Lord Germain, October 6, 1777, in *Documents of the American Revolution, 1770–1783*, 21 vols., ed. Kenneth G. Davies (Dublin: Irish University Press, 1972–79), 14:194; Alexander McGillivray to Estevan Miró, August 20, 1788, Lockey Collection, University of Florida; Alexander McGillivray to Benjamin James, August 10, 1792, in Caughey, *McGillivray of Creeks*, 334.

13. Abigail Adams to Mary Cranch, August 8, 1790, in *New Letters of Abigail Adams, 1788–1801*, ed. Stewart Mitchell (Boston: Houghton Mifflin, 1947), 57; Timothy J. Shannon, "Dressing for Success on the Mohawk Frontier: Hendrick, William Johnson, and the Indian Fashion," *William and Mary Quarterly*, 3rd ser., 53 (January 1996): 13–42.

14. Royal Cedula, December 13, 1783, East Florida Papers, P. K. Yonge Library, b44, E4; David B. Mitchell to John C. Calhoun, February 3, 1818, in *The Territorial Papers of the United States*, 28 vols., ed. Clarence Edwin Carter (Washington, DC: Government Printing Office, 1934–49), 18: 244; Albert James Pickett, *History of Alabama and Incidentally of Georgia and Mississippi, from the Earliest Period*, 2 vols. (Charleston, SC: Walker and James, 1851), 190.

15. Thomas Henderson, "Indian Education," in *American Baptist Magazine* 7 (February 1827): 49; Joe R. Goss, ed., *The Choctaw Academy: Official Correspondence, 1825–1841* (Conway, AK: Oldbuck Press, 1992).

16. Benjamin Griffith, "Lt. David Moniac, Creek Indian, First Minority Graduate at West Point," *Alabama Historical Quarterly* 43 (1981): 104; "David Tate to Cadet David Moniac," *Alabama Historical Quarterly* 19 (1957): 407–8.

17. Thomas Woodward to Albert J. Pickett, August 12, 1858, in Thomas Simpson Woodward, *Woodward's Reminiscences of the Creek, or Muscogee Indians, Contained in Letters to Friends in Georgia and Alabama* (Montgomery, AL: Barrett and Wimbish, 1859), 73; Benjamin Hawkins to William Eustis, August 27, 1809, in *LBH*, 2:566; Harry Toulmin to Ferdinand L. Claiborne, July 23, 1813, Harry Toulmin Papers, Alabama Department of Archives and History, Montgomery.

18. Harriet Turner Corbin, "A History and Genealogy of Chief William McIntosh, Jr. and his Known Descendants," 23–24, typescript, Mississippi Department of Archives and History, Jackson.

19. John Fleming to David Green, January 23, 1836, Papers of the American Board of Commissioners for Foreign Missions, Missions on the American Continents, 1811–1919, Library of Congress; William Capers to William McKendree, August 27, 1822, William McKendree Papers, Special Collections and Archives, Robert W. Woodruff Library, Emory University; *Annual Reports of the Commissioner of Indian Affairs, 1824–31* (New York: AMS Press, 1976), 26, 33; "Extracts from Rev. Mr. Compere's Journal, Sent to the Corresponding Secretary, November 5, 1826," *Baptist Missionary Magazine* 7 (May 1827): 145; Carolyn Thomas Foreman, "Lee Compere and the Creek Indians," *Chronicles of Oklahoma* 42 (Autumn 1964): 291–99; Jane Lyon (Compere) Pipkin, "E. L. Compere, Border Missionary," Southern Baptist Historical Library and Archives, Nashville, TN; "Notes Furnished A. J. Pickett by the Rev. Lee Compere of Mississippi Relating to the Creek Indians among Whom He Lived as a Missionary," Albert James Pickett Manuscripts, Alabama Department of Archives and History.

20. Joseph G. Smoot, "An Account of Alabama Indian Missions and Presbyterian Churches in 1828 from the Travel Diary of William S. Potts," *Alabama Review* 18 (April 1965): 139; *Niles Weekly Register*, August 3, 1822; William Capers to John C. Calhoun, May 17, 1824, Crowell to Calhoun, March 18, 1824, and A. Hamill to Capers, March 25, 1823, all in Letters Received by the Office of Indian Affairs, 1824–1880, Creek Agency, National Archives, Washington, DC, Microcopy M-234, rolls and frames 219:37, 219:55–76, and 219:204 respectively.

21. For a discussion about the connection between marriage and the deerskin trade, see Kathryn E. Holland Braund, *Deerskins and Duffels: Creek Indian Trade with Anglo-America, 1685–1815* (Lincoln: University of Nebraska Press, 1993), esp. 83–86.

22. Benjamin Hawkins's Journal, February 21, 1797, in *LBH*, 1:49; interview with Thomas Barnett, June 24, 1937, Indian Pioneer History Collection (ed. Grant Foreman), Western Historical Collection, microfilm at Florida State University, 5:6479; Benjamin Hawkins to Thomas Pinckney, September 5, 1814, in *LBH*, 2:695–701.

23. James C. Bonner, "Journal of a Mission to Georgia in 1827," *Georgia Historical Quarterly* 44 (March 1960): 81.

24. George Galphin's will, April 6, 1776, in Creek Indian Letters, Georgia Department of Archives and History, Atlanta, 8; Saunt, *New Order of Things*, 168–71.

25. John Swanton, *Indians of the Southeastern United States* (Washington, DC: Government Printing Office, 1946), 718–29, esp. 724; Swanton, *Early History*, 373–74; Christopher B. Rodning, "Mortuary Ritual and Gender Ideology in Protohistoric Southwestern North Carolina," in *Archaeological Studies of Gender in the Southeastern United States*, ed. Jane M. Eastman and Christopher Rodning (Gainesville: University Press of Florida, 2001), 77–100.

26. Laws of the Creek Nation, June 12, 1818, David B. Mitchell Papers.

27. Louis François Benjamin Dumont de Montigny, *Mémoires historiques sur la Louisiane* (Paris: Chez Cl. J. B. Bauche, 1753), 248.

28. James M. Crawford, *The Mobilian Trade Language* (Knoxville: University of Tennessee Press, 1978); Pamela J. Innes, "Demonstrating That One Can Work within Two Communities: Codeswitching in Muskogee (Creek) Political Discourse," *Florida Anthropologist* 50 (December 1997): 203.

29. Aron, "Pigs and Hunters," 175–204.

30. William Gilmore Simms, "The Broken Arrow: An Authentic Passage from Unwritten American History," *Ladies Companion,* January 1844, 111. For an alternative view of literacy, see Saunt, *New Order of Things,* 186–204.

31. Stiggins Manuscript, 54–55, Alabama Department of Archives and History; John H. Moore, "Mvskoke Personal Names," *Names* 43 (September 1995): 187–212; Thomas Woodward to Albert J. Pickett, June 21, 1858, in Woodward, *Woodward's Reminiscences,* 59.

32. *Message from the President of the United States, Transmitting an Extract from the Occurrences at Fort Jackson, in August 1814, during the Negotiations of a Treaty with the Indians and Recommending the Ratification of Certain Donations of Land Made by the Said Indians to Gen. Jackson, Col. B. Hawkins, and Others Therein Named* (Washington, DC: William A. Davis, 1816); Statement of Josiah Gray, an Indian half-breed, July 3, 1825, *American State Papers, Indian Affairs,* 2:837; interview with Loney Hardridge, January 1, 1937, Indian Pioneer Historical Collection, University of Oklahoma, Norman, 38:5163; T. Frederick Davis, "Milly Francis and Duncan McKrimmon: An Authentic Florida Pocahontas," *Florida Historical Quarterly* 21 (January 1943): 256; J. Leitch Wright Jr., *Creeks and Seminoles: The Destruction and Regeneration of the Muscogulge People* (Lincoln: University of Nebraska Press, 1986), 81.

33. Andrew K. Frank, "The Rise and Fall of William McIntosh: Authority and Identity on the Early American Frontier," *Georgia Historical Quarterly* 86 (2002): 18–48.

34. Thomas Woodward to J. J. Hooper, November 3, 1858, in Woodward, *Woodward's Reminiscences,* 109–13; Arturo O'Neill to Estevan Miró, December 22, 1788, Archivo General de Indias, Papeles de Cuba, Seville, microfilm at P. K. Yonge Library, University of Florida.

||||||||||||||||||||||||||||||||||||||||||||||||||||||||

6

A Child Shall Lead Them

Children and New Religious Groups in the Early Republic

Todd M. Brenneman

King Benjamin, one of the characters in the Book of Mormon, warned his people that to experience salvation individuals had to become like little children. Children were "submissive, meek, humble, patient, full of love, [and] willing to submit." Furthermore, it was not possible for children to sin. Among human beings, children alone were "found blameless before God." They were the example for others of what type of lives to lead. "As a child doth submit to his father," human beings had to submit to God.[1]

The Latter-Day Saints, however, were not the only group in the early republic who conceptualized human relationships to the divine through children. In the new American nation religious leaders created identities through ideas about children and what it meant to be a child. They connected their constructions of children to their constructions of ways to be religious, and in the early republic there was no shortage of such ways.

Historian Jon Butler has referred to the early republic as a "spiritual hothouse" that nurtured the development of many religions. A multitude of emerging denominations contended with each other for members as established churches lost their government sanction and people began to work out the meaning of religious freedom. Successful groups and leaders were able to provide beliefs, practices, and experiences that other groups did not. With these differences in the constructions of spiritual life came differences in conceptualizing children. Religious people of the late eighteenth and early nineteenth centuries recognized the importance of children to their own group's survival, but as leaders questioned how groups should be organized, how people and God interacted, and how religiosity affected other areas of life, they reconceptualized children and identity in the context of ideals fostered by the American Revolution. Historian Nathan Hatch postulated that in the early republic populist religious movements filled a void left by Presbyterians, Congregationalists, and Anglicans who did not immediately adapt to a democratic atmosphere. Groups that developed the ideals of the Revolution (particularly, for Hatch, individualism and antiauthoritarianism) grew very quickly as they emphasized the ability of each individual to connect directly with the supernatural through scripture study, preaching, and prayer.[2]

Three new faiths demonstrated this mixture of religion, children, and revolutionary ideals: the Disciples of Christ (often called "Christians"), the Church of Jesus of Latter-Day Saints (the Mormons), and the United Society of Believers in Christ's Second Coming (the Shakers). These groups illustrate that the unique doctrines that differentiated them from other groups stemmed at least partly from their understanding of children. By comparing how these groups conceptualized children, we reveal how religious leaders reconceptualized theologies of salvation and the afterlife, philosophies of education and economics, and ideologies about family while also incorporating American ideals like individualism, equality, and antiauthoritarianism into their ecclesiological systems. Through children's lives, Disciples created a new type of Christian primitivism, Mormons developed distinctive doctrines shaped by distinctively American sensibilities, and Shakers struggled with an ambivalence about the nature of children that dramatically affected the movement's subsequent generations.

Conceptions of American children were changing for many people in the early republic as romantic and Enlightenment ideologies reshaped the thinking of the colonies and provided the philosophical foundation for groups like the Disciples, Mormons, and Shakers. These new groups, however, were not necessarily creating new conceptions of children on their own. In his history of Protestant child-raising beliefs, historian Philip Greven noted that different conceptions of children existed in America from the colonial period. These types, which were deeply connected to ideas about the self and child raising, developed further in the young United States as people introduced new ideas about children from Enlightenment and romantic sources that complemented ideas John Locke had presented.

Although there was a great religious diversity in the colonial period, the doctrine of original sin tainted children in the eyes of many

Christians. According to various Christian theologies, children had inherited the sin of Adam and Eve from birth. Infant baptism, a practice from late antiquity, was practiced by Christian groups as a means to remove original sin. While groups like the Baptists practiced adult baptism, other Christians at the time believed that only baptism in infancy could avert the theological consequences of original sin. As Greven noted, however, even Christians who held notions of the sinfulness, or "total depravity," of children struggled with ambivalence: Were children "embryo-angels" or "infant fiends"? Strict Calvinists chose the latter. Their doctrine of total depravity stated that all human beings were tainted with original sin from birth. Infant baptism removed the stain of original sin and indicated that the child would be raised in a Christian home. The practical experience of parents, however, often operated against this theological tenet. In the forms and faces of infants and young children, parents and others saw not the demonic but the divine. Operating against the idea that infants who died outside the elect went to hell was the idea that children were gifts from heaven bearing the likeness of God.[3]

Strict Calvinism, however, was not the only theological option available to Americans, many of whom fit into Greven's "moderate" and "genteel" categories. The Calvinist theory of total depravity held sway for many from a Reformed Protestant background, but the burgeoning romantic view that children were entirely innocent began to make headway. In the middle of the competition for ideological supremacy Arminian and Lockean views also developed. In the nineteenth century, then, conceptions of children existed on a continuum from totally depraved to completely innocent. The notion of children as blank slates with their own wills fell between the two extremes. As the 1840s dawned, however, a romantic sensibility about childhood spirituality began to hold sway. With the production of Horace Bushnell's *Views on Christian Nurture* and the work of the Beecher sisters Harriet and Catherine, a Victorian view became prominent that enshrined domesticity and elevated children to the place of spiritual guide.[4]

In between the Calvinism of many people in the colonial period and the romanticism of new Americans in the antebellum period was the philosophical and religious diversity of the early republic. New groups had to compete with more established religious groups, but this competition was not just relegated to the realm of differing interpretations of Christian scriptures and histories. New movements constructed shifting ideologies of religion in the new nation. In this creation of identity, these groups and their leaders incorporated changing notions of childhood and children into their identity construction. Thinking about the nature of children, the question of their relationship to the divine, and the need to educate them affected the developing ecclesiologies of the Disciples of Christ, the Mormons, and the Shakers.

Even from the beginning, revolutionary ideals, religious identity, and children were intertwined in the thoughts of the Disciples' leaders as they attempted to create a theology that emphasized individualism, condemned infant baptism, and relied on Lockean ideas about children's education. In 1809 Thomas Campbell tried to explain the ideas guiding the group gathering around him. In "Declaration and Address," Campbell argued that Holy Writ alone should be the source of faith and practice. All Christian practices must follow an explicit command or approved precedent in the Bible. Campbell framed this stance in the context of American ideals that affirmed the individual's ability to discern truth on the basis of scripture alone. Furthermore, argued Campbell, since scripture alone was the source of Christian doctrine, human beings were all equal in relationship to it. Although individualism and equality could lead to pluralistic interpretations of sacred texts, Campbell believed that it would lead to unity—people approaching scripture with no intermediaries would come to one conclusion, because, he believed, there was but one interpretation of scripture. The United States was the perfect place for this union of Christianity to occur because it was "[a] country happily exempted from the baneful influence of a civil establishment of any peculiar form of [C]hristianity."[5]

When Campbell first read "Declaration and Address" to an audience, the implications of his argument were debated immediately after he finished. Andrew Munro and Thomas Acheson, two of the individuals present at the time, expressed concern about the consequences for children of such beliefs. If Campbell's hermeneutic was followed closely, Munro argued, infant baptism would have to be discarded. Campbell responded that if Christians could not demonstrate that infant baptism had divine warrant they should eliminate it. Acheson retorted, "I hope I may never see the day when my heart will renounce that blessed saying of the Scripture, 'Suffer little children to come unto me, and forbid them not, for of such is the kingdom of heaven.'" James Foster, also present at the time, answered that this saying had nothing to do with infant baptism.[6]

In the wake of "Declaration and Address," Thomas's son Alexander, who would soon after become the principal figure in the movement, began to question whether infant baptism was consistent with their new hermeneutic. Although Thomas had been a Presbyterian minister and had raised Alexander and his other children in the Presbyterian Church, both Thomas and Alexander began to doubt the Presbyterians' scriptural reasoning for the practice.[7]

The birth of Alexander's first child, Jane, in March 1812 solidified his opposition to infant baptism. Although prior to this time Campbell had avoided making any firm commitment to whether infant baptism should be practiced, Jane's mother, Margaret, and Campbell's in-laws were still affiliated with the Presbyterian Church. With Jane's birth making the issue concrete for him, Campbell made what was probably a difficult decision not to baptize Jane. Shortly after this he began to question whether he should consider his own baptism as a child valid. Deciding that it was not, Campbell asked a Baptist minister to immerse him in June 1812. The Campbells associated with the Baptists for a short time but eventually dissolved this arrangement as well. While the Baptists practiced adult immersion, the Campbells believed that God required baptism for salvation, which Baptists did not espouse. Their distinctive views on baptism would eventually separate the Campbell movement from other Christian groups (even those who practiced adult immersion), and three of Campbell's five public debates would be about baptism.[8]

Campbell's discourses on infant baptism reveal his attitudes about children and their place in his movement. For Campbell the Calvinist doctrine of the total depravity of humanity (which included children) was scripturally unwarranted. Anyone could see from experience, argued Campbell, that children and adults differed in their moral nature. Children by nature generally appeared to be more believing and nobler than adults. Campbell also argued that the notion of "total" depravity was illogical because that would mean human beings were like Satan, who could not be anything more than "*totally* depraved."[9]

In other writings Campbell was much more explicit about his opposition to infant baptism. "Infant sprinkling" was founded on human opinion, argued Campbell, and "as, then, we have no *testimony* that it is a divine institution, we can have no divine faith in it . . . . It is certainly a human institution, and founded wholly upon human opinion." For Campbell, infants had no need for baptism simply because "the Lord never commanded" it. If human opinion created infant baptism and the attendant doctrine of original sin, what did this practice accomplish? asked Campbell. Infant baptism, he claimed, "is a pretty good expedient for trammeling the conscience of minors, and getting them into a sect before they can judge for themselves."[10]

Campbell also worked out his ideas about the nature of children by discussing education. In the first issue of his second journal, *Millennial Harbinger* (1830), Campbell noted that one of the subjects to be covered in this new periodical was "the inadequacy of all the present systems of education, literary and moral, to develope [sic] the powers of the human mind, and to prepare man for rational and social happiness." Within a few months Campbell addressed the subject of children and education. In it he demonstrated his indebtedness to John Locke, someone who had made a large impact on him in many ways, especially in Locke's view of children as "a blank slate upon which experience and environment would draw the lines of character."[11]

One of the ways Campbell showed his indebtedness to Locke was in his views on education. Children had to be taught about God, argued Campbell, and the religious education most children received alienated them from God instead of bringing them closer. Drawing on his antipathy for the Calvinist view of total depravity, Campbell argued that teaching children that they were depraved made them hate God, not love him. Instead of the Calvinist view, Campbell espoused a Lockean view concerning education. People learn to love or hate someone, according to Campbell. If they do not know about God, they "cannot naturally hate him, fear him, or love him. Whether a child shall love or hate God is *educational*, and not natural." What children learned determined how they related to God. Campbell went on to conclude, "That the minds of children are capable of being shaped after almost any model and cast into any mould, universal testimony and observation prove."[12]

Because children were blank slates or empty molds, it was especially important for the Disciples of Christ to shape children in godly ways through education. Campbell was concerned that this was not being done. Not only did the success of the movement depend on the indoctrination of children, but their souls depended on it as well. Campbell argued that this made education all the more important. "The children of all disciples should be taught the oracles of God from the first dawning of reason." If children were educated early, according to Campbell, they would be less likely to allow "the strong seeds of vice" to become a part of their character. Campbell bemoaned that "most saints, in this generation, appear more zealous that their children should shine on earth, than in heaven—and that they may be rich here, at the hazard of eternal bankruptcy." Educating children in religion affected not only their eternal destiny but how society operated. If parents made the effort to teach children "to fear God and keep his commandments, how many more virtuous, solid and useful citizens . . . would be found in all the corners of the land."[13]

Campbell's ideas about soteriology, education, and good American citizenship demonstrate the interconnection between identity, children, and the ideals of the new nation that shaped the Disciples. In the Campbell movement, conceptions of children were important because they helped separate the Disciples from other nineteenth-century Christian denominations. Although theologically the Campbells determined that infant baptism had no scriptural warrant, it was not until Jane Campbell was born that Alexander Campbell had to make the decision to discontinue the practice. Furthermore, as the Disciples movement developed, Alexander Campbell's ideas about the blank-slate nature of children became important in encouraging members to organically grow the movement. These issues were founded upon ideals of individualism, equality, and nationality formed by the Revolution. An approach to the Bible shaped by American ideals led to theologies about church and children that made the Campbell movement distinct.

The beginnings of the Church of Jesus Christ of Latter-Day Saints, like that of the Disciples, demonstrate how children, religious identity, and the American ideals of liberty, religious freedom, and nationalism were interwoven in complex ways as Mormons attempted to carve out a place for themselves in the American landscape. When Joseph Smith encountered the Father and the Son in a grove of trees, he was not much past childhood himself. Smith was only fifteen when these two personages appeared to him and told him not to join any of the Christian "sects." He was eighteen when the angel Moroni appeared to him and told him that he would be given access to golden plates that would help him restore true Christianity in these latter days. Because of his youth when he accepted God's commission to serve, it is perhaps no surprise that children would find an important place within Mormonism.[14]

Like Alexander Campbell before him, Joseph Smith opposed the baptism of infants. The Latter-Day Saints, however, based their doctrine not on the silence of scripture like the Disciples but on the teachings in the Book of Mormon. In Moroni 8, the longest treatment of the subject, Mormon (supposedly writing around 400 CE) decried the practice of infant baptism. Mormon called it a "gross error" that had developed among the people of antiquity. Little children were "whole" and "not capable of committing sin." Anyone who baptized children mocked God.[15]

Mormon went on to say that "those who are accountable and capable of committing sin" (people older than the age of eight) should become like "little children." Anyone who said that little children needed to be baptized because of original sin demonstrated that he or she "hath neither faith, hope, nor charity; wherefore, should he be cut off while in the thought, he must go down to hell." It was "wickedness to suppose that God saveth one child because of baptism, and the other must perish because he hath no baptism."[16]

Mormons attempted to explain children's innocence through the atonement of Christ. "Every spirit of man was innocent in the beginning," declared Joseph Smith in an 1833 revelation, "and God having redeemed man from the fall, men became again, in their infant state, innocent before God." Original sin, then, was something children suffered prior to Jesus Christ's atonement. Smith claimed that Jesus had told him this in an 1830 revelation: "But behold, I [the Lord God] say unto you, that little children are redeemed from the foundation of the world through my Only Begotten." In 1832 Smith was more specific: "Little children are holy, being sanctified through the atonement of Jesus Christ." Children did not even have the ability to sin. Furthermore, Smith also revealed that "all children who die before they arrive at the years of accountability are saved in the celestial kingdom of heaven."[17]

Children were important not only in the Latter-Day Saints' opposition to infant baptism but also in another distinctively Mormon doctrine: baptism for the dead. In section 128 of *Doctrine and Covenants,* Joseph Smith laid out the reasons for baptism for the dead and how it was to be performed. Baptism for the dead, originating from 1 Corinthians 15:29, was a way for Mormons to bring salvation to those who had died "without a knowledge of the gospel." According to Smith, it was necessary for baptism for the dead to be instituted under the restored church. If it was not, "the earth will be smitten with a curse." Such a curse could be avoided through "a welding link of some kind or other between the fathers and the children." That welding link was the Mormon practice of baptism for the dead. Parents, children, and those who had died without knowing the "gospel" were all interconnected. Children were vital to saving parents, and parents were vital to saving children: "For we without them cannot be made perfect; neither can they without us be made perfect." The welding together of parents, children, and the departed would bring about "the fulness *[sic]* of time." In this period "those things which never have been revealed from the foundation of the world, but have been kept hid from the wise and prudent, shall be revealed unto babes and sucklings in this, the dispensation of the fulness *[sic]* of times."[18]

Because parents and children were interconnected throughout Mormon sacred history, parents had certain responsibilities toward their children. First of all, of course, all parents were expected to provide materially for their children until adulthood, and if parents died without an inheritance, children were to receive "maintenance" from "the Lord's storehouse." Parents were also to instruct their children in church doctrines "of repentance, faith in Christ the Son of the living God, and of baptism and the gift of the Holy Ghost by laying on of the hands, when eight years old." When children reached the age of eight, they were prepared to become church members.[19]

Mormon parents had other special responsibilities that were connected to liberty, religious freedom, and American exceptionalism. Because of the harassment that Latter-Day Saints faced everywhere they went, parents needed to make their unjust persecutions known to the world. While in prison in Missouri, Smith encouraged the saints to record their maltreatment, including the property they lost, the abuses they faced, and the "names of all persons that have had a hand in their oppressions." The recording of such an event was "an imperative duty" that saints owed to God, to themselves, and "to our wives and children, who have been made to bow down with grief, sorrow, and care, under the most damning hand of murder, tyranny, and oppression." Smith hoped that such records would help future generations see the truth and nobility of the Latter-Day Saints.[20]

The Mormons were noble, in Smith's mind, because they understood that protecting the American ideals of religious freedom and liberty was vital to protecting children. In nineteenth-century America, Mormons looked to what they considered ancient texts as well as contemporary revelation and saw that liberty, children, and the American nation were tied together. Their destinies were united in a deep spiritual bond. In the Book of Mormon this connection was highlighted in the words and actions of Moroni, a man from early Christian antiquity who became the angel who had spoken to Joseph Smith. In the book of Alma, Moroni and his army battled with the Lamanites, a rival tribe that supposedly peopled North America in the early centuries CE. In an attempt to avert bloodshed, Moroni offered Zerahemnah, the Lamanite leader, an opportunity for peace.

The Lamanites could not win, Moroni argued, because God was on his side. Moroni and his fellow soldiers represented "the true faith of God." God had provided Moroni and his army the ability to defeat the Lamanites "by our faith, by our religion, by our rites of worship, and by our church, and by the sacred support which we owe to our wives and our children, by the liberty which binds us to our lands and our country; yea, and also by the maintenance of the sacred word of God." Moroni could make such a boast because, according to the narrator of Alma, "The Nephites [Moroni's tribe] were inspired by a better cause, for they were not fighting for monarchy nor power but they were fighting for their homes and their liberties, their wives and their children, and their all, yea, for their rites of worship and their church." How comforting these words, which echoed the sentiments that fueled the American Revolution, must have been to a group persecuted in the nineteenth century because of their distinctive beliefs! If, as they believed, God had helped Moroni defeat the evil Lamanites, he would surely help the Mormons in their struggles against those persecuting his nineteenth-century church.[21]

A final way that Mormons connected children to their distinctiveness was through plural marriage. While Smith's revelation of plural marriage was based on a biblical primitivism, the doctrine had important political ramifications for Mormons later in the nineteenth century. The doctrine, laid out now in *Doctrines and Covenants* 132, takes its foundation from the polygamous relationships of Old Testament figures like Abraham, Jacob, David, and Solomon. Only a few passages relate directly to children, but they form the foundation for later Mormon eschatology and pneumatology.[22]

Ideas about Mormon marriage, whether plural or not, were connected to Mormon ideas of the afterlife. In Mormon eschatology, men could achieve godhood, also called "exaltation." Mormon men who entered into a marriage "sealed unto them by the Holy Spirit of promise," who lived by the "new and everlasting covenant" of God, and who did not murder or "shed innocent blood" had the opportunity to achieve "their exaltation and glory in all things." According to Smith's revelation, after death "then shall they be gods, because they have no end; therefore shall they be from everlasting to everlasting."[23]

Children were vital to plural marriage and exaltation because it was important that Mormon men produce many children. God gave women to Mormon men for this purpose: "They [virgins] are given unto him [a Mormon male] to multiply and replenish the earth . . . for their exaltation in the eternal worlds, that they may bear the souls of men; for herein is the work of my Father continued, that he may be glorified." God warned Smith's wife Emma against interfering with this revelation so that God could "bless him and multiply him and give unto him an hundredfold in this world, of fathers and mothers, brothers and sisters, houses and lands, wives and children, and crowns of eternal lives in the eternal worlds."[24]

Even elements of the theology of plural marriage had connections to American ideals. Nathan Hatch has argued that many of the populist groups arising in the early republic sought to restore the primitive order of first-century Christianity to the United States. The Campbell movement and the Mormons were two such groups. Although Christian restorationism had been part of Christian history for hundreds of years, in the new nation the "sharp blows of the democratic revolutions" in Europe and America separated people not only from past ideas about politics but also from ideas about religious traditions and structures. The severing of the "taproots of orthodoxy" combined with "the disconcerting reality of intense religious pluralism" provided a unique medium for Christian primitivism to grow. For the Mormons, however, the Old Testament patriarchs were part of that primitivistic turn. This American Christian tendency toward primitivism was wrapped up with theologies about marriage and children to create a distinctively Mormon teaching.[25]

In contrast to the Disciples of Christ, Mormons had conceptions of children that were much more intricately tied to unique Mormon doctrines. Conceptions of children in Mormon ideology also connected disparate ideas like religious freedom and the importance of the American nation. Both ideas were extremely important to and definitive of Mormons, and in children they were joined to create a distinctively Mormon identity in the early republic. The freedom of religious expression that allowed these distinctive doctrines to develop was not the only way American ideals formed a part of Mormon theology. God had blessed the very land of the United States and the Mormons who lived there. The ideals of the new nation formed the ideological foundation upon which Joseph Smith (and later other leaders) built a church that tied religious identity, children, and American ideals together.

Although the United Society of Believers in Christ's Second Coming (the Shakers) also intertwined revolutionary ideals with children and religious experience, they relied on revolutionary ideology to a lesser extent than the Disciples of Christ or the Mormons. Individualism and equality were important facets of Shaker social life, but although freedom of religious expression allowed them to develop and thrive, persecution often drove Shakers into communities largely separated from other Americans.[26]

Formed by "Mother" Ann Lee in late eighteenth-century England, the Shakers came to prominence in the era of the early republic after Lee had decided that their "limited success in Manchester, growing pressures on the sect, and the promise of different circumstances in North America" necessitated a move. Lee would barely live out the revolution that divided her old homeland from her new one. Leadership of the then declining group passed from Lee to others who were able to reshape the Shakers into a more communitarian society that achieved some success in the early republic and antebellum periods.[27]

One of the ways that those leaders (Joseph Meacham and Lucy Wright especially) shaped the movement was the way they conceptualized children. Four of Lee's children had died at very young ages. Some scholars of the movement suggest that this might have led to "an emotional attachment to and concern for children" that marked the early Shaker period. Children in the early Shaker movement were considered "innocent in nature," demonstrating a proto-romantic view of childhood, but as the Shakers developed in the early nineteenth century, this view began to change.[28]

In the early republic period the Shakers had ambivalent ideas about children. The Shakers practiced celibacy, so many of the children who became part of Shaker communities came with parents who converted. Adopting Mother Ann's concern for children, Shakers viewed children as "true and pure gifts of God." After 1820, however, attitudes toward children began to change. Family studies scholar Judith Graham has argued that "as the nineteenth century progressed, Shaker leaders placed less emphasis on children's spiritual commitment to the group than on their contributions to the economic well-being of the society." Children became important not because of a connection to the divine but because of their necessity to the community's survival numerically and economically. With this sociological shift came an ideological one as well. No longer were children innocent in nature, as Mother Ann had thought. Instead, during the 1820s children became the physical evidence of humanity's evil nature. They were "the sinful results of concupiscence, of adults failing to take up the cross of celibacy."[29]

Attendant on these shifts was the separation of children from the parents and from the larger Shaker community. Shaker Children's Orders had been in place to divide up the community since about 1800. Prior to this time children had been a very small portion of Shaker communities. They experienced a large growth in the percentages of children and teenagers between 1800 and 1820. A Children's Order that separated children from adults concretized the dissolution of bonds Shakers thought God desired.[30]

Children came into the Children's Order in a variety of ways. As mentioned previously, many children came in with parents who converted. As adults joined the Shakers, they were placed into specific families, or orders, "based on the dedication, faith, and commitment of individuals." Shakers shunted any children of these individuals into the Children's Order, where they divided them by sex. At other times parents might leave children with the Shakers because the parents could not provide for them. The Shakers would also find children as they traveled. The revivals of the Second Great Awakening brought additional children and youth into the Shaker fold.[31]

No matter how the children entered the Shakers, all of them under the age of sixteen were "indentured" to the community. Indentures were made between the parents or guardians of the children and the deacons or trustees of the order. Under the indentures the Shakers provided the necessities of life for the children while the parents were excluded from the children's lives, unless the children failed to behave according to Shaker standards, in which case they might be returned to their parents.[32]

While children did provide for the economic well-being of the community through their indentured status and their manual labor, Shakers were also concerned that children be properly educated. In the early 1800s proper education meant making sure children knew how to behave in Shaker communities. Gradually, the Shakers began to add more academic subjects to their concept of education. The reason for this shift was the aging of the second generation of American Shakers, who realized that the younger generation had to be educated to assume their place.[33]

Even in education the ambivalence of Shaker attitudes toward children was evident. Mother Ann's ideas about childhood innocence marked one aspect of thought, but Shaker leaders also believed that children had to be disciplined to act morally. Shakers had to provide good examples for children so that they would not follow their inclination toward immorality. Education was a double-edged sword, however: while it promised the opportunity to develop a new generation of Shakers who could continue to grow the movement, it also prepared those who became adults to leave

Shaker communities and become members of the world with the skills they had acquired.[34]

Part of the reason for the destructive nature of education for the Shakers was the way Shaker education developed in the 1830s. Seth Wells, the superintendent of Shaker schools, encouraged an educational program that closed the gaps between Shaker communities and the rest of the United States. As historian Stephen J. Stein notes, "The practical effect of [Wells's] work was to move the [Shakers] closer to the educational standards of the larger culture." Just as the larger culture began to focus on education to create good citizens of the new nation, the Shakers looked to education to prepare children to take their places as good citizens of Shaker communities.[35]

Toward the end of the early republic period, Shaker ideas about children began to shift again. After 1837 the Shakers experienced a preponderance of visions and ecstatic experiences that connected the spirit world to the natural one. Known as "Mother's Work" (because of the interactions between some Shakers and the deceased Mother Ann) or the "Era of Manifestations," increased trances and messages from beyond the natural world disrupted Shaker communities as the 1840s arrived. In the midst of this heightened spiritualism, children took on a different role. Quite often spirits, including deceased American political leaders, spoke to and through children, particularly girls. At one time marginalized and separated from the community (although still vitally important), some children now began to take on a more central role as instruments of the spirit world. By the early 1840s, however, the leadership of Shaker communities attempted to control the messages of the spirits, once again demonstrating the ambivalent conceptions Shakers had of children—were children innocents or were they markers of immorality that needed to be controlled?[36]

The Shaker ambivalence about children was mirrored in the ambivalence children began to have about Shakers. As Judith Graham noted for the years 1821–50, 71 percent of girls and 87 percent of boys left Shaker communities when they became adults. These young adults had a variety of reasons for leaving the movement, but one could say that because the Shakers could not decide how children should be viewed they were unable to develop relationships with children that would encourage them to remain in Shaker communities upon reaching adulthood.[37]

As the Disciples, the Mormons, and the Shakers entered the 1840s and 1850s, monumental changes occurred. Institutional decisions among leaders in the Stone-Campbell movement led to rifts that would eventually split the group. When Joseph Smith died in 1844, Brigham Young moved the Mormons west to Utah. The end of the Era of Manifestations led to a reassertion of centralized authority for the Shakers as they dealt with defection and apostasy.[38] While some of the identities of these groups were already fixed, the antebellum period led to further changes. As first generation of leadership gave way to a second or, in the case of the Shakers, a third generation of leaders, there were concerns about children.

An example from Alexander Campbell's life illustrates how movements worried about their ultimate success even after they had formed their identities. In 1847 Campbell visited Europe. When he returned to the United States, he discovered that his son Wickliffe, age ten, had drowned. Campbell's son-in-law, W. K. Pendleton, was the first to write about Wickliffe's death in the Millennial Harbinger. While Campbell was still ignorant of his son's fate, Pendleton wrote that Wickliffe had been "a boy of remarkable and peculiar character." This character had made him "the object of special hope," but Pendleton did not say what that hope was. He concluded that Wickliffe's mother and father would experience "more than ordinary bereavement." Even though it is completely understandable that a poetic tinge would color Pendleton's remarks on the death of a child, his words suggest more than simple grief over the death of a child, even a family member. Perhaps since Wickliffe died at such a young age, the idea of lost opportunities presented itself to Pendleton's mind.[39]

Two months after Pendleton's obituary for Wickliffe appeared in the Harbinger, Campbell penned his own memorial. Calling him "a child of more than ordinary promise," Campbell noted that Wickliffe "was a child not only beloved by all his relatives and acquaintance, and dear to his parents, but one on whom clustered many a hope of eminent usefulness to society in coming years."[40] While grief over lost opportunities could surely be coloring these sentiments, something else is underlying these words. Campbell believed that Wickliffe had some special destiny that he might have fulfilled had he not died.

While such words are historically contextualized in Wickliffe's death, they could probably have been written, in slightly modified form, about other children in other movements. Children, as Campbell and others realized, were vital to the survival of religious movements. Parents and other adults recognized that their faith would not last past their death if children were not initiated into the group to provide sustained growth. Americans in the early republic especially saw the reality of the fact.

It is now taken for granted that the American religious experience was different after the War of Independence. The First Amendment, especially, offered Americans the opportunity to define themselves without official coercion. The "Second Great Awakening" provided opportunities for the development of diverse forms of Protestant Christianity, while at the same time Jews and Catholics, as well as Native Americans, experienced revivals of religious feeling and practice.

Among the groups that developed in the early republic were the Disciples of Christ, the Mormons, and the Shakers. Exploring how new religious movements thought about children helps us understand not only how these groups responded to conditions in the early United States but also how spiritual people defined themselves by measuring their children's lives in relation to children in other communities. Instead of examining how these groups actually raised their children, I have attempted to demonstrate how children often provided a framework for, if not a challenge to, the developing ideologies of religious Americans. Previous scholars have paid little attention to how adults negotiated their identity as differently religious Americans through children.[41] Yet their youngest members played integral roles as these new religious movements invented themselves in the early republic.

NOTES

1. Mosiah 3:16–21.

2. Jon Butler, *Awash in a Sea of Faith: Christianizing the American People* (Cambridge, MA: Harvard University Press, 1990); Nathan Hatch, *The Democratization of American Christianity* (New Haven: Yale University Press, 1990).

3. Philip Greven, *The Protestant Temperament: Patterns of Child-Rearing, Religious Experience, and the Self in Early America* (New York: Knopf, 1977), esp. 28–31.

4. Anne M. Boylan, "Growing Up Female in Young America, 1800–1860," in *American Childhood: A Research Guide and Historical Handbook,* ed. Joseph M. Hawes and N. Ray Hiner (Westport, CT: Greenwood Press, 1985), 154–55. Also see Jacqueline S. Reinier, *From Virtue to Character: American Childhood, 1775–1840* (New York: Twayne, 1996), esp. ch. 4.

5. Thomas Campbell, *Declaration and Address of the Christian Association of Washington* (Washington, PA: Washington Christian Association, 1809), www.mun.ca/rels/restmov/people/tcampbell.html.

6. Robert Richardson, *Memoirs of Alexander Campbell* (n.p., n.d.; repr., Germantown, TN: Religious Book Service, n.d.), 1:237–38.

7. Ibid., 250.

8. Ibid., 391–96.

9. Alexander Campbell, "Reply to Bro. Semple," *Millennial Harbinger* 1 (August 1830): 355.

10. "The Bible," *Millennial Harbinger* 3 (August 1832): 356–59.

11. "Prospectus," *Millennial Harbinger* 1 (January 1830): 1; Boylan, "Growing Up Female," 155.

12. Alexander Campbell, "Education—No. 2," *Millennial Harbinger* 1 (June 1830): 253–54.

13. "Regeneration," *Millennial Harbinger, Extra,* 4 (August 1833): 364.

14. See Jan Shipps, *Mormonism: The Story of a New Religious Tradition* (Urbana: University of Illinois Press, 1985), for a more complete examination of the origins of Mormonism.

15. Moroni 8:4–9.

16. Moroni 8:14–15.

17. *Doctrine and Covenants* 93:38, 29:46, 74:7, 29:47, 137:10. The celestial kingdom is the highest place one can attain in the Mormon afterlife.

18. Ibid., 132:5, 17–18.

19. Ibid., 68:25–27.

19. Ibid., 123:2–3, 7, 11–15.

21. Alma 44:1–5, 43:45.

22. See Lawrence Foster, *Women, Family, and Utopia: Communal Experiments of the Shakers, the Oneida Community, and the Mormons* (Syracuse: Syracuse University Press, 1991), 153, and *Religion and Sexuality: The Shakers, the Mormons, and the Oneida Community* (Urbana: University of Illinois Press, 1981), 139–46.

23. *Doctrine and Covenants* 132:20.

24. Ibid., 132:63, 55.

25. Hatch, *Democratization*, 167–70; Shipps, *Mormonism*, 67–69.

26. See Stephen J. Stein, *The Shaker Experience in America: A History of the United Society of Believers* (New Haven: Yale University Press, 1992).

27. Ibid., 7; Judith Graham, "The New Lebanon Shaker Children's Order," *Winterthur Portfolio* 26 (Winter 1991): 215–16.

28. Graham, "New Lebanon," 215; Priscilla J. Brewer, *Shaker Communities, Shaker Lives* (Hanover, NH: University Press of New England, 1986), 74.

29. Graham, "New Lebanon," 226.

30. Brewer, *Shaker Communities*, 23–24, 30; Graham, "New Lebanon," 218.

31. Graham, "New Lebanon," 216–18.

32. Edward Deming Andrews and Faith Andrews, "The Shaker Children's Order," *Winterthur Portfolio* 8 (1973): 202; Graham, "New Lebanon," 218.

33. Andrews and Andrews, "Shaker Children's Order," 205–6.

34. Graham, "New Lebanon," 222–24.

35. Stein, *Shaker Experience*, 160–61; for education in the early republic, see Reinier, *From Virtue to Character*, 43–44.

36. Amanda Porterfield, *The Protestant Experience in America* (Westport, CT: Greenwood Press, 2006), 73–75; Sally M. Promey, *Spiritual Spectacles: Vision and Image in Mid-nineteenth-century Shakerism* (Bloomington: Indiana University Press, 1993), 46–48, 161; Jean M. Humez, ed., *Mother's First-Born Daughters: Early Shaker Writings on Women and Religion* (Bloomington: Indiana University Press, 1993), 214; Andrews and Andrews, "Shaker Children's Order," 208; Stein, *Shaker Experience*, 185.

37. Graham, "New Lebanon," 219–20.

38. See Stein, *Shaker Experience*, 183–200.

39. W. K. Pendleton, "Death of Wickliffe E. Campbell," *Millennial Harbinger*, 3rd ser., 4 (October 1847): 595–96; Joseph R. Jeter Jr. and Hiram J. Lester, "The Tragedy of Wickliffe Campbell," *Lexington Theological Quarterly* 22 (July 1987): 87.

40. Alexander Campbell, "Obituary," *Millennial Harbinger*, 3rd ser., 4 (December 1847): 713–14.

41. I am particularly thinking of Hatch, *Democratization*, as well as other standard and revisionist histories of American religion, such as Sydney E. Ahlstrom, *A Religious History of the American People* (New Haven: Yale University Press, 1927); Paul K. Conkin, *American Originals: Homemade Varieties of Christianity* (Chapel Hill: University of North Carolina Press, 1997); and Charles H. Lippy, *Being Religious, American Style: A History of Popular Religiosity in the United States* (Westport, CT: Praeger, 1994).

III

Taking a Flying Leap
Educating Young Republicans

"I learned my letters in a few days," recalled Lucy Larcom, "standing at Aunt Hannah's knee while she pointed them out in the spelling-book with a pin, skipping over the 'a b abs' into words of one and two syllables, thence taking a flying leap into the New Testament, in which there is concurrent family testimony that I was reading at the age of two years and a half."

Larcom's early education in the apartment over her father's general store, above a garden where the students marveled at the daily opening of the "many-tinted four o-clocks," was a pretty informal operation. Her teacher, "Aunt" Hannah, was an ageless neighbor—not really an aunt. Although generally kind, she was known to threaten naughty students with a ruler and "numskulls" with a rap on the head with her thimble. Holding school in her kitchen or sitting room, she often supervised her students while cooking, cleaning, or spinning, "wetting her thumb and forefinger at her lips to twist the thread, keeping time, meanwhile, to some quaint old tune with her foot upon the treadle." The curriculum was simple and aimed largely at getting children educated enough to read the Bible. Hannah took children as young as two—she acted as a community child care provider as well as teacher—and set up makeshift beds for the sleepiest toddlers.[1]

Larcom's village school was more dame's school than public school. Yet it was part of one of the great republican projects in the new nation: creating an educated citizenry capable of capable of carrying out the responsibilities and worthy of the benefits of democracy. Led by Horace Mann and others, educational reformers believed that publicly funded schools, regulated teacher licensing, and mandatory attendance would play vital roles in the survival of the Republic.

The essays in this section explore the ways in which educators and students responded to the needs and imperatives of the Revolution. The founders and students at the Philadelphia Young Ladies' Academy, as A. Kristen Foster shows, engaged in a lively debate about the extent to which girls—who would soon be young women and mothers—needed to be exposed to the full range of subjects and learn the entire package of skills their male counterparts would need to participate in political life. On a broader scale, Gretchen A. Adams examines how schoolbooks published in the United States imparted not only knowledge but also patriotism.

Lucy Larcom would eventually move on to a better, more formal school when her family moved to Lowell. But her memories of her first syllables and words—following the pointing pin of Aunt Hannah—would remain among the central images of her early life. For her, and for most Americans of the period, education was not simply a privilege of wealth but a necessary part of life in the nation.

NOTE

1. Lucy Larcom, *A New England Girlhood: Outlined from Memory* (Boston: Houghton Mifflin, 1889), 39–40, 41–42.

||||||||||||||||||||||||||||||||||||||||||||||||||||||

7

"A Few Thoughts in Vindication of Female Eloquence"

The Case for the Education of Republican Women

A. Kristen Foster

"We have it in our power to begin the world over again," proclaimed Thomas Paine in his precedent-shattering pamphlet *Common Sense*. Indeed, once American patriots made the leap from resistance to revolution, they embarked on a journey into the unknown. To be sure, military victory brought political independence from Great Britain, but what Americans fashioned out of their newfound autonomy would define them as a people and a nation. At no time in American history, save perhaps for the first colonial settlements, did the people themselves have such an opportunity to envision their world anew. How would they define their revolution? Was it simply independence, or would there be more? While historians have debated and will continue to debate the depth and breadth of American social change in the wake of American independence, Gordon Wood has argued that the Revolution's radicalism lay not in what it had wrought during the war or the ensuing constitutional era but in its potential, in the very language that promised more than the founding generation was willing to give. While the nation's political architects constructed a government that brought moderate changes to the lives of most Americans, some women wondered at the extent to which they had been left behind. "Remember the ladies," counseled Abigail Adams when she wrote to her husband John in March 1778, but this advice is as well known as the fact that the Revolution brought limited change to the lives of American women. Yet over the course of the early republic, American girls learned the language of the Revolution and found their own radicalism in the female academies that grew out of attempts to build the new United States into a classical republic. In educating republican girls to be virtuous citizens, American girls found an independent voice that would eventually redefine both virtue and citizenship.[1]

Many in the revolutionary generation understood that the war that won them independence from Britain would not in itself create a nation. They understood that the job of building a nation was in their hands. "Americans," exhorted Noah Webster, "unshackle your minds and act like independent beings. You have been children long enough. . . . You have now an interest of your own to augment and defend: you have an empire to raise and support by your exertions and a national character to establish and extend by your wisdom and virtues."[2] Philadelphia's patriot doctor Benjamin Rush understood the weightiness of this opportunity, as he called in 1787 for his fellow Americans to rescue the revolutionary experiment from the chaos of the Confederation years. "There is nothing more common," he wrote, "than to confound the terms *American Revolution* with those of the *late American War*. The American war is over: but this is far from being the case with the American revolution. On the contrary, nothing but the first act of the great drama is closed. It remains yet to establish and perfect our new forms of government; and to prepare the principles, morals, and manners of our citizens for these forms of government."[3]

Benjamin Rush moved in elite circles with other classically educated men who believed that republican government would best serve this new United States. What made republics unique and fragile, however, was the necessity that citizens place their country's interest before their own. Each citizen, therefore, would need to possess extraordinary virtue, or independence of mind, in order to make this experiment work. In other words, a republican nation would be only as good as its citizenry. Many wondered, however, if such selflessness came naturally to human beings. Certainly the fires of revolution had forged a new kind of American, committed to a government without monarchs or aristocrats, independent and sturdy perhaps, and willing to experiment with change. Yet as Rush himself pointed out in 1787, Americans would need to "prepare" their "principles, morals, and manners" for republican government. "Americans must *believe* and *act* from the belief that it is dishonorable to waste life in mimicking the follies of other nations and basking in the sunshine of foreign glory," argued Noah Webster.[4] Americans had to create the world anew—this would be their revolution.

For many Americans, including Rush and Webster, the school stood unparalleled in its importance for shaping a republican citizenry. In the nation's new academies, young boys and girls would be taught to think and act like republican citizens, no longer the subjects of outmoded European monarchical hierarchies. While republican government supported hierarchies of its own, the nation found ways to justify unequal citizenship. Republican theorists argued that dependents, anyone without their own financial means, could not participate equally in the republic because their votes could be coerced by those with power over them. So women, servants, workers, and children, having few if any property rights, found themselves on the margins of republican citizenship.

The voices from the margins, however, spoke articulately during and after the war, and they grew louder over time. Abigail Adams understood that her revolution was ripe with possibilities for women. Why not change the legal status of women? she asked her husband John, when he and the other founders met to draft laws for their new government. Others wondered about property requirements for voting, and some questioned the morality of slavery in this new nation. Clearly, the founders understood that they would need to reconcile the Revolution's egalitarian language with republican hierarchies and economic realities. Fearing the chaos of a full-scale social revolution, America's founders steered the republic's ship on a moderate course. On this journey, women, who were left without property rights and thus the vote, would still have an important role as equal guardians of republican virtue, and education would be the key to their preparation.

While historians have embraced Linda Kerber's thesis that, among other things, female academies were intended to educate American girls to be republican mothers, Margaret Nash has offered a more nuanced look at the goals of these academies. She argues that educating girls to raise the next generation of republican citizens was one of many impulses for these founding academic trustees. *Republican womanhood*, she argues, would be a more appropriate term. A close look at both the major proponents of female education in the early republic and the application of their ideas in the founding of the Young Ladies' Academy of Philadelphia shows that the idea of republican womanhood had a life of its own in the hands of these young women. In spite of efforts to define gender-appropriate republican citizenship, the girls of the academy took their lessons and began to think of themselves not only as women but as individuals.[5]

The Importance of Republican Education

In 1786, as the young United States suffered from the convulsions of inexperience and a problematic frame of government, Benjamin Rush sought to further the cause of education in Pennsylvania, perhaps in part to instill virtue in a citizenry that seemed to teeter on the brink of chaos. In his "Plan for the Establishment of Public Schools," Rush argued that "a free government can only exist in an equal diffusion of literature" and that "without learning, men become savages or barbarians." Finally, he argued that where only a few people have access to education, "we always find monarchy, aristocracy, and slavery." The health and future of the republic itself, argued Rush, depended not on virtue born from faith but on virtue carefully nurtured by both secular and spiritual learning. Republican schools would become the "nurseries of wise and good men" who would grow up to protect the republic with their virtue. "Next to the duty which young men owe to their Creator," said Rush, "I wish to see a SUPREME RE-GARD TO THEIR COUNTRY inculcated upon them." In this way, American men could be converted into "republican machines" that "perform their parts properly in the great machine of the government of the state."[6] Rush's plan thus manifested his affinity with the Enlightenment. Boys should receive a classical education that included the "learned or dead languages," "eloquence," history and chronology, commerce and money, chemistry, the art of war, and practical legislation. For Rush and other enlightened architects of early American education, republican learning should be orderly and purposeful; his plan was scientific and clear.

Benjamin Rush also took tremendous interest in the education of young women, since he understood them, as familial actors, to be equally important for the health of the republic. As he closed his "Thoughts upon the Mode of Education Proper in a Republic" in 1786, he begged his audience to pardon him for delaying his thoughts on "the separate and peculiar mode of education proper for WOMEN in a republic," asserting that women had to be part of all plans for educating young men, "or no laws will ever render them effectual." Thus he argued that women had to learn "the usual branches of female education" but should also be instructed in the "principles of liberty and government, and the obligations of patriotism." Rush was not suggesting radical social change; rather, he was arguing that because women had so much power over the "opinions and conduct" of men they had to understand republican virtue. In keeping with this traditional construction of female social roles, Rush also argued that as mothers of the next generation of citizens, women must be learned. Because "the *first* impressions upon the minds of children are generally derived from the women," he said, these women needed to "think justly upon the great subjects of liberty and government."[7]

True to his word, then, Rush became a founding member of one of the first female academies in the United States. In both Rush's explicitly outlined plan and the speeches given by the trustees at the first graduation ceremonies, these men defined republican womanhood within the boundaries of traditional female social roles centered on God and family. In the spring of 1787, John Poor opened the Young Ladies' Academy of Philadelphia. This academy educated adolescent girls from Philadelphia families who could afford the tuition (four dollars per quarter by 1794), as well as girls from Georgia, Carolina, Virginia, Maryland, Delaware, New Jersey, New York, Connecticut, Rhode Island, Massachusetts, Maine, Nova Scotia, Canada, and "several of the West-India islands."[8] Along with the other founding trustees, Rush helped formulate the school's plan to educate republican women.

In July 1787, at the close of quarterly exams at Philadelphia's new academy, trustee Benjamin Rush delivered a speech entitled "Thoughts upon Female Education" in which he argued that educated women were essential to a republic. "It is incumbent upon us," he said, "to make ornamental accomplishments yield to principles and knowledge in the education of our women." He argued first that American women required a unique education to be "accommodated to the state of society, manners, and government of the country." According to his list of American peculiarities, though, republican women are defined, even confined, by their familial roles as mothers or as wives. Rush argued that early marriages necessitated a "useful" education and that as "stewards" of their husbands' property women needed to learn how to discharge these duties effectively. He emphasized that as partners in parenting American women needed appropriate schooling and "that our ladies should be qualified to a certain degree, by a peculiar and suitable education, to concur in instructing their sons in the principles of liberty and government." Finally, he argued that because American servants were more ignorant and less tractable than those in Europe, American women had to learn to manage their households.[9]

Rush's sense of America's domestic peculiarities, then, shaped his plan for female education. For these republican women to fulfill their obligations, they would need to learn the English language, have a "fair and legible hand," learn figures and bookkeeping, have an "acquaintance with geography and some instruction in chronology" (so that they could be "an agreeable companion for a sensible man"), learn some astronomy and natural philosophy to prevent superstition, become proficient in vocal music to take part in public worship and "soothe the cares of domestic life," and take some dancing lessons for physical health. Young women should also be encouraged to read history, travel narratives, poetry, and moral essays rather than frivolous novels. And crucially for Rush and most Americans of the time, including the young ladies at the academy, "It will be necessary to connect all these branches of education with regular instruction in the Christian religion." As he neared the close of his address, he reminded his audience (trustees and students) that "to be the mistress of a family is one of the great ends of a woman's being." In the end, republican women were family women, and the health of the republic could be measured by their virtuous dispensation of these duties. "The first marks we shall perceive of our declension," warned Rush, "will appear among our women. Their idleness, ignorance, and profligacy will be the harbingers of our ruin."[10]

Benjamin Rush was not alone in his assessment of the importance of female education. Not surprisingly, the trustees of the Young Ladies' Academy of Philadelphia also discussed the benefits of and boundaries for educating young women. Between 1788 and 1794, these men took turns proctoring and grading exams for the girls and then delivering what was called the Visitor's Address at the graduation ceremonies. As it did for Rush, the Enlightenment greatly influenced these men. They all stressed the importance of female education that could be applied to life in the new republic. Girls would acquire "useful knowledge" to lead useful lives. Throwing off the frivolous shackles of Europe included educating American women to be more than accoutrements in the lives of American men. Indeed, the school's official seal centered on a pile of seven books, each emphasizing one of the branches of education taught at the academy, encircled by the words "THE PATH OF SCIENCE." At the top of the seal the "eye of Science" emitted "rays over the whole."[11]

While these trustees did not imagine American women beyond their social roles as wives and mothers, they were influenced by the Enlightenment and the Revolution to suggest a more rigorous education for girls that included subjects well beyond what would be necessary for domestic duties. The seven books portrayed on the academy's seal dealt with spelling, reading, writing, English grammar, arithmetic, geography, rhetoric and composition. While the girls would take these subjects in unexpected directions, the trustees' speeches clearly placed limitations and qualifications on the application of these subjects in the lives of women. Women who could read, write a clear script, and cipher competently were not particularly threatening to the social order, and it made sense for women to do these well so that they could help their husbands run family economies. But why have "a general knowledge of the . . . terraqueous globe," of the "planets that compose the solar system," of "the rise, progress, declension, and final extinction of the most remarkable states, kingdoms and empires"? How would a familiarity with the cultures of the world, the workings of the solar system, and the ebb and flow of history help women run families? "Let it suffice to say," argued Presbyterian minister and trustee James Sproat, "that such academical improvements, tend to mol[l]ify the temper, refine the manners, amuse the fancy, improve the understanding, and strengthen virtue—to lay a foundation for a life of usefulness and happiness here, and if rightly improved, for a blessed immortality hereafter." In 1792, another trustee, the Rev. Dr. Samuel Magaw, took this practical education one step further, arguing that as long as women learned useful subjects and not abstract ones, all would be well in the Republic. "The most useful [subjects]," he told the girls, "are certainly the most estimable." Setting clear boundaries, he added that "the abstract and abstruse come not properly within *your* line."[12]

The trustees certainly took seriously their responsibility for educating American girls, but as the young republic redefined male citizenship they remained limited in their vision for American women. Sproat, in describing the "foundation for a life of usefulness and happiness," and Magaw, in speaking of a female "line," saw women in the same roles they had assumed prior to the Revolution—wives, mothers, and Christians. Knowing arithmetic, Dr. Benjamin Say told the girls in 1789, "will enable you to buy or sell advantageously—cast up accounts, and in general to transact such business as may be found occasionally necessary for yourselves, and as assisting companions of the other sex." The 1792 commencement ceremony so moved an anonymous gentleman that he wrote the following lines in celebration:

> To teach th' aspiring faculties to soar,
> And the bright realms of science to explore;
> To form the maiden for th' accomplish'd wife,
> And fix the basis of a happy life!

As accomplished wives, American women would accept the responsibilities of mothers. These mothers, wrote John Swanwick, would teach their children of the glories of American laws and government; consequently "all the obligations contained in the invaluable name of mother, will be secured as a bulwark round our inestimable constitution."[13]

To be sure, as stewards of republican education, the trustees of the academy emphasized secular content, but not because they intended to separate republican education from Christian education. Instead, these men heartily believed that a solid classical education would rid American girls of superstition and better prepare what the Rev. Pilmore called their "immortal souls" for heaven. Christianity remained central to definitions of female republican virtue. As the "illuminating rays of celestial science" had rid the world of "gothic rudeness, and barbarity of manners," these men believed that education would also sharpen the minds of American women so that they could better understand divine providence. "Education and religion disperse the clouds that hide the glory from us," said Rev. Joseph Pilmore. Geography, argued Benjamin Say, would help students "admire the wonderful works of an Almighty hand." Rev. Pilmore reminded his audience that the girls were perpetually in the "utmost danger of seduction" by "the prince of darkness," who was always at work in the world. Diligent instruction and a watchful eye would be their weapons. The Young Ladies' Academy thus would provide American girls not just with the practical instruction aimed at educating useful mates and mothers but also with the Christian instruction that would lend a moral weight and a higher purpose to their studies. "May the smiles of Providence, and the influences of grace, ever attend this seminary . . . and while the fair youth are led by the gentle hands of their worthy instructors, in the paths of useful learning, may the purest morals be here cultivated and maintained, and the holy religion of Jesus recommended," instructed Rev. Sproat, so that instructor and pupil alike would "be happy in heaven for ever."[14]

A Female Perspective

While the Enlightenment and its child the American Revolution had inspired the trustees of the Young Ladies' Academy of Philadelphia to open the doors of advanced learning to girls, these events would lead the girls to consider themselves not only as part of a republican community but as individuals. Women had already begun to imagine more inclusive, less dependent roles for themselves in society. A transatlantic group of thinkers that included historian Catharine Macaulay and intellectual Mary Wollstonecraft counted some notable American women among their ranks. Lucky enough to have had a father who valued learning for his daughters, Abigail Adams wrote to her husband in 1778 that he "need not be told how much female Education is neglected, nor how fashionable it has been to ridicule Female learning." Her friend Mercy Otis Warren wrote an important history of the War for Independence. In Philadelphia, Esther Reed and Sarah Franklin Bache organized a very public fund drive for Washington's army, while Judith Sargent Murray of Massachusetts, who seemingly stood alone in her proposals for female economic independence, remains the most significant female theorist of the early republic.

In a series of publications that include the famous *Gleaner* articles, Sargent Murray wrote at length about the abilities of women, female education, and the forces that had historically kept women from intellectual excellence. Like others, she exposed the hypocrisy of those men in power who had historically kept girls from extensive education and then had called them inferior for their intellectual limitations. If women did not measure up to the intellectual standard set by men, argued Murray, the cause was not an inferior intellect but an inferior education. "I have conceived that the distinction male, and female, does not exist in *Mind*," she wrote to one Rev. Mr. Redding in 1801, "and it appears to me that my opinion is sanctioned by the imposing authorities of nature, and scripture—I have thought that the disimilarity confessedly apparent, was merely artificial, entirely the result of education, variety of pursuits, and uncounted accidental occurences." Like Benjamin Rush and the various trustees of the Young Ladies' Academy, however, Murray's own construction of republican womanhood is at one level confined by her acceptance of women's social roles as wives and mothers. "A mother," wrote Murray, "is certainly the most proper preceptress for her children, and it [is] for this reason that I would educate a daughter upon the most liberal plan." She also argued that education made women better, more interesting wives and that this allowed for happier marriages. "By strengthening the body and exercising the mental capacities," she wrote, "we shall be rendered more capable of managing our families, of systematizing morality, and of becoming the friends of our husbands."[15]

Although sharing the spotlight with Benjamin Rush as the nation's primary theorist of republican motherhood, at another level Sargent Murray courageously tested the limits placed on American women. She dared to imagine and write about women as independent actors and public beings; and, like her European counterpart Mary Wollstonecraft, she found herself pushed to the margins of acceptable discourse. Murray herself had experienced the insecurity of poverty, and in spite of her obvious abilities she knew that if her husband John died before her she could be left destitute. As such, she agitated in her writing for female economic independence. "THE SEX," she wrote, "should be taught to depend on their own efforts."[16] Murray hoped that education, by proving American women's equal abilities, would help them gain some economic independence in addition to personal happiness. Murray's economic ideas, however, were too radical for most of the architects of the young United States.

Although her calls for female economic independence remained unanswered, Murray continued to pursue the topic of inequality. In fact, she was at her most passionate when she discussed female equality. She addressed her readers as if she had been personally affronted. In a pathbreaking essay entitled "On the Equality of the Sexes," published in two installments in the *Massachusetts Magazine* in March and April 1790, Murray made her most articulate defense of women's education. Asking her readers to consider with her whether nature had been partial in the distribution of intellectual abilities (giving the lion's share to men), Murray pointed out that she had seen excellence and its opposite in both sexes. Then she invited her readers to make a comparative examination with her of the "four heads" of "intellectual powers" (imagination, reason, memory, and judgment) in both men and women. She argued first that imagination had "long since been surrendered up to us [women], and we have been crowned undoubted sovereigns of the regions of fancy." In memory, however, men and women were equal. And in her discussion of reason and judgment, Sargent Murray got to the heart of historic discrimination. Are women deficient in reason? she asked. Such a deficit could not be adequately assessed, she answered, since women had not had equal access to education: "We can only reason from what we know, and if opportunity of acquiring knowledge hath been denied us, the inferiority of our sex cannot fairly be deduced from thence." Logically, Sargent Murray tied judgment to reason, again arguing that education was the root cause of the discrepancy between men and women. "Our judgment is not so strong—we do not distinguish so well," she acknowledged, but she continued to explain that a lack of female education was to blame. "From what doth this superiority, in thus discriminating faculty of the soul, proceed?"

she asked. "May we not trace its source in the difference of education, and continued advantages?" Using her powers of reason, she asked her reader to compare the judgment of children. At the age of two there is little difference between a boy and girl, she said. From that time on, however, one was "exalted and the other depressed, by the contrary modes of education which are adopted! the one is taught to aspire, and the other is early confined and limited. . . . Grant that their minds are by nature equal, yet who shall wonder at the *apparent* superiority, if indeed custom becomes *second nature*; nay if it taketh place of nature."[17]

Sargent Murray wanted her readers to understand that America's belief in female inferiority had become second nature and thus more difficult to combat. As she built her case for female education in her argument for the equality of the sexes, she became angrier and angrier. She directly condemned male arrogance for degrading women by forbidding the latter to acquire any knowledge but "the mechanism of a pudding, or the sewing of the seams of a garment." "Yes, ye lordly, ye haughty sex," she declared, "our souls are by nature *equal* to yours; the same breath of God animates, enlivens, and invigorates us." But according to Sargent Murray, men had used their superior physical strength to justify the advantages they had in all facets of life. Cleverly, however, she also exposed the faulty logic involved in equating male physical superiority with intellectual dominance. "I know there are who assert [sic], that as the animal powers of the one sex are superiour, of course their mental faculties also must be stronger. . . . But if this reasoning is just, man must be content to yield the palm to many of the brute creation, since by not a few of this brethren of the field, he is far surpassed in bodily strength." Only eight years later, Sargent Murray would celebrate the rise of the female academy. "I may be accused of enthusiasm," she wrote in 1798, "but such is my confidence in THE SEX, that I expect to see our young women forming a new era in female history."[18]

While Judith Sargent Murray had no direct connection to Philadelphia's Young Ladies' Academy, her challenges to the limits placed on American women were echoed in the youthful speeches of a few of the school's graduates. Indeed, Benjamin Rush, the trustees of the academy, and the female students themselves seemed to agree with Sargent Murray on the importance of female education. They all hoped to help the young United States succeed in building a republican society that relied not only on its male citizenry but also on its women to maintain the virtue necessary for the republic to flourish. But as Rush and the academy's trustees envisioned republican women as companionate citizens not to be trusted with independence, Murray's work suggested the direction in which the girls themselves would take their studies. While the girls' public graduation addresses reveal echoes of the trustees' mission to prepare the graduates for "useful" Christian lives, they also reveal whispers and sometimes shouts of anger and independent thinking.[19]

Most of the girls began their orations modestly by first acknowledging their humility. Ann Loxley told her audience that when she actually thought about speaking in public at her age it caused her to "tremble at the task." Eliza Shrupp also told her audience that she was afraid to speak publicly but that she knew her sense of duty would help her overcome this. The following year, Molly Wallace made it clear to her listeners that female humility was of the utmost importance: "Our improvements will be best shewn in the exercise of humility. Charity and modesty are the best evidences of a highly cultivated mind." And in 1793 Eliza Laskey chose to devote her entire speech to the topic of modesty, which she carefully distinguished from ignorance, saying that modesty "does not insist on that dull and rigid silence, which so often reigns in some stiff and uninlightened [sic] companies, where silence passes current for virtue, ignorance sometimes for religion, and affectation for politeness." Laskey best embodied the goals of the trustees. She argued for female education on the grounds that it would improve the quality of female companionship and "add beauty to its original." Modesty, as she described it, offered educated women a middle ground between ignorance and arrogance: it "teaches us deference and respect to our superiors; it imposes profound silence on us, when such persons are speaking in our presence. It at all times restrains us from any unbecoming and indecent speech, or behaviour, but more especially in company." Like her fellow students, Laskey rarely talked about motherhood, but she did argue that the purpose of their education should be to make women more sophisticated members of their communities.[20]

While the theorists of classical republicanism often juxtaposed masculine virtue with effeminate vice, the girls and their teachers at Philadelphia's Young Ladies' Academy suggest another construction of republican womanhood. The students clearly understood the goals of republican education. Echoing the trustees, a number of Eliza Laskey's classmates stressed that education brought respect, happiness, and salvation. After pronouncing that all of their future actions should be "seasoned with virtue, guided by wisdom, and crowned with modesty," Ann Loxley went on to explain that educated women would be "admired and esteemed" by all who knew them and that learning would be "conducive to a happy life here, and a blessed immortality." In addition to these weighty goals, an educated woman, they argued, would be freed from the frivolous distractions that brought dissipation and ruin to a fragile republican society. "The love of ease, and indolence, is opposed to every valuable acquisition," said Eliza Shrupp. "Put on, then, the helmet of discretion. Accustom yourselves to some of the duties of self-denial. . . . Never depart from the path of truth and sincerity. . . . Remember that youth is the fittest season for a foundation upon which a glorious superstructure may be erected, and if this season is given up to pleasure and dissipation, you will sustain a loss not easily retrieved." John Adams might have been proud of Eliza Shrupp. Ann Laskey also understood the community benefits of a well-educated woman, arguing in 1793 that the girls should take "fast hold" of their instruction. "Let her [education] not go," she warned, "keep her; for she is thy life." With education, Laskey told her classmates, they would be like warriors for virtue: "With modesty your shrine, and innocence your strongest shield, you shall repel the attack of vice and folly. So shall the tongue of slander be dumb, and envy vex itself: Flattery, and ingenious deceit shall give place to truth and virtue, and fortune smile at length on innocence."[21] Students like Shrupp and Laskey did not focus explicitly on educating themselves for their roles as wives and mothers (neither did they explicitly exclude these roles); instead they understood themselves to be contributing members of a larger community in which they had to uphold virtue by avoiding the pitfalls of frivolous behavior so often associated with women.

Like Benjamin Rush and the trustees, the girls never wavered from their desire to use their education to bring them closer to God. In fact, as Rush himself pointed out, a knowledge of science would dispel the ignorance and superstition that kept people from truly knowing God. Molly Wallace closed her oration with a reminder to her classmates to join her in consistent humility before Christ: "*Blessed* Jesus! be *thou* our living guide—may virtue and its tract be our daily and delightful path, which leads upward to the regions of love and joy." Molly Barker also reminded her classmates that the vanity of youth would lead them away from God if they were not vigilant. "Alas," she told her friends, "how little do they know of the dangers which await them.—Neither human wisdom nor human virtue, unsupported by religion, are equal for the trying situations which often occur in life." Wisdom and virtue alone, according to Barker, would be inadequate in life's struggles against temptation and hardship.

"Correct this ill-founded arrogance. Expect not that your happiness can be independent of him who made you." The United States would be a Christian republic. In the words of one anonymous student, "The man who in his youth has been taught his duty, and how to perform it will . . . dedicate his time to the advancement of the glory of his God and the benefit of his fellow creatures."[22]

The girls of Philadelphia's Young Ladies' Academy had learned their lessons of virtue and usefulness well, but their studies also gave them an opportunity to think in new ways about who they were and about their lives as women in America. As much as they echoed the goals of Benjamin Rush and the other trustees, the girls of the academy began to think about themselves as individuals. This was the unexpected impact of female education in the early republic. Eliza Laskey thanked the school's founders and teachers for the opportunity to learn, saying that their work had "delivered" the girls "from the shackles of custom, and dispelled from our minds those clouds of ignorance and darkness, in which our sex has been too long involv'd." Molly Wallace echoed Laskey's appreciation for the chance they'd been given, saying to her graduating class that "we must be sensible, that we are favoured with opportunities of improvements, of which thousands of our sex are denied." These girls understood, too, that the world was watching, some cheering perhaps, while others waited to watch the girls fall short of their male counterparts. "It is our duty then nobly to exert ourselves," urged Molly Wallace, "and to shew, that the labour and care which have been bestowed upon us have not been bestowed in vain, and to prove that the female mind will reward the most assiduous culture." Eliza Laskey may have understood best how much some observers were waiting like hungry wolves to see them fail, warning her classmates that "the least departure from the path of virtue, will be the more exposed to the eye and tongue of the critical observer. Envy ever seeks to enrich itself by detracting from the virtues and magnifying the faults of others." And although she knew this was "contemptible," the girls had to be vigilant.[23]

In the graduation orations of Molly Wallace and Priscilla Mason, the radical social potential of both the Enlightenment and the American Revolution is most apparent in spite of the more moderate aspirations of the academy's trustees. Molly Wallace took the podium in 1792 for her valedictory oration and told her audience that her sex, youth, and inexperience all conspired to make her tremble as she stood there. But as if this was merely pro forma, she wasted little time skillfully asserting herself thereafter. Like Judith Sargent Murray, Wallace argued that the ignorance of women should be proof that girls needed education, not that they were incapable of using it. She focused her condemnation, then, on the inability of women to speak in public and the reasons given for keeping them from such tasks. Some people, she argued, had questioned whether women "ought *ever* to appear in so public a manner. Our natural timidity, the domestic situation to which by nature and custom we seem destined . . . are urged as arguments against what I have now undertaken." So, why, she asked, should women learn the art of public speaking? "That she should harangue at the head of an Army, in the Senate, or before a popular Assembly, is not pretended," Wallace made clear, "neither is it requested that she ought to be an adept in the stormy and contentious eloquence of the bar, or in the abstract and subtle reasoning of the Senate." "We look not for a female Pitt, Cicero, or Demosthenes," she admitted. Women needed to learn the art of elocution, not for politics or statecraft, but for the habits of mind that it created. Personifying her own argument, Wallace used her education to lead her audience logically through her point. "Why is a boy diligently and carefully taught the Latin, the Greek, or the Hebrew language, in which he will seldom have the occasion, either to write or converse?" she asked. Or why is he taught Euclidian geometry, and why are girls taught to dance? Her answer: not so they will become Euclidian mathmaticians or dancers; rather, "these things are commonly studied more on account of the habits, which the learning of them establishes, than on account of any important advantages which the mere knowledge of them can afford."[24]

In the following year, a young Priscilla Mason stunningly asserted not only that women had been ill-treated by men but that they deserved better. She began her salutatory oration as did the other girls, asking for the audience's indulgence: "A female, young and inexperienced, addressing a promiscuous assembly, is a novelty which requires an apology, as some may suppose. I therefore . . . beg leave to offer a few thoughts in vindication of female eloquence." Although Mason argued that women had an uncontested right to be heard in public, she carefully softened her assertion by saying that women should leave their oratorical skills resting "like the sword in the scabbard, to be used only when occasion requires." Having said this, though, Mason continued to enumerate the ways that women not only were skilled orators but might even surpass their male counterparts at the podium. "Our right to instruct and persuade cannot be disputed," she began, adding that women had "in eminent degree" the "power of speech, and volubility of expression." Women also brought "personal attractions" to public oratory, she argued, adding "charms to eloquence, and force to the orator's arguments." In the end, however, Mason stressed the emotional complexity of women as an attribute, arguing that the "tender passions" of the female heart "enable the orator to speak in a moving and forcible manner." In fact, this ability to emote, according to Mason, was "confessedly ours," and in conjunction with their powers of persuasion and their "personal attractions," women were "in all these respects. . . equal,—nay, on *superior* ground." Mason thus argued that the very characteristics that most Americans assumed made women into unreasonable creatures actually proved to be strengths for public speaking.

Like Judith Sargent Murray, the young Priscilla Mason was at her angriest when she discussed the reasons that women had remained uneducated. She was the most direct, even confrontational, as she blamed men for the inequity. "Our high and mighty Lords (thanks to their arbitrary constitutions)," she said, "have denied us the means of knowledge, and then reproached us for the want of it." And like Sargent Murray as well, Mason claimed that superior physical strength had given men the false belief that they could make laws that "denied women the advantage of a liberal education" and "forbid them to exercise their talents . . . which would serve to improve them." According to Mason, then, men had willfully subjugated women to aggrandize their own power. "They doom'd the sex to servile or frivolous employments, on purpose," she continued, "to degrade their minds, that they themselves might hold unrivall'd the power and pre-eminence they had usurped." Citing a number of accomplished women, Mason suggested that her sex had already proven itself more than capable of eloquence. "The Church, the Bar, and the Senate are shut against us," she declared. "Who shut them?" Her answer: "Man; despotic man." In closing, Mason asked her audience to look to the Society of Friends, her own denomination, for a lesson in female eloquence. She explained that while other churches continued to give women what she called "mock pre-eminence in small matters," the Quakers "look to the soul, and allow all to teach who are capable of it, be they male or female."[25] In the end, Priscilla Mason did not ask that these public arenas be opened to women, but she did suggest that women were capable of having a more public social role and so deserved the respect to which these skills entitled them. Looking at the youthful oratorical skills of young Molly Wallace and Priscilla Mason, perhaps Judith Sargent Murray had reason to feel confident that educated girls would form "a new era in female history."[26]

Had American revolutionaries begun the world over again, as Thomas Paine suggested? They had certainly set in motion more radical change than many expected or wanted. While a majority of the founding fathers hoped to contain and thus moderate the radicalism embodied in revolutionary words like *liberty* and *equality*, they could no more contain this tide than England could contain colonial unrest once the Stamp Act had passed Parliament. The seeds had been sown, and only time would reveal what had been planted. While many founders tried to construct a limited role for women in the new republic, the growth of enlightened education for girls set in motion changes in the ways that women thought about themselves and their lives as women. For the girls at Philadelphia's Young Ladies' Academy, education brought with it a desire for expanded possibilities and a denial of the legitimacy of their second-class status.

NOTES

1. Scholars have recently begun to qualify Linda Kerber's groundbreaking study on what she termed republican motherhood. See Linda Kerber, "The Republican Mother: Women and the Enlightenment, an American Perspective," *American Quarterly* 28 (1976): 187–205, and *Women of the Republic: Ideology and Intellect in Revolutionary America* (Chapel Hill: University of North Carolina Press, 1980). Both Margaret Nash and Mary Kelley argue that republican motherhood was one of a number of goals of female education in the early republic. See Margaret A. Nash, "Rethinking Republican Motherhood: Benjamin Rush and the Young Ladies' Academy of Philadelphia," *Journal of the Early Republic* 17 (Summer 1997): 171–91, and *Women's Education in the United States, 1780–1840* (New York: Palgrave Macmillan, 2005); and Mary Kelley, *Learning to Stand and Speak: Women, Education, and Public Life in America's Republic* (Chapel Hill: University of North Carolina Press, 2006). For an older study of female education, see Thomas Woody's multivolume *History of Women's Education in the United States* (New York: Science Press, 1929).

2. Noah Webster, "On the Education of Youth in America" (Boston, 1790), reprinted in *Essays on Education in the Early Republic*, ed. Frederick Rudolph (Cambridge, MA: Harvard University Press, 1965), 77.

3. Benjamin Rush, "The Defects of the Confederation" (Philadelphia, 1787), in *American Patriotism: Speeches, Letters, and Other Papers Which Illustrate the Foundation, the Development, the Preservation of the United States of America*, comp. Selim H. Peabody (New York: John B. Alden, 1886), 147.

4. Ibid., Webster, "On the Education," 77.

5. Nash, "Rethinking Republican Motherhood," 171 and 178. In *Learning to*

Stand, Kelley argues that female education gave young women the opportunity to imagine themselves as civic actors, not only helpmates, and thus makes the link between these early female academies and women's activism in antebellum America.

6. Benjamin Rush, "Plan for the Establishment of Public Schools" (1786) and "Thoughts upon the Mode of Education Proper in a Republic" (1786), both reprinted in Rudolph, *Essays on Education*, 3 and 9, 13 and 17, respectively.

7. Ibid., 21–22, 22.

8. *The Rise and Progress of the Young Ladies' Academy of Philadelphia: Containing an Account of a Number of Public Examinations & Commencements; The Charter and Bye-Laws, Likewise, a Number of Orations Delivered by the Young Ladies and Several by the Trustees of Said Institution* (Philadelphia: Steward and Cochran, 1794), 3 and 118. See also Marion B. Savin and Harold J. Abrahams, "The Young Ladies' Academy of Philadelphia," *History of Education Journal* 8 (Winter 1957): 58–67.

9. Benjamin Rush, "Thoughts upon Female Education, Accommodated to the Present State of Society, Manners, and Government in the United States of America," speech given to the visitors of Philadelphia's Young Ladies Academy, July 28, 1787, reprinted in Rudolph, *Essays on Education*, 36, 27–28. Margaret Nash argues that Rush saw American women as enlightened beings and that "historians have overstated the impact of republican motherhood." While this is true, I do think that the republic's male theorists did not think about women's roles or obligations much beyond domestic duties. While Nash importantly qualified the emphasis on educating mothers, arguing that the trustees focused on educating the girls to have the pleasure of learning, to create a heightened relationship to God, to lead useful and virtuous lives, and to perform business functions, I think that these men stressed these goals within the context of women's domestic relationships. See Nash, "Rethinking Republican Motherhood," 171 and 182, and *Women's Education in the United States*.

10. Rush, "Thoughts upon Female Education," 28–31, 35, 37.

11. Description of the seal of the Young Ladies' Academy of Philadelphia in *Rise and Progress*, 68, found in the collections of the Library Company of Philadelphia. While the Young Ladies' Academy endured well beyond 1794, the first publication of these addresses covered the years 1788–94, and this publication provides the basis for this study.

12. Address by the Rev. Doctor James Sproat (June 9 and 10, 1789), and Address by the Rev. Dr. Samuel Magaw (Fall 1792), both in *Rise and Progress*, 25–26 and 83 respectively.

13. Address delivered at the Young Ladies' Academy by Dr. Benjamin Say (December 3 and 4, 1789), Poem by an Anonymous Gentleman (1792), and Address delivered at the Young Ladies' Academy by John Swanwick, Esq. (1790), all in *Rise*

and Progress, 32, 79, and 23 respectively. Published separately but found with *Rise and Progress* in the collections of the Library Company of Philadelphia.

14. James Armstrong Neal, *An Essay on the Genius and Education of the Fair Sex* (Philadelphia, 1795), 1; addresses by Joseph Pilmore, Benjamin Say, and James Sproat, all in *Rise and Progress,* 9–10, 32, and 27–28 respectively.

15. Judith Sargent Murray to Rev. Mr. Redding, May 7, 1801, Letterbook, 11:287–88; Judith Sargent Murray to Winthrop Sargent, Sept. 1803, Letterbook, 12:878; Judith Sargent Murray to Mrs. K____, April 21, 1802, Letterbook, 11:350, all in Sheila L. Skemp, *Judith Sargent Murray: A Brief Biography with Documents* (Boston: Bedford Books, 1998), 174–75, 88, and 89, respectively.

16. Judith Sargent Murray to Maria Sargent, March 16, 1793, Letterbook, 8:103, in Skemp, *Judith Sargent Murray,* 89.

17. Judith Sargent Murray, "On the Equality of the Sexes," (1790), in Skemp, *Judith Sargent Murray,* 177–78.

18. Ibid., 179–80; Judith Sargent Murray, "The Gleaner Contemplates the Future Prospects of Women in This 'Enlightened Age'" (1798), in Skemp, *Judith Sargent Murray,* 183.

19. While I agree with Margaret Nash at a basic level that "the school did not produce docile women willing to assume subordinate roles in life" ("Rethinking Republican Motherhood," 186), I would not suggest that school made the girls discontented. Certainly the graduates express some reservations about traditional domestic roles, but most of them advocate changes in degree only. The girls suggest that they want to be enlightened Christian members of their communities. What they do, however, is suggest new directions for women. In *Learning to Stand,* Kelley looks more extensively at female academies in the early republic and argues that the academies prepared these girls to think about themselves as civic actors with rights and responsibilities. Indeed, the girls at the Young Ladies' Academy show some early inclinations to question male authority and wonder at the possibilities for the own lives.

20. Ann Loxley, valedictory oration, June 1790; Eliza Shrupp, valedictory oration, September 1791; Molly Wallace, valedictory oration, June 1792; and Eliza Laskey, valedictory oration, May 1793, all in *Rise and Progress,* 30, 49, 77, 96, respectively.

21. Valedictory orations of Loxley, Shrupp, Laskey, all in *Rise and Progress,* 41, 51, and 101 respectively.

22. Wallace, valedictory oration; Molly Barker, "A Funeral Oration on the Death of Miss Molly Say," February 1794; anonymous student, "On the Importance of an Early Application to Study," December 1788, all in *Rise and Progress,* 78–79, 111–12, and 22 respectively.

23. Valedictory orations of Laskey, Wallace, and Laskey, all in *Rise and Progress,* 97–98, 76–77, and 102 respectively.

24. Wallace, valedictory oration, *Rise and Progress*, 73–75.

25. Priscilla Mason, salutatory oration, May 1793, in *Rise and Progress*, 91, 92.

26. To date, only Mary Kelley has looked at the public lives of many American women who were educated in some of the young republic's earliest female academies. While young women like Philadelphia's Molly Wallace and Priscilla Mason invite further study, such research has yet to be done. Kelley herself has furthered our understanding of this field by looking back from the adult lives of notable women, but there is still room for a social history of the lives of the earliest graduates of the republic's first female academies.

‖‖‖

8

"Pictures of the Vicious ultimately overcome by misery and shame"
The Cultural Work of Early National Schoolbooks

Gretchen A. Adams

J. Orville Taylor's 1834 edition of his popular manual for the creation and operation of local school systems set forth the primary responsibility of educators within the context of a republic in clear terms: "It is our duty to make men moral." Any educator who failed to produce scholars who were both "virtuous and intelligent," he continued, was no less than a "traitor to liberty" itself. Orville Taylor was no radical. By the 1830s, the pairing of the concepts of "virtue" and "liberty" was one that would be familiar to any adult in the United States as a distillation of the fundamental principles of a distinctly American education. Educating the "rising generation" in a manner that would cultivate the affective bonds of nationalism while defining the obligations of the citizen was a source of endless conversation in the first decades after the American Revolution. The education of children, as Orville Taylor understood by 1834, was a political duty. Although historians of postrevolutionary America have long recognized the crucial role of print in the project to create a collective national identity, the emphasis has been on the political and performative efforts directed at adults. Such a perspective has resulted in a comparative neglect of the vast effort of the postrevolutionary generations to inculcate the same affective bonds of nationalism in the children of the republic. Even more than the campaign directed at American adults, the political socialization of American children relied on print.

As early as 1786, Philadelphia physician Benjamin Rush advanced a widely circulated plan for the proper education of children in the new republic. It was plain that just as adult men and women had roles to play in the new political order, so did children. Americans would be wise to "secure to the state all the advantages that are to be derived from the proper instruction of youth," Rush argued in his proposal for the general establishment of public school systems. For only through the creation of such "nurseries of virtue and knowledge" would youth best be turned into the "republican machines" who could ensure the future security and prosperity of the nation. Dr. Rush's plan was one that was frequently quoted with approval but seldom made real. Even in the communities that did create common schools, poor teacher training and prevailing ideas about effective methods of instruction made the elementary or "common school" book vitally important as the primary vehicle for instructing the nation's youngest republicans in American political ideals. Consequently, the neglect of these texts obscures a powerful influence in the creation of American nationalism between the Revolution and the Civil War. By putting the narratives meant for the education of American children at the center of the nationalizing project in the early United States, we can see how schoolbooks became not merely the "guardians" of revolutionary ideology as it was transformed into national ideology but one if its most important creators.[1]

Benjamin Rush was not alone in his concern about children's centrality to the creation of a reflexive republican consciousness or the role that education could play in that process. Noah Webster also promoted education along the lines of proper republican principles so that children would grow to adulthood with a strong "attachment to their own country." Nor was the "preoccupation" with education confined to men in the public sphere. Abigail Adams, writing to her own married daughter, impressed upon her the political imperatives that fell even to a young mother in the new order. You will, she wrote, "be responsible for a great share of the duty and opportunity of educating a rising family, from whom much will be expected." Benjamin Rush had similar ideas about women's role in the political education of children. It was they who most often provided the "first impressions upon the minds of children." Therefore, he argued, women needed to be "instructed in the principles of liberty and government." The idea of a political role for women, though one that was still subordinate and largely ensconced in the private sphere, was nevertheless a recognition that they indeed had a political role and one that required intellectual capabilities. So too, in a practical sense, did children. Education certainly presented the ideas and behaviors expected by adults, but they were directed toward explicitly political ends. The republican child had a special destiny to fulfill the promise of the Revolution and to secure the nation. For boys, this included the understanding that they would one day be citizens, but girls too had a role to fulfill as wives and mothers who would influence husbands and raise the next generation of Americans.[2]

The political implications of educating the new republic's children were consistently expressed not only in terms of creating patriotic attachment to the United States but in terms of defining the type of virtuous citizen that a republic required. The term *virtue* expressed a cluster of core values that included familiar moral lessons about piety and honesty but specifically stressed sacrifice, frugality, industry, self-discipline, and, above all, avoiding individual "interest" in preference to "disinterested" service to higher ideals that would serve the commonweal. Americans took the ideology of the European Enlightenment and, "dulling its radical and skeptical edge," found a middle ground by mingling it with "traditional moral and religious values." Lessons in "civics" were hardly necessary in a government where citizenship itself was defined by gender and property. A citizen was a man with enough standing to vote. The duties of a citizen, therefore, were defined by his attention to his moral character. Maintaining virtue in the service of the commonweal was a product of moral training. Failure of character, particularly acting with selfish "interest," had consequences not only for the individual but for the republic. Schoolbook morality was predicated on directing the child toward a moral adulthood where he could use the lessons learned in youth in the service of the nation. Noah Webster, one of the first to produce books meant to build an expressly American mentality, elaborated on the crucial relationship between virtue and citizenship. In his *Grammatical Institute of the English Language* (1783) he addressed parents and teachers who were assumed to be the potential buyers of the book by reminding them that "the virtues of men are of more consequence to society than their abilities." The idea reflected a mind-set that dominated not only late eighteenth-century political ideology but the resultant nineteenth-century American theory of education and informed every line of every schoolbook.[3]

Schoolbooks became important not only for their central philosophies in tune with republican ideals but for their centrality to the American system of education in and out of the formal classroom. Before 1830 in most settled areas (and before 1860 in most regions), childhood education was a varied and often highly individualized proposition. Despite the schemes for widespread public schools made by Benjamin Rush and others, few systems were in operation prior to the mid–nineteenth century. Local or district schools on a "fee" or a "free" basis arose as communities chose, but regulated state systems were much later to develop. Massachusetts was the first to create a free public school system in 1827. The long tradition of organized education in New England and other northern states was as much a product of geography and demographics as it was of philosophy. From the original settlement of the region in the seventeenth century through the Revolution, the influence of the steady migration of English Protestant families who valued literacy for religious salvation and commercial success promoted the establishment of schools and the production of juvenile texts. Well into the nineteenth century, New England authors coming out of this tradition also dominated the schoolbook market in every subject. Other states, even in long-settled regions with a similar tradition of local common schools, were slower to set up formal structures for state oversight or standardization. For instance, Pennsylvania established a similar system in 1834 and Vermont only in 1850. Despite repeated attempts by individual educators and legislators in North Carolina to establish similar public systems, they were defeated by the same practical obstacles that slowed the development of public education in all the southern states. The southern states could build on no long-standing tradition of public education at the town level, possessed a smaller middle class, and had greater distances between settlements. The result in the southern states was the predominance of private academies as the primary location of any formal classroom instruction for white students through much of the nineteenth century. As the western territories were settled, the remoteness of individual farmsteads and the rigors of frontier life made the education of children living there an even more personal and sporadic endeavor. With such a wide variety of settings for the education of American children, the schoolbook often provided the only elements of commonality in a nation determined to unite culturally as well as politically.[4]

Even in communities with public or private schools, teacher training remained an equally individual and unregulated enterprise. Those seeking teaching positions offered as their credentials their own successful completion of a basic (or occasionally advanced) education in the standard subjects and their own good character. Imperfectly or poorly educated teachers responsible for the entire range of young scholars, from beginners barely past toddlerhood to adolescents with experience nearly equal to their own, relied on the more advanced to serve as "monitors" for the instruction of the youngest. Where no schools existed at all, basic instructional duties fell to any literate adult in the household. The realities of the nature and location of instruction led to a widespread reliance upon a pedagogical approach that stressed recitation and, above all, rote memorization of lessons from whatever textbooks the individual students attending owned or could borrow from neighboring families.

The common link between young Americans of the private academy, the district schoolroom, and the frontier cabin was not the "general and uniform system of education" that Benjamin Rush envisioned to "render the mass of the people more homogenous" but that found in the elementary schoolbook. The schoolbook was, "along with the Bible, the 'stock book' in the bookshops and general stores of the village." As William Gilmore showed in his study of literacy in rural Vermont in the first decades of independence, even the "hardscrabble" farmers of the region very often had among their few possessions listed on probate inventories a book or two. As reading became "a necessity of life" even in these rural settings, the contents of the inventories often reflected that of the general store's shelves: a Bible and an elementary textbook. Publishers and authors noticeably recognized that instruction was just as likely to take place at the hearth after a day of work for both the child and his instructor as in a schoolroom. Titles of books frequently included the words "for schools and academies" or a more generic "for children and youth," but equally prevalent were titles that included "for home and school" or "for schools and families."[5]

The impetus to create a truly "American" body of knowledge commenced immediately following the Revolution. Noah Webster was in the forefront of an effort to create an "American language" as the only appropriate vehicle to express distinctly American ideas free from the "corruption and tyranny" of Europe and its "debased" culture. Webster's *Grammatical Institute of the English Language* (1783) signaled the beginning of the Massachusetts schoolteacher's lifelong project to produce a dictionary of the American language. Webster's various publications for the adult and the juvenile markets expressed his belief that it was "the business of *Americans* to select the wisdom of all nations . . . to add superior dignity to this infant Empire and to human nature." A few European selections might be appropriate within readers, Noah Webster believed, but the practice of importing books from Europe or reprinting them in America without alteration was clearly not compatible with promoting American nationalism. Shortly afterward, fellow Massachusetts resident Jedidiah Morse, a Congregational minister and teacher, published his own contribution to the emerging national literature with the wildly popular *American Geography,* an expansion of his original 1784 schoolroom textbook, *Geography Made Easy.* As the *American Geography* went through its many editions and revisions, Americans were encouraged to visualize themselves as one nation through maps offering familiar territory with new political boundaries. The financial success of these early efforts to provide practical knowledge with American content and the general enthusiasm for involvement in the nation-building effort animated many others to enter the field of authorship over the next few decades. Where Noah Webster had once appealed to the patriotism of those who might write such books, by the 1830s authors were directing the language of patriotism to the customer in hope of capturing a larger share of the burgeoning market. Lyman Cobb, author of the popular *North American Reader,* scolded the parent who might be browsing his book's preface about the scandalous popularity of *Murray's English Reader* in America fifty years after independence. Cobb challenged his British competition by appealing explicitly to buyers' sense of patriotism. Would a wise American parent provide a reader for his child that "does not contain a single piece or paragraph written by an American citizen? Is this good policy? Is it patriotism?"[6]

Prefaces like Cobb's clearly functioned as opportunities for textbook authors not only to assert the superiority of their own book over the competition but also to promote various educational philosophies, establish their own credentials as authors, and preemptively answer potential concerns. For every well-educated textbook author like Noah Webster or Jedidiah Morse there were increasingly many more like Lyman Cobb and Samuel G. Goodrich, whose own formal education was more limited. The decades following the War of 1812, in particular, marked the rise of a class of self-made men and women who offered their fidelity to the notion of disinterested public service as their credentials. That men and women of limited educational backgrounds could credibly offer books for the education of children reflected not only the emphasis on content that promoted patriotism and the development of moral character but the nature of textbook writing itself in the antebellum period.

"Compiling," which consisted of what was essentially wholesale adoption with little or no abridgment or modification of other texts on the same subjects, required little knowledge about the subject. Many authors like Benson Lossing or Samuel Goodrich referred to themselves as specifically as "compilers." Lossing used it as a way to promote his history of the United States as containing the best available information on the subject in his preface by saying: "We freely appropriated to our use the fruits of the labors of others." Not everyone found the marketplace to be the ideal arbiter about what was appropriate content. By 1842 John Yeomans, president of Lafayette College, complained that "books are rather *made* than written. . . . The whole thing has become an affair of money-making." Nevertheless, changes in commercial culture in the decades after the Revolution caused a shift in the production of schoolbooks as the democratization of literary culture reached into all areas of publishing. Despite this influx of men and women with poor or unknown qualifications to the ranks of authorship (or perhaps because of it), schoolbooks remained profoundly conservative, stressing an aggressive nationalism grounded in the individual virtue of its citizens.[7]

Whether textbook authors should concentrate on the rewards of virtuous behavior or the consequences of vice was a vital question that many authors sought to answer. That a child might learn bad habits from such examples or even that "familiarized with vice, they will view it with less abhorrence" was regularly addressed in authors' appeals to parents and teachers. J. L. Blake, in the preface to his *Historical Reader,* argued that such people should not blame the book but instead look to "themselves or their teachers." Finding a guide to vice in stories that detailed the consequences of bad behavior was simply a failure of the teacher to make "suitable moral reflections" a part of the lesson. Charles A. Goodrich took the middle ground on the issue. He wrote that the study of history presented "striking instances of virtue, enterprise, courage, generosity, [and] patriotism" and that by reading them the child was invited "to copy such noble examples." Goodrich, however, thought there was equal value in presenting children with "pictures of the vicious ultimately overtaken by misery and shame." Those lessons, by contrast, "solemnly warn us against vice." His younger brother, Samuel G. Goodrich, who had enjoyed fewer opportunities for education in his own youth, was a determinedly self-made man who often saw the world in harsher and simpler terms. Master of the vivid historical example in his many books under his own name and within his popular "Peter Parley" series, Samuel Goodrich believed that children were fully familiar with vice long before any schoolbook passage suggested bad behavior. Ordinary socialization, he said, taught children that theft (for example) was wrong. Parental or other adult moral guidance being absent, the child only had to turn to a newspaper to read of a thief having been "seized and hurried away to prison" or "an account of some pirates being hung." The majority of authors, like Emma Willard, offered parents and teachers a history that would "sow the seeds of virtue, by showing the good in such amiable lights, that the youthful heart shall kindle into desires of imitation." The reality, however, even within Willard's juvenile history, was what J. Merton England called "tendency to see things in terms of their opposites" in schoolbooks published prior to the Civil War. Moral choices, schoolbook authors appeared to believe, at least in the antebellum decades, were most firmly impressed upon a child by showing the dire consequences of the failure of virtue for both the individual and his community.[8]

Within the textbooks themselves the most basic and straightforward lessons about virtue directed at the child were found in the readers and spellers. The first lessons in reading lent themselves to the simple proverb, platitude, or short tale that offered a clear moral lesson about virtue rewarded or vice punished. The various editions of Noah Webster's books provided hundreds of examples that ranged from the simple instruction ("A good child will not lie, swear, nor steal") to the warning ("A bad life will make a bad end"). Longer passages provided for the more advanced reader featured vignettes with disobedient children who were punished swiftly and often brutally. In one typical lesson a man sees a boy stealing apples and orders the boy to stop. When "the young Sauce-box told him plainly he would not," the man "pelted him heartily with stones." This, the young reader was assured, cured the bad boy. Bad conduct was always a product, in the schoolbook, of bad character or bad parenting. Including such colorful examples of punishment, authors apparently believed, made their books more interesting and marketable. In doing so, they also marked the acceptable ideas and behaviors that adults hoped the child, in the pedagogical fashion of the day, would memorize and carry through life.[9]

Histories, or historical selections within readers, offered more elaborate opportunities for authors to illustrate desirable values in combination with pointed lessons in nationalism that might serve the future citizen. As in every type of schoolbook, histories written for the juvenile market started with an appeal to the adult buyer. The introductions and prefaces offered testimonial passages that attested to the importance of a child's early exposure to the story of the founding of the United States. Each author not only touted the superiority of the United States over all other countries but promised that the early study of appropriate illustrative incidents and persons from its history would lead to "improvement in individual and national virtue." Emma Willard was especially fervent about the importance of children studying American history in preference to that of any of the "old and wily nations" of Europe. The examples of virtue found in the American child's own national history were "ennobling" to the young "future statesman," who, she promised, would one day look back upon his lessons and conclude: "My country was the most virtuous among the nations." American history was also a safer course of study for the child's overall moral development. Here the American schoolchild would find no "tales of hereditary power and splendor" that might "inflame the imaginations of youth with desires for adventitious distinction." Willard might have waxed more poetic about the promise of American history within a curriculum of study than many other authors, but all the promoters of American histories for children made similar claims. American history (and their own textbooks in particular) bred not only sturdy patriotism in a child but appreciation for simple, sturdy virtue.[10]

Despite all the claims made for the benefits of the study of American history, providing volumes with "American" content was complicated by the fact that there was as yet little "national" history to draw upon for the appropriate lessons. The Revolution itself was, naturally, the centerpiece of any adult or juvenile American history. As the event that created the political nation, the Revolution was mined by textbook authors for emblematic moments of unity and instances of heroism. Nowhere was the convergence of the twin desires of promoting the nation and promoting virtuous character in its future citizens more evident than in accounts of the Revolution itself. George Washington was the personification of those values and was given ever-increasing coverage in the books. A favorite device was to contrast the pinnacle of virtuous character Washington displayed with the nadir exemplified by Benedict Arnold. Authors seeking illustrations of the consequences of vice and the rewards of virtue had a unique treasure in the story of Arnold's treason. If the revolutionary experience defined virtuous national character, Benedict Arnold, whom fellow general Nathanael Greene had called "once his country's Idol, now her horror," became the standard for American schoolbook villainy. Willard's *History of the United States* echoed Greene's sentiments in a way that similarly appeared in all juvenile histories: Benedict Arnold had "bartered his honor, his peace, and his fame; changing the high esteem of the public into general detestation."[11]

Arnold, the hero of Ticonderoga and one of the most trusted of George Washington's generals, shocked the country in 1780 when it was revealed that he had spent more than a year negotiating with the British to sell the information necessary to take control of the American fort at West Point. Arnold's ongoing troubles with the Continental Congress, rumors of debt, and subsequent mismanagement of his command at Philadelphia had little credibility with those who saw "politicians" hounding a great man or with those whose own support for the war wavered with the fortunes of the army. But the capture of Arnold's British contact, Major John Andre, and Arnold's own flight from capture provided unequivocal evidence and provoked widespread outrage. Benedict Arnold escaped to the British lines and got his promised commission in the British army, his payment, and a reputation that later lent itself to American patriotic narratives as the most irredeemable individual since Judas Iscariot. As such, Arnold was not simply "evil"; his actions and character were consistently expressed in terms that stood at the opposite pole from those explicitly assigned to the nation and its patriots like Washington. In the sort of grand statement that nationalist narratives claim for their subject, the whole world and not only American patriots despised Arnold: "His conduct has stamped him with infamy, and like all traitors, he is despised by all mankind." His sins were repeatedly described in terms used as warnings against antirepublican behavior in other adult and juvenile literature. Arnold's actions had been predicated on "self-interest," love of "extravagance," "vice," and "greed." His "enslavement" to self-interest embodied the general fear of the "surrender of independent judgment" for "corrupt riches." Benedict Arnold's ultimate political degradation in the schoolbook moral universe was the sacrifice he made in "resignation to the tyrant's will" by accepting the British military commission. His reported attempts to induce other Americans to follow him out of "liberty" and back into similar "enslavement" resulted, it was "rumored," in failure. Arnold did not even have the dignity of commanding regular British soldiers, Charles Goodrich reported, but only a regiment "consisting chiefly of American deserters." The child was assured that even those who had bought Arnold's honor inevitably shunned him as dishonorable for selling it.[12]

Benedict Arnold's reputation was so debased that even within the common schoolbook's anti-British narratives of the Revolution it could rehabilitate the character of his British contact Major John Andre by its contrast. Certainly when the earliest juvenile histories were published, living memory of the contemporary praise for Andre's comportment during his imprisonment and execution was well known. Within the schoolbook, Major Andre might have an incomprehensible fidelity to the British cause and an equally incomprehensible desire to defeat American "liberty," but it was one held honestly and honorably to the moment of his execution. Even the passionate nationalist Noah Webster found reason to praise John Andre's character in his 1807 edition of *Elements of Useful Knowledge*. In a passage that was repeated in elementary histories for generations afterward, Webster wrote that Andre's crime required his execution but that his "fortitude and amiable deportment . . . endeared him to the officers of the American army, who regretted the necessity of his fate." The lesson then for the student was not only that the disgraced Benedict Arnold had a more ignoble character than a convicted enemy spy but that Washington and the other officers charged with carrying out the sentence acted with admirable disinterest when compelled to do so by their duty to the nation.[13]

Major John Andre was useful in highlighting the virtue Arnold lacked, but American authors of early national juvenile histories preferred their virtue to be American born. George Washington was often featured as particularly burdened by his duty in the Andre affair, but in the event that Washington seemed too high a standard for the average child to meet, there was a more homely example in the episode. Salma Hale promised young readers that there was tangible reward in honesty and loyalty if they followed the example of the men who captured Andre. As models of American honesty and virtue, the three New York militiamen (John Paulding, Isaac Van Wart, and David Williams) were particularly useful. One author, R. Thomas, used as his frontispiece illustration for his *Pictorial History of the United States* (1847) the capture of Andre by the three men (figure 4). As examples of what any American could do for his country, the three New York citizen-soldiers were ideal. Set in contrast to Arnold's sale of his honor, the choices of the poorer young soldiers exemplified the highest form of "disinterested" patriotism. Authors made it clear that in their unsupervised late-night sentry duty it would have been easy for the men to look to their own "interests" when Andre attempted to bribe them with "a purse of gold and a valuable watch." Unlike Arnold, however, the soldiers spurned the offer and showed both their loyalty to the patriot cause and their own virtuous character. Such men, the child was assured, gained a greater more enduring reward than any "tempting offer" Andre could have made. They "were not then, nor can they ever be, forgotten by a country which owes so much to their fidelity."[14]

Since the short history of the nation provided only a limited supply of native examples, textbook authors also enthusiastically mined the British colonial past both for the lineage of the qualities that rose to the

Capture of André.

Figure 4 The capture of Major Andre. R. Thomas, *A Pictorial History of the United States of America: From the Earliest Discoveries, by the Northmen in the Tenth Century, to the Present Time* (Hartford, CT: E. Strong, 1847), title page and 493.

challenges of revolution and as a useful measure of moral progress from subject people to independent citizens. As John Frost reminded students, the study of the settlement of their own country was important because, ultimately, "the character of the republic was determined by its founders." The potential for any valorization of the British colonial past to contradict the same narratives that stressed the eventual need for the Revolution itself was always a danger. Schoolbook authors navigated this problem with the same dexterity others did in adult histories and even political oratory: virtue was located in "the people" and any vice just as firmly located in the British government and institutions or in ideas brought from Europe.[15]

The predominance of New England natives among the authors of schoolbooks solved any questions about where in the colonies the first American "school of independence" was located. According to *The North American Reader*, it was by "every settler's hearth," and the reader of any American history book soon understood that those hearths were invariably located in New England. Not coincidentally, authors from the same region produced the majority of the 113 schoolbooks (on all subjects) published in the United States up to 1860 and provided most of the content "compiled" in the creation of other books of the same type. In fact, the six best-selling authors of histories for the classroom between 1821 and 1861 (Salma Hale, Charles A. Goodrich, Samuel G. Goodrich, Jesse Olney, Emma Willard, and Marcius Willson) were all native New Englanders. The Revolution and the nation it produced followed in a direct line in all of these books and those compiled from them. American virtue flowed from "the principle of liberty and resistance to arbitrary power, in the breasts of the Puritans." The presentation of the founding of Virginia in contrast with that of the two colonies that would become the state of Massachusetts offers a particularly vivid example of both regionally driven historical narratives and the evolving nationalist claim for an inherent American impulse toward liberty from the founding of the British colonies.[16]

Virginia's founding and settlement in the histories produced for children prior to the Civil War could be summed up by a page heading in Emma Willard's 1846 *Abridged History of the United States*: "Bad Settlers." And although Puritans in her section on Anne Hutchinson's trial for heresy receive the heading "Religious Feeling. May become Perverted," the text leaves no doubt as to her meaning. Puritans made errors but only by taking a good quality (piety) to its extremes. Jamestown's "bad settlers," however, when left alone by Captain John Smith, fell to "feeding on human flesh." The schoolchild was told that when they were faced with the consequences of their actions "the spirits of the people were broken." Abiel Holmes described the colony as a place "of punishment and disgrace" for the "vicious and profligate" of England. Samuel Goodrich, as he so often would in his many juvenile histories, colorfully regaled the reader with the perfidy of Virginia's first colony, which (in his telling) "miserably perished." Goodrich built his narrative, he claimed, on an account of the colony attributed to John Smith himself. The Virginia settlers were "poor gentlemen, tradesmen, servingmen, libertines, and such like," so he was no more surprised than Willard that the Virginia colonists fell into a general mood of "despair." That such men had no resilience in the face of hardship was a result of their characters, which in turn reflected upon their motives for immigration. Virginia's men came to the New World not out of virtuous motives but out of the "self-interested" motives of "extravagant hopes of sudden and brilliant wealth."[17]

According to the antebellum school histories of Virginia, only John Smith's "persuasions and threats" could get work out of settlers otherwise prone to the "disorder and confusion" generated by their "raging passion for gold." In his account of the founding of Virginia, Noah Webster provided a terse narrative conducive to the memorization and recitation of facts, but among those facts was his judgment about the character of Virginia's first colonists as "disobedient and refractory." These common narratives display the regionally driven effort to construct a national past with Massachusetts's founders at the center, but they also display in their similarity not so much a sinister conspiracy as a similar set of sources, home-region biases, and the desire to find in every historical illustration a clear marker of future national virtue or to call its lack a "vice."[18]

Virginia's saving factor in all the schoolbooks was that it was English and Protestant and that it eventually established the rudiments of representative government with the establishment of the House of Burgesses in 1619. Although this was a year before Plymouth Colony was settled, the disapproval of the initial Jamestown settlers for merely accepting a royal council rather than setting up a local government was seen in these nationalist texts as dangerously passive submission to "the tyrant's will." Failure to show a resistant spirit was a failure to show a desire for "liberty." Clearly, beyond John Smith's brisk imposition of order there was little for the American child to emulate in this settler group, according to the average school history.

The construction of the Massachusetts colonial past in histories and readers for the juvenile market resembles that of Virginia's founding only in that it too is at heart a morality tale. The Massachusetts colonial past of the schoolbook, however, was a narrative of founding that not only was celebratory but had examples of noble character ready for emulation by the republican child in nearly all of its parts. As a symbolic ancestor of the contemporary American school child, the Puritans and Pilgrims were proto-republican models of virtue. Faith, self-discipline, and sacrifice were all highlighted, and their motives for immigration and conduct in the early years of settlement all stood in clear contrast with those described in accounts of Jamestown's early years. When Massachusetts' settlers met "incredible sufferings from cold, snow and rain," they, unlike the unfit Virginians, "were not discouraged." When "disease and hardship thinned their ranks," they did not "despair" like the Virginia schoolbook settlers but (the reader was assured) "bore all with equal firmness." It was the underlying moral condition of the Massachusetts settler, the child was constantly reminded, that provided his strength. Such character was, naturally, rewarded with "stability and prosperity," and the child was left to assume that the "greedy" residents of Jamestown had continued to starve as punishment for their "licentiousness."[19]

Because the founders of New England were tested and found virtuous in the common schoolbook narrative, that region was worthy of being called "a nursery of men." The manly business of building a desirable political and social structure that foreshadowed the one the schoolchild himself enjoyed was also a sign of that generation's virtue. While the schoolbook Virginian passively accepted a governing council imposed upon them, the Mayflower passengers were shown creating "a voluntary government before landing, upon purely democratic principles." The impulse for that organizing principle was in the Plymouth colonists' resistance to "oppression in England." Resistance by the colonists (or the "people") to the oppressing English government was presented as instinctive and was always framed as an obvious parallel to their descendants' own later rebellion. Looking for national virtue in all its forms within British colonial settlement led all the books to the same conclusion: colonial Virginians were unfit for national leadership even of the symbolic kind because their founding was by "self-interested" men while New England in the form of its Massachusetts colonists was fit through its long history of self-sacrifice for principle.[20]

In portraying the Massachusetts settler as the proto-American, there was still the problem of accounting for why such liberty-loving people hadn't thrown off colonial rule sooner. The idea that the present age was especially "enlightened" in terms of political philosophy was easily (and often) explained. But, as in other subjects that were staples of the school histories, even the heroic example had elements that could be used to teach lessons about "error" and moral progress. In the case of colonial Massachusetts, "Salem Witchcraft" in particular offered more opportunities to compare the dark colonial past with the bright progressive national present. If the otherwise admirable Puritans were in error for legislating and enforcing such laws as those against witchcraft, it was an error that was an inescapable product of European influences and their own entrapment in a backward age—circumstances that the contemporary American child had the good fortune to have escaped.

More than any other event in British colonial America, Salem's "witch-hunt" offered authors of juvenile histories the opportunity to emphasize the importance of a wide variety of values that underpinned American nationalism by their absence in preindependence times. Whether the emphasis was on contemporary ideas about "reason" versus the rampant "superstitions" of the past, a condemnation of English laws, courts, and all things "foreign," or even the dangers of self-interested actions, Salem's episode of witchcraft in the seventeenth century provided useful cautionary tales with implications for the present. More importantly, it was also one of the few historical episodes where children could be placed at the center of the narrative. Most particularly, as moral narrative, the story of Salem's witch-hunt stressed the proper place of the child in the social order and showed the dire consequences for the entire community when that natural order was disturbed.

The execution of nineteen men and women convicted of practicing witchcraft in 1692 Massachusetts Bay Colony began with the complaints of two little girls. No author failed to mention the "fits" of Abigail Williams and Elizabeth Parris as the origin of the tragedy. Their claims of being tormented by "invisible agents" and the way other children were soon brought in to make their own charges against adults in the community launched the witchcraft trials. Each account made it plain that even if Puritans had believed in such a ridiculous notion as witchcraft, the children had incited the arrests and trials either by lying or by making a convincing display of hysteria brought on (consciously or unconsciously) by witnessing the attention the other child accusers were receiving. The children of Salem, wrote Salma Hale, were "hardened by impunity and success" as they expanded their circle of accused witches. William Grimshaw did not disguise his horror that "children, not twelve years old, were allowed to give their testimony." The whole thing, Jedidiah Morse claimed, was a result of "fraud and imposture, began by young girls, who at first thought of nothing more than exciting pity and indulgence." Certainly the schoolchild was told that adults were lax in their responsibilities because of their own fears, but at the heart of the story was the moral lesson that cunning or unstable children had been permitted to testify and that as a result their innocent neighbors had been imprisoned or even hanged (figure 5).[21]

The eternal schoolbook warning about the dangers of "self-interest" was also highlighted in the schoolbook narratives about Salem. While each author found a variety of disturbing elements within the episode to serve as moral lessons, acting for the preservation of oneself at the cost of others was highlighted. Children were taught that in 1692 "the most effectual way to avoid an accusation was to become an accuser." Such a conclusion could only leave the student with the distinct impression that what drove the Salem witch-hunt was not religious belief but the cowardly act of saving oneself at the cost of others. In terms of an example of the dramatic consequences of the vice of acting out of "interest," it was difficult to find a more craven example than that presented by schoolbook authors about the children of Salem.[22]

As disturbing as the disruption of adult authority was in 1692 Salem, the underlying belief in the possibility of witchcraft was another sign of dangerous backwardness and foreign ideas. This element of the witchcraft

Salem witchcraft.

Figure 5 A schoolbook's portrayal of one of the hangings that followed the Salem witch trials. R. Thomas, *A Pictorial History of the United States of America: From the Earliest Discoveries, by the Northmen, in the Tenth Century, to the Present Time* (Hartford, CT: E. Strong, 1847), 203.

trials narrative was enthusiastically used to support the idea that the present-day society and government of the United States was in all ways superior to that which had come before it or that which still existed in Europe. Jedidiah Morse's popular *American Geography* (1789) reminded readers that Salem witchcraft was "the practice of the courts . . . regulated by English law and custom." Hannah Adams did the same in her 1807 *Abridgment of the History of New-England,* and Samuel Goodrich regularly stressed to the readers of his various school histories that New England witch-hunting "was not an invention of their own. They received their notions from England." Even when Massachusetts colonists were not reported to be directly under the influence of English customs or law, children were instructed that witchcraft persecutions had been "common in Europe for centuries" and that, as sorrowful as the nineteen executions at Salem were, "thousands were executed in England and other countries" contemporaneously with the Salem outbreak. And so, John Hinton concluded, however distressing the events at Salem in 1692 might be, "neither England nor any other nation is entitled to cast the first stone at them."[23]

The British colonist within the antebellum American schoolbook had a deliberately fluid identity. When his actions showed an impulse to form representative government, defy British authority, or demonstrate qualities like industry, thrift, or piety, he was easily cast as a proto-republican model of an evolving but unquestionably "American" virtue. When less admirable qualities were on display, as in the accounts of the early years of Jamestown or even within the two Massachusetts colonies during episodes like that at Salem, the same authors framed the colonist as trapped within a web of British customs and beliefs that had yet to be transformed by his experience on the American shore. The schoolbook colonist would become truly "American" only with the Revolution, but in the minds of the schoolbook authors and their young readers the colonial past was merely a resource to be selectively excavated for appropriate character traits to label essentially British or American as suited the requirements of the moral lesson to be learned.

The importance of schoolbooks in the early national cultural landscape ultimately lay not only in their content but in their reach. The practice of "compiling," the personal acquisition and ownership of schoolbooks, and the realities of a diverse and highly individualized system of instruction not only kept old favorites in print but in their infrequent alteration kept the definitions of a distinctly postrevolutionary virtue alive for decades after they ceased to be critical. The estimated twelve million volumes of the popular Goodrich-authored "Peter Parley" series alone sold from the 1820s through the end of the nineteenth century testifies through sheer numbers to the influence of the schoolbook in American life. As early as 1845, author Marcius Willson recognized this when he praised the importance of the elementary-level history book in national life. From the perspective of more than two generations of independence, he said that clearly it was from "those unassuming companions of the schoolroom, and not from those more elaborate writings which grace the libraries of the men of wealth and the professional scholar, that the great mass of our citizens must ever derive their knowledge of the character, toils, and privations of our fathers, and the origin and nature of our free institutions."

Willson, himself the author of a popular school history, naturally had an interest in promoting the continued sale of such books, but he also was describing what his audience knew as a reality in American life in the decades between the Revolution and the Civil War. Most Americans had gotten all of their knowledge of national history from elementary school history books. And although Willson called them "companions of the schoolroom," many of the educators in his audience may well have gotten their own introduction to the books or even their entire education outside a formal classroom. If the "nurseries of virtue" that Benjamin Rush envisioned in 1786 to sustain the new nation did not exist for many decades afterward in the form of the schoolhouse, they did exist between two cardboard covers in the form of the schoolbook.[24]

NOTES

1. J[ohn] Orville Taylor, *The District School* (New York: Harper and Brothers, 1834), 317, 116; Gordon S. Wood, *The Radicalism of the American Revolution* (New York: Vintage Books, 1993), 190; Benjamin Rush, "A Plan for the Establishment of Public Schools and the Diffusion of Knowledge in Pennsylvania; to Which Are Added, Thoughts upon the Mode of Education Proper in a Republic," in *Essays on Education in the Early Republic,* ed. Frederick Rudolph (Cambridge, MA: Harvard University Press, 1965), 10, 17.

2. Noah Webster, *A Grammatical Institute of the English Language . . .* (Hartford, CT: Huntington and Hopkins, 1784), 45; Mary Beth Norton, *Liberty's Daughters: The Revolutionary Experience of American Women, 1750–1800* (Boston: Little, Brown, 1980), 248, 250; Rush, "Plan for the Establishment," 22.

3. Donald H. Meyer, "The Uniqueness of the American Enlightenment," *American Quarterly* 31 (1979): 172; Webster, *Grammatical Institute,* 14.

4. Ruth Miller Elson, *Guardians of Tradition, American Schoolbooks of the Nineteenth Century* (Lincoln: University of Nebraska Press, 1964), 9, 5. On the importance of moral education in early national America, the establishment of public and private schools, and the nationalist orientation of schoolbooks, see especially Carl F. Kaestle, *Pillars of the Republic: Common Schools and American Society, 1780–1860* (New York: Hill and Wang, 1983); Elson, *Guardians of Tradition;* Wood, *Radicalism;* David Waldstreicher, *In the Midst of Perpetual Fetes: The Making of American Nationalism 1776-1820* (Chapel Hill: University of North Carolina Press, 1997); and Melvin C. Yazawa, "Creating a Republican Citizenry," in *The American Revolution: Its Character and Limits,* ed. Jack P. Greene (New York: New York University Press, 1987), 282–308.

5. Rush, "Plan for the Establishment," 10; William J. Gilmore, *Reading Becomes a Necessity of Life: Material and Cultural Life in Rural New England, 1780–1835* (Knoxville: University of Tennessee Press, 1999), 295, 297.

6. Introduction to Webster, *Grammatical Institute,* n.p.; Lyman Cobb, *The North American Reader* (New York: Harper and Brothers, 1835), v.

7. Benson J. Lossing, *A Pictorial History of the United States for Schools and Families* (New York: F. J. Huntington–Mason Bros., 154), iii; John Yeomans, "Address Delivered in Easton, Pennsylvania, August 18th, 1841, on the Occasion of the Author's Inauguration as President of Lafayette College," *Biblical Repertory and Princeton Review* 14, no. 2 (1842): 218.

8. J. L. Blake, *The Historical Reader: Designed for the Use of Schools and Families, on a New Plan* (Concord, NH: Horatio Hill, 1825), 3; Charles A. Goodrich, *A History of the United States of America, on a Plan Adapted to the Capacity of Youth,* rev. and enl. from 44th ed. (Boston: Jenks, Palmer, 1834), 4; Samuel G. Goodrich, *The Young American: Or, Book of Government and Law* (New York: William Robinson, 1844), 12; Emma Willard, *History of the United States, or,*

Republic of America (New York: White, Gallagher, and White, 1828), introduction to Webster, *Grammatical Institute*, n.p.

9. Noah Webster, *The American Spelling Book* (Albany, NY: Websters and Skinners, 1822), 44, 45, 83.

10. Emma Willard, *History of the United States, or, Republic of America* (Philadelphia: A. S. Barnes, 1843), v–vi.

11. Charles Royster, "The Nature of Treason: The Revolutionary Virtue and American Reactions to Benedict Arnold," *William and Mary Quarterly* 36 (1979): 166, 175–78, 183, 186; Willard, *History* (1843 ed.), 240.

12. Elson, *Guardians of Tradition*, 207; Moses Severance, *The American Manual; Or, New English Reader* (Geneva, NY: R. Robbins, 1832), 259; C. Goodrich, *History*, 210.

13. Webster, *Elements of Useful Knowledge: Containing Historical and Geographical Accounts of the United States, for the Use of Schools*, 3rd ed. (New London: Ebenezer P. Cady, 1807), 1:48.

14. Salma Hale, *History of the United States: From Their First Settlement as Colonies, to the Close of the War with Great Britain, in 1815*, 2nd ed. (Keene, NH: J. and J. W. Prentiss, 1838), 204–5; "Capture of Andre," in R. Thomas, *A Pictorial History of the United States of America: From the Earliest Discoveries, by the Northmen, in the Tenth Century, to the Present Time* (Hartford, CT: E. Strong, 1847), frontispiece and 493.

15. John Frost, *The Pictorial History of the United States of America: From the Discovery by the Northmen in the Tenth Century to the Present Time* (Hartford, CT: Case, Tiffany, 1849), vi.

16. Lyman Cobb, *The North American Reader* (New York: Harper and Brothers, 1835), 102; Charles F. Heartman, *The New England Primer . . . a Bibliographical Checklist* (Metuchen, NJ: Charles F. Heartman, 1922), xvii.

17. Emma Willard, *Abridged History of the United States* (New York: A. S. Barnes, 1846), 114, 42, 46; Abiel Holmes, *American Annals: Or, A Chronological History of America* (Cambridge, MA: W. Hilliard, 1805), 1:205; Samuel G. Goodrich, *A Pictorial History of North and South America* (Hartford, CT: House and Brown, 1848), 362, 374; Charles Goodrich also made the claim of cannibalism in Jamestown. C. Goodrich, *History*, 34.

18. Hale, *History,*17–19; Webster, *Elements of Useful Knowledge*, 89.

19. Webster, *Elements of Useful Knowledge*, 92; Goodrich, *History*, 21; Samuel G. Goodrich, *Peter Parley's Pictorial History of North and South America* (Hartford, CT: Peter Parley, 1858), 405, 408, 401; Jedidiah Morse, *The American Geography* (Elizabethtown, NJ: Shepard Kollock, 1789), 144, xx.

20. C. Goodrich, *History*, 83; Hale, *History*, 48.

21. Hale, *History*, 44; William Grimshaw, *History of the United States from their First Settlement as a Colony to the Cession of Florida* (Philadelphia: Benjamin Warner, 1821), 60; Morse, *American Geography*, 191. An illustration of one execution

was included in some schoolbooks for lower grades. See, for example, Thomas, *Pictorial History*, 203.

22. Morse, *American Geography*, 191.

23. Ibid.; Hannah Adams, *An Abridgment of the History of New-England* (Boston: Etteridge and Blos, 1807), 105; Samuel G. Goodrich, *First Book of History: For Children and Youth* (Boston: C. J. Hendee, 1837), 37; See also Joseph Worcester Emerson, *Questions and Supplement to Goodrich's History of the United States* (Boston: Richardson and Lord, 1829), 100; [Frances Lister Hawks], *History of the United States* (New York: Harper and Brothers, 1835), 210; John Howard Hinton, *The History and Topography of the United States of North America, Brought Down from the Earliest Period*, 2nd ed. (Boston: Samuel Walker, 1843), 71.

24. M.[arcius] Wilson *[sic]*, "Review of American Common School Histories," *Biblical Repository and Classical Review*, 3rd ser., 1 (July 1845): 517; Rush, "Plan for the Establishment," 17.

||||||||||||||||||||||||||||||||||||||||||||||||||

Part IV

A Hard World

Child Welfare and Health Reform

The Larcom family was never rich, but when Lucy's shopkeeping father died the family's resources declined precipitously. Their new situation affected everyone in the family. Even the three youngest children, including Larcom, could see "that it was a hard world for my mother and her children to live in at present. . . . The older members of the family found occupations by which the domestic burdens were lifted a little; but . . . there was still much more outgo than income, and my mother's discouragement every day increased." The family hung on in Beverly for a time, but her mother decided to follow a plan originally proposed by her father: to relocate to Lowell, Massachusetts, where the burgeoning textile factories were creating economic opportunities of all kinds. Mrs. Larcom moved most of her brood to Lowell and opened a boardinghouse. But she could not make enough money to support her family. Lucy had to go to work in the mills, where she became one of the famous "Lowell girls"—girls and young women recruited to operate the machinery in the new factories along the Merrimack River. "I thought it would be a pleasure to feel that I was not a trouble or burden or expense to anybody," Larcom later wrote, "So I went to my first day's work in the mill with a light heart." She was twelve years old. The work was easy, in fact, although the hours could be long. But millwork interfered with her education; her mother simply could not afford to lose even Lucy's meager wages by allowing her to attend the local grammar or high schools full time.[1]

Larcom and her family would, in fact, survive their hard times. Mixing work with school, Lucy flourished in Lowell, where she was a "mill girl" for several years. Most importantly, she would finally be able to practice her passion for writing by publishing some of her poems in the *Lowell Offering*, a literary magazine edited by other millworkers. But she would always remember the hard choices forced upon her mother—Lucy had gone to the mills instead of her older sister because she was bigger and could stand the work, for instance—and the shortened childhood she experienced due to her family's straitened circumstances.

Countless Americans experienced similar dilemmas in the early republic. Few safety nets existed to help out families faced with the loss of breadwinners and parents; like Larcom's mother, most American women of modest means would face tremendous hardships after losing a husband and father. But the political, social, and religious democratization of the period introduced new concepts about caring for dependent children. Although it would be many generations before governments created coherent programs to care for children, modest attempts to standardize treatment and to educate the public about children's welfare did emerge.

The pair of essays in this section examine two very different ways in which American society began to take responsibility for the well-being of its youngest members. Nancy Zey shows the transition from colonial to republican attitudes about orphans in her essay on dependent children in Natchez, Mississippi, where traditional and rather ad hoc responses eventually gave way to a more structured—more "American"—way of dealing with them. Rebecca Noel explores a very different, almost abstract way of contributing to the health of children through the public school systems that were so much a part of the public agenda in the new republic. Their new emphasis on secularized textbooks produced by "experts" with the intent of educating children about the ways their bodies worked foreshadowed the early twentieth-century campaigns of Progressive-era scientists.

NOTE

1. Lucy Larcom, *A New England Girlhood: Outlined from Memory* (Boston: Houghton Mifflin, 1889), 142, 153.

Children of the Public

Poor and Orphaned Minors in the Southwest Borderlands

Nancy Zey

Elizabeth Alston of Natchez died in the spring of 1781, leaving behind six minor children whose welfare became the responsibility of a government in transition. Founded by the French in 1716 and seized by the British in 1763, Natchez remained a predominantly Anglo-American colony even when the Spanish captured the settlement as a war prize.[1] War still raged in the East when Charles de Grandpré took control of Spain's new, unruly possession in 1781, and one of his first actions as civil and military commandant was deciding what to do with the Alston children: Henry, Lucy, Solomon, Jacob, William, and Anne, who ranged from five to fourteen years of age. Under English law, the guardianship of minors belonged to their father, yet John Alston had lately disappeared into Indian country. Consequently, Grandpré regarded Alston's four sons and two daughters as "orphans"—in other words, as though the man were well and truly dead. With no father and now no mother, the Alston children thus became wards of the state. Fortunately for scholars, dealings with them became a matter of public record.[2]

The government's handling of the Alston siblings reveals much about the community at that point in time. Life on the frontier necessitated improvisation, and Spanish officials relied on their own jurisprudence while also drawing from British and French practices to cobble together an ad hoc system of child welfare. Then at the end of the eighteenth century the United States took over the region, and what was known as the Natchez District became the city of Natchez, also the seat of Adams County and onetime capital of Mississippi. Under this new government, the treatment of minors became streamlined and codified according to American legal custom, which held pauper apprenticeship as the primary method of relief. However, child welfare in Natchez did not remain static. A group of charitable women founded an orphan asylum in the 1820s, and eventually this female-run institution assumed authority over the support and education of poor young white children in the community. While orphans from the nearby Indian nations did not receive juvenile assistance, they became objects of sympathy among many white Americans during the early nineteenth century. Of the three racial groups in and around Natchez, black children generated the least public concern, and their situation grew only more precarious. As we shall see, shifting American attitudes toward children and childhood informed these changes in the way that poor and orphaned minors were viewed and treated in the southwest borderlands.[3]

As Natchez's principal official, Charles de Grandpré effectively became a father to the late Elizabeth Alston's children, assuming control over their upbringing and their inheritance. Careful management of orphans' property was always a key concern for the state, for the possession of land and material goods kept them off public assistance. In accordance with English common law, which had prevailed in Natchez for nearly two decades, Grandpré appointed a third party, Alexander McIntosh, to manage the property and the daily care of the four boys and two girls. As guardian, McIntosh governed the young Alstons in loco parentis, but in this legally constructed "family" the commandant still held ultimate authority. The guardian had to submit to Grandpré a detailed inventory of the orphans' inheritance, which included a house, acreage, livestock, and sixteen slaves. Furthermore, every financial transaction pertaining to the children's inheritance required the commandant's official approval.[4]

Through these meticulous and at times tedious recorded details, an unsavory picture of the community emerges. The generally impoverished populace abounded with thieves, liars, and brigands, posing a constant threat to the children's property and indeed their very well-being. Henry, the youngest of the siblings, soon followed his mother to the grave. A week after the boy's death, McIntosh wrote Grandpré requesting permission to effect a radical change in their situation. "The five children, his wards, are continually in company with evil disposed persons, receiving from them bad advice," warned the guardian. With his own family to tend, McIntosh was having difficulty rearing the orphans properly. In short, the Alston children were learning the wrong sort of education in this boisterous borderland outpost and at the present rate seemed unlikely to grow up as the right sort of adults. Natchez offered few alternatives. Hence, the guardian sought to remove the remaining Alstons and their property to a more civilized community, a request the commandant approved. So the children went to New Orleans; the boys were put to trades, while the girls were placed as pupils in the Ursuline Convent.[5]

Founded by a group of French nuns in 1727, the Ursuline Convent functioned as an elite boarding school as well as an orphanage. In Catholic communities, children who had lost their parents commonly found shelter with religious orders, but such a course was out of the ordinary for children like the Alston girls, Anglo-Americans who were probably Protestant. Nevertheless, Alexander McIntosh deemed a Catholic cloister in a city filled with Frenchmen and Spaniards a better environment for Anne and Lucy than the rough-and-tumble of Protestant, Anglophone Natchez. Religious differences mattered little when the company of "evil disposed persons" threatened the character—indeed, the future well-being—of two girls. The placement of William, Jacob, and Solomon with tradesmen, on the other hand, resembled the course usually followed in communities of British America. Indeed, the apprenticeship of minors, male and female, had dominated child welfare since the earliest days of colonial settlement. The Alston boys had means but not enough to ensure a life of moneyed leisure. Placed with families in the more stable and refined New Orleans, they would receive basic support, moral guidance, and vocational training so that they could earn a decent and honest living as adults.[6]

Though Natchez remained a province of Spain for nearly twenty years, Catholic religious orders never established a presence in that time, nor, apparently, did Spanish law firmly take root. When the war on the North American continent formally ended in 1783, Madrid hoped to maintain Natchez as a buffer against a new imperial rival: the United States. The Americans had once encroached upon the region and showed every indication of wishing to do so again. Therefore, to cement the loyalty of the populace, the dons granted unprecedented tolerance toward the English language and the Protestant religion as well as their legal and civil institutions. This tolerance appeared particularly pronounced under the governorship of London-educated Manuel Gayoso de Lemos, who steadily brought order to the frontier community and asserted a more stringent oversight over the welfare of poor and parentless minors.[7]

No single guardian appeared willing to take on the four Marble children when they became orphans in 1792, and the fact that they apparently inherited no property made a bad situation worse. Thus, as per the custom in Anglo-American settlements, each minor orphan was bound out as an apprentice: the boys until the age of twenty-one and the girl until age eighteen. The brief entries in the governor's record book indicate that these pauper apprenticeships included the standard contractual obligations prescribed by law. For example, each master and mistress pledged to provide basic support and schooling as well as "freedom dues" of clothing and, in some cases, tools upon completion of service. Some of the contractual language, however, departs from traditional English indentures and calls to mind an adoption rather than a business transaction. For instance, Mary Higdon promised Theophilus and Isaac Marble, both around age twelve, all the usual provisions but added that they were "bound to serve me like a mother."[8] John Arden reversed the familial reference and swore to educate seven-year-old Louisa "as I would my own daughter."[9] These curious insertions do not appear in indentures in British America, where formal adoption was, in fact, legally impermissible. Spanish law, by contrast, allowed filial bonds to be forged between adults and children where none had existed before. Mary Hidgon's assertion that she would instruct her charges "suitable to their station in life" seems to temper the expectation that Theophilus and Isaac would indeed be raised exactly as her own sons. Instead, the family references may suggest other relational expectations. Given the potential for sexual transgression in these two sets of arrangements—a woman taking on two boys and a man taking on a girl—the allusion to Mary Higdon as "a mother" and Louisa Marble as "a daughter" may have implied that the taboos of physical intimacy within natural families were to be preserved in these contractual households. At the very least, the parent-child construction implied a certain anticipated standard of treatment between master and apprentice. A violation of that standard could throw the whole arrangement into question, as was the case with carpenter David Douglas and his apprentice Stephen Marble.[10]

In 1795, the governor received a petition for the removal of Stephen from his master's custodianship. Ezra Marble, the eldest of the orphaned siblings and the only one not bound out, complained that Douglas had given the boy neither schooling nor manual training but had instead "used him as a servant."[11] A number of witnesses, including Mary Higdon, supported Ezra's claim, attesting that Douglas kept Stephen "employed in menial work such as milking cows, washing dishes and other such business, which must be a detriment to him."[12] Most frontier children endured the affliction of household chores, but Stephen Marble had been turned into a drudge by some accounts. Such treatment would have mattered little to the governor if the complaint had come from a natural son, but as the case involved a public child, Douglas had to answer for his actions. In response to the charges made against him, the master argued that concern for Stephen's tender age had guided his treatment of the apprentice:

> This boy is very small and it is true that I have not made him work much at the carpenter's trade as Your Excellency knows that in the first place children should be taught to read and write and afterwards put to work; as to my making him a servant, I can prove by those who are really my neighbors, as those who sign the certificate presented by Marble do not live near my dwelling. They are persons who wish to oblige him and the greater part do not know what they have signed, but the truth of the matter is that I have had this boy nearly four years and I have maintained him all this time when he could be of no use to me and now when he begins to be able to make me some return for the cost of his maintenance, they wish to take him from me, to aid them in their swamp where he would learn nothing but to be a vagabond, without a trade, like the others of his family.[13]

At fourteen years of age, Stephen Marble could hardly be considered "very small." If the boy's father, brother, and other relations had indeed ignored his education, his physical and mental development may very well have been below what was usual for the time. To refute the assertions of Ezra's supporters, Douglas provided the governor his own set of testimonials, including one from John Arden, the master of Stephen's sister Louisa. Arden vouched that the carpenter had "used Stephen Marble more like one of his own children than like a strange child both in the household and in schooling." A longtime neighbor shared this opinion that Douglas had treated the boy well "in every respect I think an apprentice ought to be used. I believe that he gave him as much learning as he conveniently could which was as much as the other boys got."[14]

Satisfied that the master was fulfilling the terms as well as the spirit of the indenture, and perhaps suspicious that Ezra valued his younger brother's labor more than the boy's well-being, the governor ruled in favor of Douglas, with the stipulation that the carpenter immediately commence teaching the adolescent apprentice his trade. The case did not end there. Stephen took matters into his own hands and ran away to live with his brother, but contractual bonds ultimately proved thicker than blood. The governor ordered Ezra Marble to return the boy to Douglas—his rightful guardian—or face imprisonment.[15]

In a frontier community like Natchez, many children contributed significantly to the household economy. For the first several years minors constituted a liability, but as soon as they could manage chores they became an important asset. The Stephen Marble case showed that the government viewed milking cows and washing dishes as reasonable expectations of a fourteen-year-old apprentice and as fair compensation for all the support given "when he could be of no use" to the household. In general, the government supported the notion that guardians deserved compensation for tending poor children as well as a certain degree of latitude in child-rearing methods, as evidenced by the case involving Susanna Galtney, an orphan between eleven and thirteen years of age.[16]

The claim that a poor orphan had been "used as a servant" held a range of meanings, but there was no mistaking the point of Patrick Connelly in the summer of 1795 when he accused Elizabeth Tomlinson of treating young Susanna as "a slave." According to Connelly's petition, Tomlinson had taken his wife's younger sister "through profession of humanity and good will." Now, ten years later, he sought to remove Susanna, for "she passes a painful life and is treated of a footing with a negro," an accusation that signified more than long days of labor. Connelly charged the guardian with beating the girl, even horsewhipping her. And he casts such treatment as wholly unacceptable given not only the orphan's youth but her race. The governor immediately looked into the situation and questioned the child, who complained of receiving "cruel treatment and excessive whipping" from her guardian, but Susanna's misery did not end there. "What she feels still more sensibly," noted the governor in his report, "the negro wenches are also permitted to treat her in the same manner." Despite the evidence of abuse, he permitted Tomlinson to keep Susanna, though he ordered the guardian "to treat this orphan with more decency and humanity or on the first notice to the contrary she will be taken from her, with the loss of the whole expenses."[17]

The issue of expenses had been long been a contentious one between Susanna's family and her guardian. Several years earlier an uncle, Abraham Galtney, had attempted to claim the child. Tomlinson offered to release her in exchange for $20 for her schooling and $120 for the support given when she was too young to earn her keep.[18] Though Elizabeth Tomlinson and Susanna Galtney were not bound to each other by an indenture, the governor treated the relationship between them as such and upheld her request for reimbursement. Giving the guardian the benefit of the doubt was a matter of sound policy, for few in the community would agree to take on poor young orphans if relatives could easily remove them as soon as they were old enough to be useful. But probably few would fault the governor for removing a white girl whose guardian continued treating her "of a footing with a negro," which subverted an increasingly important racial hierarchy.[19]

When the United States finally acquired the region from Spain and created the Mississippi Territory in 1798, poor and orphaned children came under greater regulation than ever before. The new governing officials simply adapted laws from other territories, which had been culled from the states. Standardizing juvenile relief helped prepare this borderland outpost for American statehood and brought it in line with the rest of the nation. As the ordering of indigent minors became codified in law, apprenticeship emerged as the primary method of relief. Chapter 36 of the territorial code, echoing its English statutory antecedents, established a permanent bureaucracy to facilitate apprenticeship transactions. The county court became the administration center for orphans and indigent minors, officials known as "overseers of the poor" located needy children and bound them out. While the apprenticeship law stipulated that masters and mistresses must be "reputable and discreet" and "willing to take them," nowhere did the statute indicate that the legal relationship created by indentures would be cast in terms of parental and filial regard, as had been the case under Spanish rule.[20]

In exchange for room, board, clothing, a bit of schooling, and freedom dues, apprentices provided their labor for a contracted number of years. Of course, the law mandated the teaching of some "business or occupation," with the understanding that the apprentices would one day become masters and mistresses themselves.[21] Gender usually determined the trades that children entered: boys became apprenticed to carpenters, saddlers, bakers, tailors, tanners, and shoemakers, while girls worked primarily as housekeepers and seamstresses. As in the time of Spanish government, a few boys were bound to women and a few girls were placed with men. In these cases, apprentices either learned a vocation from a third party or simply worked in a capacity befitting their sex and received care in return. The Adams County Court specified trades for less than half of the children bound out, probably because pauper apprentices more commonly served as menial laborers than artisans-in-training.[22] Despite the existence of statutory relief, Mississippians continued to place some poor orphans informally with caretakers, who now received a public stipend for their trouble. In 1809, for example, William Henry King collected eight dollars per month to care for Cynthia Williams, but the county found a better bargain the following year and paid Mary Hustler five dollars per month for the same task.[23] Then in 1814, the overseers of the poor found someone "willing" to take Cynthia as an apprentice, perhaps because she had finally reached an age when she could earn her keep.[24]

Guardians still answered for the way that they "used" their young charges, yet American officials differed from Spanish predecessors in the handling of reported instances of abuse and neglect. Reflective of changing attitudes toward child rearing in the United States, these officials showed less tolerance toward adults who chastised their young charges too severely. Verbal admonitions were steadily replacing physical chastisement as the preferred form of punishment, as well-to-do Americans placed greater emphasis on molding children's character than on breaking their will. In the South, correctional violence became increasingly associated with slaves, hence the distaste that overseers of poor developed for the beating of white children, whether indigent or orphaned.[25]

By law, apprentices had the right to lodge complaints with the court, usually with the assistance of a "next friend," an adult agent who sought to protect the minor's best interests.[26] Masters and mistresses found guilty of abuse or neglect received no second chances, as in the case of Margaret Gibson, alias Margaret Reed. In 1818, apprentice Benjamin Phillips, through a next friend, accused her of "ill treatment." The court summoned the mistress "to appear forthwith and show cause if any she can, why said Apprentice should not be taken from her, and the Indenture if any she had, be rendered void." When Gibson appeared and admitted the charge, the court seized Benjamin at once. In this case, unlike the cases of Stephen Marble and Susanna Galtney, the petitioner made no apparent attempt to claim the boy. Instead, the overseer of the poor subsequently bound Benjamin to a third party.[27] This new master, a brickmaker, soon took on another mistreated apprentice, thanks to the intervention of the boy's own mother. Rachel Williams complained to the court that her son's master used him in "an improper and an inhuman manner." At twelve years of age, Daniel Williams was approaching his prime laboring years; however, his mother did not seek his return. Under this arrangement, the master would reap the benefits of Daniel's assistance around the house and in the workshop, but the boy was more likely to enter adulthood with a valuable and steady trade than if he had remained at home.[28]

Though American officials demonstrated a more protective stance toward children of the public, in certain instances guardians still received the greater benefit of the doubt. Children bound to influential adults could experience difficulty with their complaints. In 1802, for instance, apprentice John Blumon petitioned against his master for "ill treatment," and after delaying the case once the court finally dismissed it altogether on the grounds that it had "not come properly before them." In fact, no other official body dealt with poor and orphaned children at the time. Court officials probably gave this particular apprentice the cold shoulder for fear of offending his master, Winthrop Sargent, the former territorial governor.[29]

Perhaps the most significant documented change in child welfare under American rule was the binding out of black children. The laws regulating relief made no exclusions based on color: all free minors settled within the county boundaries could expect public assistance. Of the black apprentices mentioned in the county records, most were designated as "mulatto" and by first name only, in the manner of slaves. Indeed, the line between short-term and lifetime bondage could be precariously thin for children of color because perceived blackness served as prima facie evidence of enslavement. The conversion of apprentices into slaves had been a problem in Natchez even under Spanish rule. In 1781, the governor received a petition from "Betty and Jude, daughters of a free woman," who had been brought from "the Carolinas" as apprentices. They had been snatched into slavery during the revolutionary turmoil and had served their apprenticeship terms in that state, but now they sought liberation from service as promised in their indentures.[30] The Superior Court of Mississippi faced a similar dilemma in 1818 when William Sutton of Delaware launched a freedom suit on behalf of his former apprentice, the son of an enslaved black man and a white woman. Though free by virtue of his mother's race, John Ham appeared dark enough to make him an easy target at a camp meeting in Maryland. Kidnapped there and then sold down the river to Natchez, John became the property of a wealthy local attorney, who held a legitimate bill of sale. The apprentice struggled for years—with the burden of proof placed entirely upon him—to reclaim his freedom.[31] For the most part, free children of color bound as apprentices in Natchez were too well known to endure the calamity of sudden enslavement. Except for racial designations in county court records, black apprentices resembled white apprentices in every way, receiving the manual training, rudimentary education, and "wholesome provisions" guaranteed by law.[32] Enslaved

boys and girls, on the other hand, fell outside the scope of public assistance altogether, for terms such as *poor* and *orphaned* did not apply to
individuals regarded as private property. Masters bore full responsibility
for the care of their slaves, and if care proved financially difficult, those
slaves could be sent to the auction block.[33]

Children in Indian country were similarly excluded from statutory relief. Along with persons of European and African descent, Indians constituted the third major population in the Old Southwest, though as inhabitants of separate nations they had their own methods of dealing with
needy boys and girls. The Choctaw nation, which flanked Mississippi
counties to the north and west, dominated this borderland at the turn
of the nineteenth century. Like many indigenous peoples, the Choctaws
took the children of conquered enemies as captives, and families either
adopted them or used them as slaves. According to European observers,
however, orphans doomed to Choctaw slavery performed the same sort
of work as their free peers, though they never faced the prospect of sale
to other peoples.[34] More often than not, orphans became regarded as sons
and daughters, for Indians tended to view those within the nation as kin
and everyone else an "enemy." Indeed, before Spanish and American em-
issaries could engage in any kind of negotiations with the Choctaws, they
had to be ceremonially "adopted" into the nation.[35]

On the whole, Choctaw families demonstrated a marked predilection
for welcoming young outsiders. Visitors to the nation remarked upon the
frequency with which couples adopted boys and girls, even when those
couples already had children of their own. And an adopted child usually
grew up as a full member of the family, according to H. B. Cushman, a
white American whose parents were missionaries to the Indians of the
Lower Mississippi Valley:

> Never have there been found among the Chickasaws or Choctaws homeless
> and friendless orphan children, thrown out to shift for themselves, and left
> "to root pig or die." I have seen, time and again, in many families among
> the Chickasaws and Choctaws from one to four adopted children; and they
> were adopted, not through mercenary motives, but to be protected, cared
> for and loved, not to be enslaved for the few dollars and cents that anticipa-
> tion whispered would be made out of them by adoption. And one might
> live a lifetime in a family of adopted orphans, and, unless told, he would
> not even suspect, but that all the children were of the same parentage.[36]

Through his praise of Indian attitudes toward orphans, Cushman makes a thinly veiled attack upon American child welfare and the exploitation of destitute minors in white communities. He implies that Americans who took on poor children viewed them primarily as servants, whereas Indians considered orphans as objects of affection. The work of Cushman's parents probably fueled his admiration of the native approach, for missionaries regularly accepted Indian children and raised them as fellow members of the Christian family. To be sure, these missions actively targeted the education of young "savages" as the surest means of bringing them into the civilized fold.[37]

Curiously, white Americans during the early republic sometimes demonstrated greater concern for the welfare of indigenous children than for that of children of their own race. Indeed, the response to one particular Indian orphan was so strong one would think she was the only child who had ever lost her parents. The "little Osage captive," as she became known, was taken by Cherokees sometime in 1817, after her mother and father had been killed in a war between the two nations. A young missionary named Elias Cornelius was traveling through Mississippi when he came across the party; according to his account, he recoiled in horror when the warriors proudly displayed the scalps of the girl's slain parents. When Cornelius offered to take the child, the warriors agreed but demanded a large sum in compensation. Too poor to free the child himself, the missionary pleaded for funds in a letter that subsequently appeared in various evangelical publications around the United States. Ultimately, his own moving narrative prompted the necessary donation: when Lydia Carter of Natchez heard him describe the orphan's plight, she gave $150 to pay the ransom.[38]

The girl became known as "Lydia Carter," but she did not go to live with her benefactress. Because white Americans generally believed that Indian children belonged in Indian country, the Osage orphan went instead to the mission at Brainerd to be raised as a Christian and to learn the ways of "civilization." Evangelical Americans continued to follow her story with interest, and the missionaries obliged them by submitting periodic detailed reports. "Our feelings on the reception of this exiled orphan, may be more easily conceived than described," they wrote of her arrival at Brainerd. "We feel ourselves bound, not only in duty, but by the feelings of our hearts, to train her as our own child."[39] One couple "adopted" the girl and reared her alongside their own daughter, with the other missionaries serving as co-parents. Lydia herself seemed to share the sentiment that a natural family had been formed, starting with the clergyman who had brought her to Brainerd: "She fixed her eyes with great earnestness upon him . . . and leaned her head on his bosom, as if she had already found a father."[40] The little Osage orphan became a regular feature in the Brainerd journal, which appeared in various religious publications and related many other examples of missionary successes among the young Indians of the wilderness.

Lydia's tale may have given hope and satisfaction to evangelicals across the United States, but that fame also led to her removal from Brainerd in 1821. When the Osage people learned of her survival, they demanded her return. Although the missionaries appealed all the way to the president of the United States, diplomacy required that they relinquish custody. Lydia fled to the woods rather than leave the family she had come to regard as her own, and when she finally acquiesced, she cried particularly hard over leaving her younger (white) sister behind. Unfortunately, Lydia fell ill on the journey to Arkansas and died before reaching her natal soil. "She had just begun to feel the value of that Christian benevolence that redeemed her from captivity," lamented the anonymous author of her obituary, "and to lisp the praises of Him who died to redeem her from the captivity of Satan."[41] A year after Lydia's death, Elias Cornelius recounted her short but instructive life in a religious tract directed at young readers. Thus, ironically, the little Indian orphan who had been found and rescued near Natchez became an example for American children to admire and emulate.[42]

Lydia Carter seems to have inspired more widespread compassion than most white orphans during the early republic. In fact, Mrs. Lydia Carter contributed more money on behalf of her Indian protégée than for the white boys and girls of Natchez. Around the time she heard Cornelius's sorrowful tale, Mrs. Carter donated $20—less than 15 percent of what she had given to ransom the Osage girl—to the Female Charitable Society for the education and support of destitute white children. Perhaps she felt that the poor children of Natchez already benefited from statutory relief and that young Indians were more in need of assistance. Whatever reasons motivated the benevolent woman to donate more for the Osage orphan than for minors of her own race, her involvement with the Female Charitable Society helped effect a transformation of the child welfare system in Mississippi and throughout the United States.[43]

Since the late eighteenth century, well-to-do women around the country had been forming philanthropic voluntary associations to benefit needy members of the community. Poor and orphaned children became a special target of benevolent activity, owing to a pervasive spiritual awakening that emphasized early religious and moral education as well as the growing perception of motherhood as the essential feminine duty.[44] The Natchez Female Charitable Society was one of many associations that established an orphan asylum in which poor boys and girls could be reared and instructed entirely by women. Mirroring the Indian missions in providing a comprehensive education that went beyond the schoolroom, institutional relief was relatively novel for American children who were white and Protestant. The Ursulines in New Orleans had operated an orphanage for nearly a hundred years when the Natchez ladies inaugurated theirs in 1821. As they cultivated maternal authority in their own homes, benevolent women sought to extend that authority over public children. They believed that statutory relief neglected the religious and moral upbringing of orphans and other poor children and exposed them to exploitation as household laborers at the expense of learning a useful, honest trade. Overseers of the poor and other county officials in Mississippi proved remarkably willing to cede jurisdiction over young indigent minors to benevolent women. In 1825, the state legislature made the transfer of authority complete by designating the Natchez orphan asylum managers as the legal guardians of the public children in their care, a power that women as individuals still lacked over their own sons and daughters.[45]

Fifty years had passed since the Spanish governor at Natchez dealt with the Alston siblings. Though public children with property continued to enjoy more leisure and greater comforts, indigent minors who were young and white now received a very different upbringing. Charitable women supervised their care and determined their fate, and a residential institution—once an anomaly in Protestant communities—became the primary means of relief. As a result, the experiences of poor children no longer varied as widely as when male officials summarily bound them to different guardians as apprentices and indigent wards. Living in the orphan asylum, poor white boys and girls now grew up more or less the same way: devoting their mornings to lessons, their afternoons to chores or sewing, and every Sunday to the Presbyterian church, the spiritual home claimed by most members of the Female Charitable Society. Older children typically returned to their families or entered new households, but only when benevolent women approved of the domestic arrangement.[46]

In 1822, for example, the members agreed to let Mr. and Mrs. Alfred Green take ten-year-old Olivia Wrice, provided that the couple sign "Articles of Agreement" outlining how the girl would be raised. Reminiscent of apprenticeship indentures, the document stipulated that Olivia would remain with the Greens until age eighteen, the statutory requirement for female apprentices. The articles also included the standard pledges of clothing, rudimentary education, and instruction in "those useful acquirements which will enable her to get an honest living," but the nature of basic provisions differed from those of ordinary indentures. For starters, Olivia's apparel was to be "genteel" rather than simply "wholesome." And the articles stated that the girl "be permitted to attend Sunday School, and divine service as often as possible," something never mentioned in the old system of relief. Of course, members hoped that the guardians would provide religious and moral instruction on a daily basis and that Sunday services would merely serve to reinforce precepts learned at home. The articles did not refer to Mr. and Mrs. Green as "master" and "mistress," and the couple made no pledge to treat Olivia Wrice as their own child. Instead, it seems that the Female Charitable Society arranged a middle ground for the girl in this new household: neither daughter nor servant, but a public child raised according to an elevated standard of care.[47]

Child welfare was changing around the United States, as was the notion of who should govern public children. Since the earliest days of colonial settlement, male officials had held authority over all wards of the state, just as fathers had absolutely ruled their "little commonwealths," but by the early republic, women challenged this patriarchal structure in the name of charity and motherhood and assumed greater control over young white minors.[48] Though overseers of the poor continued to bind out free black children as apprentices, such cases were few and far between and were often handled without any official interference. Young Indians in the Lower Mississippi Valley had once been the sole concern of their respective nations. However, as evangelical men and women established missions in the backcountry, Indian children became objects of intense interest among pious Americans, who hoped to "save" young natives from savagery. As Mississippi evolved from a borderland to a settled center in the United States during the late eighteenth and early nineteenth centuries, the Olivia Wrices and Lydia Carters of the region likewise moved more to the center of public concern. By contrast, free children of color found themselves further in the margins, relegated there by a society growing increasingly anxious about the threat that blacks—young or otherwise—posed to the ruling white minority.

NOTES

1. For a comprehensive account of this period, see Robert V. Haynes, *The Natchez District and the American Revolution* (Jackson: University of Mississippi Press, 1976); see also Clayton D. James, *Antebellum Natchez* (Baton Rouge: Louisiana State University, 1968), 25–28.

2. May Wilson McBee, *The Natchez Court Records, 1767–1805: Abstracts of Early Records* (Greenville, MS: n.p., 1954), 1–2.

3. Linda K. Kerber, *Women of the Republic: Ideology and Intellect in Revolutionary America* (Chapel Hill: University of North Carolina Press, 1980); Suzanne Lebsock, *The Free Women of Petersburg: Status and Culture in a Southern Town, 1784–1860* (New York: W. W. Norton, 1984), ch. 3; Carl N. Degler, *At Odds: Women and the Family in America from the Revolution to the Present* (New York: Oxford University Press, 1980), 74–75.

4. Degler, *At Odds*, 74–75; James, *Antebellum Natchez*, ch. 1.

5. McBee, *Natchez Court Records*, 2:2.

6. Ibid.; on the Ursuline Convent in New Orleans, see Emily Clark, *Masterless Mistresses: The New Orleans Ursulines and the Development of a New World Society, 1727–1834* (Chapel Hill: University of North Carolina Press, 2007).

7. Jack D. L. Holmes, "Law and Order in Spanish Natchez, 1781–1798," *Journal of Mississippi History* 25 (1963): 187, 190–91; James, *Antebellum Natchez*, ch. 2.

8. Entry dated September 19, 1792, in McBee, *Natchez Court Records*, 2:150.

9. Entry dated September 24, 1792, in ibid.

10. Ian M. G. Quimby, *Apprenticeship in Colonial Philadelphia* (New York: Garland, 1985); Joseph McKnight, "Legitimation and Adoption on the Anglo-Hispanic Frontier of the United States," *Legal History Review* 53 (1985): 135–50.

11. McBee, *Natchez Court Records*, 2:219.

12. Ibid., 2:220.

13. Ibid.

14. Ibid., 2:221.

15. Ibid.

16. Ibid., 2:220.

17. All of these quotations are from ibid., 2:231.

18. Ibid., 2:232.

19. Ibid., 2:231.

20. James, *Antebellum Natchez*, 75–77. The territorial law concerning apprentices was enacted in September 1799; ch. 36 reprinted in P. L. Rainwater, "Sargent's Code," *American Journal of Legal History* 11 (July 1967): 312–13.

21. Rainwater, "Sargent's Code," 312.

22. Data were compiled from the following archival records. From 1799 to 1803, apprentices were brought before the Court of the Quarter Sessions, whose records are found in Mississippi Historical Records Survey, *Transcription of County*

Archives of Mississippi, Adams County, vols. 1 and 2 (Jackson: Board of Supervisors, Adams County, 1942), as well as Orphan's Court Minutebooks I–II, which respectively cover April 1803 to January 1815 and February 1815 and January 1820, Adams County Chancery Court (ACCC), Natchez, MS. Another source of information pertaining to apprentices is the Deed Record Books A–LL, ACCC, which contain transcriptions of indentures. Not all apprentices noted in the Orphan's Court Minutebooks appear in the Deed Record Books, which feature minors bound by overseers of the poor but not recorded as having appeared before orphan's court justices.

23. Adams County vouchers for the years 1809 to 1811, Auditor's Records, Natchez Historical Society Collection, Mississippi Department of Archives and History (MDAH). Daniel C. Vogt discusses at length the business of paid caretakers in "Poor Relief in Frontier Mississippi, 1798–1832," *Journal of Mississippi History* 51 (1989): 181–99, and he mentions the vouchers pertaining to Cynthia Williams, 186–87.

24. Cynthia was bound to an unnamed individual until the age of sixteen. Orphan's Court Minutebook I, ACCC, 337–38.

25. Jacqueline S. Reinier, *From Virtue to Character: American Childhood, 1775–1840* (New York: Twayne, 1996); Philip Greven, *The Protestant Temperament: Patterns of Child-Rearing, Religious Experience, and the Self in Early America* (New York: Knopf, 1977), 269–74, 276–78.

26. Rainwater, "Sargent's Code," 312–13.

27. Orphan's Court Minutebook II, ACCC, 158.

28. Ibid., 163–64.

29. Mississippi Historical Records Survey, *Transcription of County Archives,* 2:58.

30. McBee, *Natchez Court Records,* 2:255.

31. Information pertaining to John Ham (also known as Hamm or Ben Hammett) appear in documents of the freedom suit pursued in the Mississippi Superior Court: *John Hamm v. Charles B. Green,* 1819, Drawer 108, Old Box 4, 43–76, Historic Natchez Foundation, Natchez, MS.

32. Rainwater, "Sargent's Code," 312.

33. See Marie Jenkins Schwartz, *Born in Bondage: Growing Up Enslaved in the Antebellum South* (Cambridge, MA: Harvard University Press, 2000).

34. Greg O'Brien, *Choctaws in a Revolutionary Age, 1750–1830* (Lincoln: University of Nebraska Press, 2005), 43–44.

35. Ibid., 61.

36. H. B. Cushman, *History of the Choctaw, Chicasaw and Natchez Indians,* ed. Angie Debo (1899; repr., Norman: University of Oklahoma Press, 1999), 400–401.

37. Clara Sue Kidwell, *Choctaws and Missionaries in Mississippi, 1818–1918* (Norman: University of Oklahoma Press, 1995).

38. Elias Cornelius, *The Little Osage Captive, an Authentic Narrative* (Boston: Samuel T. Armstrong and Crocker and Brewster, 1822), 23.

39. Ard Hoyt, D. S. Buttrick, and William Chamberlain, "Journal of the Mission at Brainerd," *Panoplist and Missionary Herald* 14 (December 1818): 565.

40. Ibid.

41. "The Little Osage Captive," *Boston Recorder* 6 (October 6, 1821): 164.

42. Hoyt, Buttrick, and Chamberlain, "Journal of the Mission"; Cornelius, *Little Osage Captive*; "Mission among the Cherokees," *Missionary Herald, Containing the Proceedings* 17 (January 1821): 21.

43. Her name and donation amount are listed at the end of the list of subscribers, which appears at the beginning of Minutebook I (March 1816 to December 1822), Natchez Children's Home Records (NCHR), Center for American History, Austin, TX.

44. See Anne M. Boylan, *The Origins of Women's Activism: New York and Boston, 1797–1840* (Chapel Hill: University of North Carolina Press, 2002).

45. A complete history of the Natchez Female Charitable Society and its establishment of a school and orphan asylum is found in Nancy Zey, "Rescuing Some Youthful Minds: Benevolent Women and the Rise of the Orphan Asylum as Civic Household in Early Republic Natchez" (PhD diss., University of Texas at Austin, 2007).

46. Ibid.

47. May 14, 1822, Minutebook I (March 1816 to December 1822), NCHR.

48. John Demos, *A Little Commonwealth: Family Life in Plymouth Colony* (New York: Oxford University Press, 1970); Kerber, *Women of the Republic*.

||||||||||||||||||||||||||||||||||||||||||||||||||||

Schooling and Child Health in Antebellum New England

Rebecca R. Noel

From the 1820s through the 1850s, reformers in New England launched an ambitious program to improve child health. In a further innovation, they chose the expanding system of public and private schools as their mechanism. Reformers sought to establish a hygiene curriculum complete with health textbooks, to redesign schoolhouses and school furniture, and to extend the kinds and amount of exercise children obtained in school. Children would grow up both healthier and more informed about their bodies, an investment that reformers believed would pay off in future generations as well.

Each of these elements represented a departure in early republican schooling. Although geography instruction was becoming standard by 1820, other sciences drew little attention in common schools. Private academies were introducing chemistry, astronomy, natural philosophy (physics), and botany, more widely for girls than for boys, but formal instruction in the human body and its care had made no debut. Whether students assembled in a vernacular, humble rural schoolhouse, the upstairs room of a town hall, or a grand academy building, medical opinions had contributed nothing to fashioning a healthy environment for learning. Student exercise consisted of chores, lunchtime play, and a long walk home; teachers perceived no mandate to suggest anything more deliberate. But reformers feared that the ill health of American children demanded a response. In schooling the body, they planned to attach the deep-rooted American faith in education to the budding promise of science. This vision borrowed excitement from the apparent curative power of institutions like penitentiaries and asylums, which had been partly developed by physicians. Schools too might work as complex social apparatus for the production of an enhanced child.[1]

Early republican schools were poised for overall transformation. Many Americans, especially in the urban Northeast, saw in a fresh light how schools could contribute to a booming, modernizing young nation. To prepare newly eligible voters for the electorate, aspirants for the emerging middle class, and workers for the technologically advancing economy, schooling should widen its reach. Urban charity schools merged with enlarged networks of free public schools at several levels, educating girls alongside boys; free public schools served African American children, though usually apart from whites. Reformers urged longer terms in rural and town schools and more regular attendance for more years. These and other projects of school reform, such as teacher training and state bureaucracies, found earliest coordination in New England. Gaining urgency there in the 1820s, by the late 1830s the process was well launched.[2]

By the nineteenth century, the colonial view of the child as depraved and wicked had begun to soften. Instead, people came to associate with children such qualities as moral innocence, benign (indeed healthy) playfulness, and mirth. In the late seventeenth century, Locke had suggested the moral and intellectual neutrality of the child at birth, ready to be shaped by society. Now revival religion emphasized free will rather than original sin, so that instilling moral accountability in children could defeat the impulse toward sin in the future adult. Another habit of evangelical religion, the application of sentiment to all that was meek, touched childhood too. Children were to be cherished more than chastised, actively nurtured more than controlled. Pastoral romanticism cast childhood as a natural state, with which schooling should hesitate to tamper. As one reformer conceded, a "chasm" separated "the natural life of infancy or childhood, and the artificial thing called a school." But reform that cared for the body could make schooling more natural. The reconception of the child made schooling crucial as both a moral project and a receptacle for sentimental energies.[3]

School reform's leaders included teachers and educational administrators, lawyers and legislators, ministers, merchants, industrialists, and a surprising number of physicians. Unlike the colonial and federal elite, these men (and some women) of the professions approached social problems using training and expertise, forming a nascent educated, interprofessional elite. In particular, the interest of physicians in school reform, and of educators and other school reformers in medical issues, sparked the mission of schooling the body.

Meanwhile, the industrializing economy was shaping a widening middle class of such professionals along with small business owners, white-collar workers, and their newly leisured wives. Antebellum school reform was broadly supported by the emerging middle class. Cherishing self-restraint and gasping at vice and crime, this class shaped a school system that tried to cultivate self-control in its pupils. Common school reform was also a goal of urban workingmen's organizations, especially during their most politically engaged phase from about 1825 to 1835. Amid some dissent, a spreading portion of antebellum New Englanders came to believe that schooling needed expansion and updating. Part of that renovation, many agreed, should address the child's physical well-being.[4]

Educational reformers and their middle-class peers believed that the nation's physical vigor was rapidly deteriorating. Everywhere they looked, infant and child mortality and broken health among women and men augured ill for the nation's future. In 1843, Secretary of the Massachusetts Board of Education Horace Mann reviewed the toll of suffering and death. Mortality claimed at least a fifth of children under age one, fully a third by age five, over half by age twenty. Parental mistakes and the parents' own debility wrought most of the damage before age two or three. After that, "Those children who have inherited feeble constitutions from their parents have been thinned off, and the rest have escaped the terrible slaughtering of that ignorance which presides over the nursery." Parental illness drained family resources; the sick became the poor, vice-ridden, and criminal, and all of society suffered. Worse still, in the current understanding of genetics, a sickly child would grow up to bear few, puny, and weakly offspring, suggesting a downward spiral for generations to come.[5]

Reformers believed the solution to lethal parental ignorance lay in expanded education. But here was a painful rub: schooling itself appeared to be dangerous to children's health. "It is astonishing how many perish by what has been called 'the disease of education,'" fretted the anonymous author of A Course of Calisthenics for Young Ladies in 1831. "Multitudes die every year of this disorder." Both town and country schools lacked ventilation, fluctuated in temperature, forced glare into young eyes, and damaged young bodies with their high, backless benches. Confined for hours at a time without exercise or fresh air, children wilted, especially the youngest tots. This critique tapped into reformers' preexisting (and often self-referential) worry about the poor health of sedentary adults.

"Look at the pale countenance and slender figure" of the minister, physician Abel Peirson told the American Institute of Instruction, or at the "debilitated frames" of other scholarly strivers. These were the so-called literary gentlemen, "whose studies have ruined their health . . . and will open for them an early grave." The fate of literary gentlemen would strike more adults with the economy shifting from physical, outdoor work like farming to indoor, often sedentary labor. Children might now face this danger too. If reformers succeeded in increasing school attendance, the scholars' health crisis could spread to the young.[6]

Pulmonary consumption (tuberculosis) presented a special threat to the studious. Many Americans reported a rising incidence of consumption in the Northeast after about 1810. One death in five was attributed to consumption in the antebellum years; it was the leading cause of adult death in the urban Northeast. Most New Englanders had lost at least one family member, neighbor, or friend to the disease before the century was a third gone. No one who witnessed its sufferers' terrifying thinness and macabre hemorrhages could ignore it. Physicians reassured Americans that consumption was not contagious. Instead, a predisposition ran in families, a cold and wet climate worsened the odds, and bad habits activated the tendency: lack of exercise, stagnant air, a too-stimulating diet, and (for women) tight corsets. In New England, where the climate stacked the deck, this emphasis on behavioral triggers sharply implicated sedentary indoor occupations, like teaching, the ministry, and the law. Once contracted, the disease usually took years to finish off its victims; young adults from twenty to forty died in the greatest numbers. Children and youth could permanently damage their lungs by aping those in the literary professions, pursuing their studies to the exclusion of their health. In short, all-out studenthood cost lives, perhaps years or decades later.[7]

Yet properly reformed, schools might also become mechanisms for superior child health, along with the other social improvements they bid fair to bring about. The centerpiece of the campaign to school the body was formalizing the study of human anatomy and physiology, with associated recommendations for hygiene. Preparing teachers for the subject was the first order of business. Up to the 1820s, only three self-designated schoolbooks on the body had been published in the United States. Like domestic medical guides of the previous fifty years or more, these earliest books focused on diseases rather than prevention and normal functioning. Their chapters followed the child through successive ages, quite different from later books that universalized the body as an ageless, stable specimen.

While the early books' hygiene advice varied little from later books, they did not employ the "laws of health" construct that would soon become familiar.[8]

Beginning in 1829, hygiene textbooks came thick and fast, with forty-four different texts issued by 1860. (I will refer to them as hygiene books, although authors distinguished among anatomy, physiology, and hygiene content.) Advances in print and paper technology had recently made book production cheaper; textbooks in many subjects were proliferating. Most of the hygiene textbooks were aimed at an academy or, later, high school audience, though some were suitable for common schools. The sheer number of different books implies demand, and several of them went through ten or more printings. Teacher preparation programs and normal schools proved particularly keen to teach "physiology," as they often called the subject. Most famously, teachers who were trained under Mann's influence in the Massachusetts Normal Schools, and in academies run by Catharine Beecher and Mary Lyon, carried their knowledge and their books to schools far and wide. The movement peaked with an 1850 law in Massachusetts mandating instruction in physiology at the secondary level, although enforcement varied. Surviving books from that period show signs of heavy use. Doodles, poems, autographs, and pronunciation notes suggest student consumption, while other books contain teacherly marginalia like handwritten questions.[9]

From 1834 on, the hygiene books formed a coherent genre in terms of structure, content, and philosophy. They attempted to make the body seem stable, reassuring, and familiar. The structure of the books reflected their conception as textbooks in anatomy and physiology first, hygiene secondarily. Therefore, the chapters followed the organs and systems of the body. Equally important, they discussed the body comprehensively, as earlier books had not. Though they minimized excretory functions and ignored organs of reproduction, otherwise the whole body was present, from tissues to toes. The steady march of tissues and systems would give students a sense of the body as an orderly construction of working parts. In general, the books featured the operation of the healthy adult body, plus ways to preserve health and prevent disease. Bad health mostly stayed offstage in this rosy discussion. Physical problems had brief cameo roles as curiosities whose study would prove the body's ingenuity after all. In a common example, John Hoskins Griscom reassured students that the spiky hairs inside the ear canal would entangle any insects that might invade, while the "very bitter wax" would also act as a disincentive. By dispelling this apparently prevalent fear, the hygiene books took the role of comforting debunkers of common misconceptions. Contrary to the vulnerable body children might have perceived before studying hygiene, on the brink of chaos from illnesses and earwigs, the books showed the body as reliable, safe, and normatively healthy.[10]

The urge to show the body's functionality partly accounts for the frequent comparisons of the body to a well-made machine. Like other authors, Griscom seemed to assume that children were intrigued by and familiar with machines. To explain why the body needs food, he analogized, "A steam engine, one of the most complicated machines, and made of the hardest materials, would in a few hours, cease entirely its operations, if the boiler were not regularly supplied with water, and the furnace with fuel." Elsewhere, he likened the fluid that protects joints to "oil on the joints of a machine." Whether the trope soothed all readers, especially rural ones unacquainted with steam engines, went unrecorded.[11]

Parents who had not adapted their health practices to absorb new trends might have found these books alienating in their specific advice, their structure, and their very presence. But the textbooks' guidance would be familiar to parents who were taking an active interest in their own health, perhaps participating in one of the era's health reforms. Those works published in 1834 and after lined up well with what we might call the hygienic consensus, advice tacitly agreed to among both reformist mainstream physicians and the popular alternative crowd. While few alternative healers wrote hygiene textbooks, most of the books could have come as easily from a medical sectarian as from the reform side of medical orthodoxy. Simple diet, fresh air, daily exercise, personal cleanliness, and informed self-care matched the body program of a water cure without the elaborate baths. Hygiene textbooks violated Sylvester Graham's strict regimen—regular sleep, cold-water bathing, whole-grain bread, only water to drink, and vegetarian diet—chiefly by adding a little meat. Followers of alternative therapies like the botanic Thomsonian system, which appealed to the rural working class, and low-dosing homeopathy, just reaching northeastern cities from its native Germany, would also endorse the books' preventive suggestions. Through these organized movements or just the popular study of "physiology," many in the middle class and the humbler ranks had already arrived at these hygienic precepts.[12]

Still, as children faced the grim odds represented by mortality statistics, they also now confronted an outside authority giving prescriptions in intimate areas of body management. In Lydia Folger Fowler's textbook, presented as a dialogue between a fictional teacher and pupils, the teacher frankly repudiated the supposed values of the children's parents as "foolish and untrue"—only a more honest statement of a general tension in the books. Teacher and textbook author William B. Fowle also made the alleged contest between the school hygiene curriculum and the family explicit, charging that parents did not instruct their children about health at all. "It is clearly the duty of every teacher to study the human frame so that he can advise and direct the young," he growled, "until parents are fully awakened to their duty in this respect."[13]

Textbook authors challenged parents most in their attack on tight lacing of corsets. The corset was not new, but wasp-waisted fashion beginning in the 1820s demanded that women and adolescent girls lace up their corsets too tightly to allow full breaths, let alone vigorous exercise. In treatises, lectures, and textbooks, reformers blamed tight lacing for causing consumption due to inadequate respiration and spinal curvatures, blindness, headaches, heart palpitations, fainting, feeble torso muscles, indigestion, and insanity; they hinted about impaired reproduction, insufficient lactation, and weak offspring. In their contest with the fashion of tight lacing, reformers tried to provide an alternative to the reigning middle-class female aesthetic. Like other authors, Griscom showed paired illustrations of the natural and corseted torso. In one pair, the Venus de Medici played the role of the natural chest, while the corset-damaged torso is labeled "Outline of the form of a modern belle" (figure 6). As Griscom saw it, "no one who has good taste, can think well of such an unnatural shape" as that of a corseted lady. Griscom knew that his middle-class readers prided themselves on their refinement. By opposing the warped "good taste" of middle-class students (and their parents) to an indisputable aesthetic paragon of the Renaissance, Griscom and other authors hoped to turn fashion in a healthier direction.[14]

Interestingly, while nearly three dozen different authors wrote hygiene textbooks, only four were women. Women gained a foothold in New England schools during these years, becoming the majority of teachers over the space of a generation. Girls' academies were apparently more likely than boys' to offer physiology as a subject of study. Moreover, women's roles as family caregivers and midwives, the early republican development of intensely mother-centered private family life, the era's particular concern about women's ill health, and the enthusiasm of many middle-class women about popular health reform might all have prompted more women to devote their active pens to educating schoolchildren about

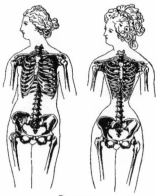

PLATE 28

Figure 6 Hygiene textbooks offered a pointed critique of "tight lacing" of corsets, a fashion trend school health reformers considered extremely unhealthy for girls. Such illustrations, though likely exaggerated, were intended to show the damage that could be done by tightly laced John H. Griscom, *First Lessons in Human Physiology: To Which Are Added Brief Rules of Health. For the Use of Schools,* 8th ed. (New York: Roe Lockwood and Son, 1847), 141. Credit: Digital copy provided by the Special Collections Department of Bailey/Howe Library, University of Vermont, with assistance from Lamson Library, Plymouth State University.

health. Nevertheless, some 90 percent of known hygiene textbook imprints were authored by men, and 80 percent by male physicians (whereas school textbooks on other subjects were usually written by teachers). Twenty-four of the thirty male authors had actual medical degrees, which marked them as newfangled and relatively well-educated physicians to boot. None of the women authors held such a degree (although Fowler became America's second female MD a few years later). Perhaps what motivated physicians to write schoolbooks was the intense competition they faced from alternative practitioners and popular health reform, which threatened physicians' livelihoods and their attempted corner on scientific knowledge. Authorial physicians may have suspected that the right hygiene book could convert young medical sectarians (and their families) into consumers of orthodox medical care. Physicians dominated school hygiene book writing far more in the nineteenth century than in the twentieth.[15]

Given this authorship and possible agenda, it is not surprising that the textbook authors frequently introduced abstract concepts, technical terms, and results of experiments and studies conducted by medical experts, often overseas. Even those meant for young children named at least a few experts, while many named fifteen or twenty, cited current articles and books that were often foreign in origin, and described complex scientific debates. George Hayward's *Outlines of Human Physiology* consisted of page after page of historic experiments and studies. This reliance on expert knowledge reveals these books as middle-class products in another way besides their congeniality to health reform. As professions like medicine gradually formalized affiliation and training, the esoteric knowledge that professionals commanded became part of their stock in trade. Grooming children to seek out and accept medical expertise, inserting such understandings as the single authoritative source of body knowledge rather than traditional lore or individual experience, hygiene textbook authors extended a middle-class professional ethos into personal, instinctive areas of experience.[16]

While the hygiene curriculum would bear fruit over time, the architectural crusade addressed both the present and future health impact of the learning environment. Here too, medical expertise shaped the reformers' program. Schoolers of the body made recommendations regarding room size and ventilation; seats, writing surfaces, and the arrangement of students in the schoolroom; the size, location, and number of windows, important for eye health; and school location, grounds, and outbuildings. All of these matters, especially ventilation, sitting posture, and eye care, impinged on the child's immediate and long-term health.

Common school reformers began clamoring for new and better public schoolhouses around 1830. In pressing for this reform, they described existing schools as shockingly shabby, unpleasant, and uncomfortable. But local taxpayers, even parents, were not easily shocked. They had lived with the current schoolhouses for years, perhaps attended the old shacks in their own youth. Prissy complaints would rarely stimulate the financial effort needed to build and outfit grander schools. Expecting resistance, reformers portrayed the buildings as dangerous to health, that ultimate inelastic good. To be sure, the expensive building program they sought would put educators in command of a larger portion of community resources. But the medical justification was not simply a manipulative ploy, as the same activists also sought hygiene instruction and exercise schemes. If common school reformers wanted all children to go to school for most of their childhood days, then for ethical reasons schools had to provide a comfortable environment—at least health-neutral and better yet health promoting.[17]

School reformers particularly plumbed late-Enlightenment scientific findings about the chemistry of air. Scientists had found that when inhaled air contacted the blood in the capillaries of the lungs, the air deposited some of its payload of oxygen and took up carbon in return. The resulting substance, called carbonic acid, was considered toxic, yet it was exhaled with every breath. For this reason, confinement without ventilation eventually led not just to suffocation but to actual poisoning. Colorless and odorless but heavier than air, carbonic acid would pool at the floor like a liquid. Reformers wrote of people drowning in their curtained beds as the tide of carbonic acid rose to the level of the pillow. The skin and lungs were constantly throwing off other noxious, if less instantly deadly effluvia as well.[18]

For help in using this knowledge to upgrade school buildings, reformers consulted with institutional physicians who, in a reform already underway, had studied closely the effects of prison, asylum, and hospital environments on the people inside. Horace Mann possessed his own knowledge base on the subject. A former legislative champion of the Worcester Lunatic Asylum, he remained active on its board. He also received detailed guidance on ventilation from his friend Dr. Samuel Gridley Howe, member of the Boston Prison Discipline Society and founder of the Perkins Institution for the Blind, and from Dr. Samuel B. Woodward, the first superintendent of the Worcester Asylum. In his "Supplementary Report on School Houses," attached to his First Annual Report in 1838, Mann claimed to have evaluated about 1,800 Massachusetts schoolhouses, nearly half through personal visits. He pronounced many substandard: hazardous to children's health and ineffectual for learning. Citing physicians throughout the report, he discussed the processes of circulation and respiration, the importance of pure air, and how poor seats and desks led to skeletal deformities, inviting consumption.[19]

In *The School and Schoolmaster* (1842), George Emerson similarly described air chemistry, carbonic acid, and respiratory effluvia. "The amount of corruption produced by these [human] sources is astonishing," he warned. "From 1400 to 2000 cubic inches of oxygen are every hour withdrawn from the air by each pair of lungs." A working scientist and teacher, Emerson also took a highly scientific approach to classroom heating. Particles of carbon in air convert to carbonic acid in contact with hot iron, he asserted, so he preferred a sophisticated fireplace to an iron stove. Emerson indulged in loving detail on ventilation systems and recent chemistry experiments. Mann, Emerson, and other reformers used expert knowledge about the medical aspects of indoor environments to shape their guidelines for school buildings. Under Mann's pressure, Massachusetts towns soon began upgrading their schoolhouses. Other New England states proceeded more slowly, but large banks of windows, transoms, and more comfortable desks evident over the next decades testify to the eventual success of schoolhouse reform.[20]

Interest in school exercise grew alongside momentum toward hygiene instruction and architectural improvements and in some cases appeared a little earlier. Reform channels like the *American Journal of Education*, founded in 1826, lectures before the American Institute of Instruction, and soon hygiene textbooks added to this ongoing discussion. Virtually all of the textbooks advocated frequent outdoor exercise as a health necessity for children. A few, like John Lee Comstock's *Outlines of Physiology* (1844), went further, suggesting a range of exercises. Comstock advocated a playground with "gymnastic apparatus for exercising the muscular activities of the young of both sexes," such as "swings, poles, hoops, see-saws, pulleys, balls, and similar articles." Activities should include "walking, skipping, running, leaping in height, length, or depth, swinging, lifting, carrying, [and] jumping with a hoop or pole," gardening, and pedestrian excursions to collect scientific specimens. For boys, he added hunting with dogs and guns, angling, and carpentry.[21]

Of all the elements of the emerging school health program, exercise for boys demanded the least alteration in prior practice. Evidence points to a lively culture of sport among boys, pursued on their own initiative. School hours limited boys' opportunities for exercise but also facilitated sport by bringing boys together and providing release time from family labor. Recognizing that most boys would play anyway, educational reformers promoted deliberate school-based exercise for new reasons: to develop habits of purposefulness, contribute to military readiness, and redress the unhealthiness of schooling. Boys' own play could not preserve their health once they had spent nearly all their time at study. The notion that exercise promoted health, and that school-sponsored exercise benefited students, predated the nineteenth century. But calls for exercise grew more pressing and more linked to education as consumption, especially, took an ever greater toll. If schooling seemed easier on the body than arduous factory work, it compared most unfavorably with outdoor manual trades and occupations, farming above all, that actually gave the body vigor. School exercise could address the health dilemma that expanded schooling created.[22]

Boys' school exercise programs took several forms in the antebellum era. Military exercise received its most thorough trial at Norwich Academy in Vermont. German gymnastics was first pursued at the Round Hill School in Northampton, Massachusetts, from 1824 to 1833. Other schools tried manual labor programs, for exercise and other reasons. After some fifteen years of experimentation in academies, the movement spread to public schools; by 1860, there were over one hundred exercise programs in New England schools.[23]

The health of girls presented a bigger problem. School health reformers vehemently decried the new mystique of the tightly laced, housebound lady, the physical manifestation of what historians have called the "cult of true womanhood." The emerging middle class's sharp distinction between male and female lives led to special health problems for the inhibited female body. William B. Fowle, headmaster of the Boston Female Monitorial School, lamented the high contrast between boys' and girls' physical condition and urged its erasure through exercise. "It would be difficult to point out any physical exercise that would be beneficial to one sex and injurious to the other," he argued, or "to give a philosophical reason why females should not be able to run, climb, swim and skate as well as boys." In fact, "far better would it be for them to excel in all these, than to be the feeble, helpless and dependent things they generally are." Fowle believed that parents intentionally inhibited girls' exercise. "The fear is, that girls will become romps and lose much of that feminine delicacy which is the charm of woman," he allowed. But girls' exercise with proper supervision could demolish "the false notion that female delicacy consists in general debility of body and sickly affectation of manners."[24]

Hygiene textbook authors underscored the connection between exercise and health and the need to combat cultural restraints on girls' movements. They probably suspected that most of their readers were girls, likely to rear and even teach children themselves one day. Author J. V. C. Smith charged bluntly, "Boys generally lead an active life, enjoying a free exercise of all their limbs in various pastimes. Girls, by a perverse custom, are taught that they were made for the house, and not for the open air." Smith believed girls ought to take "nearly as much exercise as boys, but," he added, posing the dilemma of girls' physical education, "of a less violent kind." Beginning in the 1820s, the search for appropriate girls' exercises formed a major project of the early school health movement. While a few reformers, especially women, argued that female domestic tasks naturally worked the muscles women most needed to develop, most observers sought purposive exercises. Among these, walking earned the most frequent recommendation. Authors also encouraged gardening, jumping rope, swimming, horseback riding, marching, singing, running and jumping, and skating, then primarily a male activity. Ball games and sports like hoop toss, battledore (similar to badminton), and archery were beneficial and suitable.[25]

Some reformers were not satisfied with these options. While girls' schools quickly adopted walking, the group promenade became notorious for its lethargy; one author called it "that most melancholy of all processions." At best, walking only addressed the lower body anyway. Several writers recommended more abstract, invented exercises for the sake of girls' health. Fowle gained inspiration from an 1825 lecture on physical education delivered by a prominent physician. Fowle had long "noticed the feeble health of many of my pupils, and encouraged them to take more exercise, but they wanted means and example, and little or nothing was effected." Now the headmaster set up a gymnasium with bars and pulleys. "Besides the ordinary exercises of raising the arms and feet, and extending them in various directions," he explained, "we have various methods of hanging and swinging by the arms, tilting, raising weights, jumping forward, marching, running, *enduring*, &c. &c." Except for a few blistered palms, his students had gained in both health and vigor. Sickly girls had "at least doubled their strength," he boasted, while "some very dull children have become more animated, and some over sprightly ones have found an innocent way of letting off their exuberant spirits." He also avowed that he had won over the few skeptical parents. However, Fowle later recalled the demise of his gymnastic program after a few years. Apparently, numerous parents refused to dress their children in loose enough clothes for exercise, and he took their recalcitrance, probably correctly, as a lack of support for the endeavor. He grudgingly dropped the gymnastics, hired a dancing master weekly to teach graceful movement, and devoted recesses to posture practice.[26]

Although Fowle turned to dance lessons as a less controversial, more aesthetically pleasing alternative to his gymnastic exercises, the antebellum years witnessed a vigorous debate over the morality and wholesomeness of dancing as exercise. The anonymous author of *The Young Girl's Book of Healthful Amusements and Exercises* (ca. 1840) favored dancing: "Children must have exercise; and dancing is healthy, innocent, and elegant." Beginning in 1807, Emma Hart, later Emma Willard, used quick-paced reels to warm her girls up when she ran the Middlebury (Vermont)

Female Academy in an ill-heated room. Famed teacher-physician William Alcott directed his female students to dance indoors at recess for exercise, with boys sent outside. But dance never caught on widely as school-sponsored exercise, as conservative educators considered it immoral and too nearly associated with unhealthy evening amusements. As Catharine Beecher explained, young people at dances, dressed in tight clothing, grew overheated, breathed impure air, ate rich food, stayed out too late, then emerged into cold and damp night air, meanwhile developing an unfortunate "relish and desire for high excitement." She concluded, "It is probable, that there is no single thing that can be pointed out, which combines so many injurious particulars, as this amusement, so often defended, as [being] so healthful." Genteel parents who endorsed dancing provided lessons for their children anyway.[27]

For girls, exercise must cultivate health and graceful carriage without sacrificing modest manners. Calisthenics, a European novelty, combined movements from gymnastics and dance with these gendered goals in mind. Beecher introduced calisthenics (and professed coining the word itself, from Greek roots for "beauty" and "strength") at her Hartford Female Seminary in 1827 to considerable acclaim. Before long, her students interrupted study for calisthenics twice a day. Around the same time, Zilpah Grant and Mary Lyon commenced a calisthenics program at Ipswich Female Seminary in Massachusetts. By 1835, nine New England schools reported that they offered calisthenics, and ten more added programs by 1845.[28]

Mary Lyon went on to found Mount Holyoke Seminary in 1837, installing a physically rigorous three-part exercise program from the outset. Both for exercise and to save money, students and faculty handled all the cleaning and cooking tasks in the large residential and academic building, at least an hour per day for each student. On Mondays, students and faculty rose at three a.m. and began boiling water to wash clothes, bedding, tablecloths, and every surface in the building, which they accomplished by noon. A student remembered the domestic program as "real genuine working exercise." In the school's catalogs, the explanation of the domestic system's benefits always listed exercise first—a marketing decision, perhaps, but also a firm commitment. Every day, students and faculty were also required to walk a brisk mile, in any weather; Mount Holyoke's catalog told students to come equipped with rubber footwear, an umbrella, and warm undergarments. Calisthenics, too, figured as a daily requirement from the start. After learning various individual steps, the students formed group patterns representing "'stars, crescents, wreaths,

and crosses,'" keeping time by singing popular songs but carefully avoiding any appearance of dancing. Hygiene instruction delivered the exercise
message too.[29]

At first glance, Mount Holyoke's program, with its embrace of domestic chores, walking, and graceful display, might seem not to ruffle the
mainstream surface of middle-class women's roles. Indeed, during public
demonstrations, the students wore flowing white dresses decorated with
flowers, supporting the dominant aestheticized view of women. Still, the
vigor and planfulness of Lyon's program show that this was not women's
business as usual but an innovative scheme calculated to develop women's
health beyond customary levels. Years after graduating, an alumna recalled Lyon's emphasis on performing the movements with muscular exer-
tion and erect posture. "'I hear again her urgent encouraging voice, "Now,
young ladies, try that again! a little more force! ah, yes, I knew you could!
Now, that is better. Stand erect!"' The elderly woman added that the wands
used in the exercises were "not fairy wands, but quite substantial affairs."
Lyon took the exercise program at her school very seriously, forbidding
study during recreation hours and participating in exercises herself. Some
students and teachers collapsed under the regime. Those who mastered it
drew a bashful pride from their hard-won physical stamina. "I think any
one with quite delicate health might go through a whole course here, and
go away with better health than she entered [with]," one student wrote to
a friend. "I know I should laugh if I were at home, to start out before sun
rise and walk a mile in the keen cold wintry air, but I do it here quite often and think nothing of it."[30]

A generation of experience showed school reformers that girls and
even boys required actual exercise programs, not just release from study
into ordinary activities. By the late 1850s, Boston's school system and others were making calisthenics for both boys and girls a daily inclusion,
standardizing recess times, and building playgrounds—often sex segre-
gated, but with play equipment on both sides. Many private academies
went further, carrying the Round Hill model into the athletically intense
boarding school still known today.[31]

Educational reformers were hardly alone in believing that the new
nation needed more widespread, advanced schooling, but body-focused
reformers worried that expansion of schooling would threaten children's
health. However, if the schools could be enlisted in improving health,
rather than posing a hazard to it, the linked mandates of school reform
and the republic's growth could proceed. The common denominator of

antebellum school health reform measures was the effort to install expert knowledge as a mediator between children and their bodily self-perception, and at times between parents and children's bodies. Congruent with the development of the middle-class professions, the antebellum arrival of expert knowledge in the realm of schoolchildren's corporeal experience made schooling deliberate, scientific, and middle class in a way most serviceable to the new republic.

NOTES

1. Kim Tolley, *The Science Education of American Girls: A Historical Perspective* (New York: RoutledgeFalmer, 2003), 13–53; David J. Rothman, *Discovery of the Asylum: Social Order and Disorder in the New Republic* (Boston: Little, Brown, 1971), 79–108, 130–54, 206–36.

2. Carl F. Kaestle, *Pillars of the Republic: Common Schools and American Society, 1780–1860* (New York: Hill and Wang, 1983), 30–136.

3. Quoted in ibid., 123–24, and see 109–10; Bernard Wishy, *The Child and the Republic: The Dawn of American Child Nurture* (Philadelphia: University of Pennsylvania Press, 1968), 22; Mary Lynn Stevens Heininger, "Children, Childhood, and Change in America, 1820–1920," in *A Century of Childhood, 1820–1920*, ed. Mary Lynn Stevens et al. (Rochester, NY: Margaret Woodbury Strong Museum, 1984), 1–32.

4. Kaestle, *Pillars of the Republic*, 136–81; David Tyack and Elisabeth Hansot, *Managers of Virtue: Public School Leadership in America, 1820–1980* (New York: Basic Books, 1982), 3–72.

5. Horace Mann, *Sixth Annual Report to the Board* (Boston: Dutton and Wentworth, 1843), 57–58; Jan Todd, *Physical Culture and the Body Beautiful: Purposive Exercise in the Lives of American Women, 1800–1875* (Macon, GA: Mercer University Press, 1998), 24–25.

6. *A Course of Calisthenics for Young Ladies, in Schools and Families. With Some Remarks on Physical Education* (Hartford: H. and F. J. Huntington, 1831), 14; Abel Peirson, *On Physical Education. A Lecture Delivered before the American Institute of Instruction, at Its Annual Session, Holden in Springfield, August, 1839* (Boston: Marsh, Capen, Lyon and Webb, 1840), 9.

7. Sheila M. Rothman, *Living in the Shadow of Death: Tuberculosis and the Social Experience of Illness in American History* (Baltimore: Johns Hopkins University Press, 1994), 1–74, 78, 81–82, 106.

8. Rebecca R. Noel, "Schooling the Body: The Intersection of Educational and Medical Reform in New England, 1800–1860" (PhD diss., Boston University, 1999), 176–80.

9. Ibid., 168–244, 445–46; Charles E. Rosenberg, "Catechisms of Health: The Body in the Prebellum Classroom," *Bulletin of the History of Medicine* 69 (1995): 175–97; Michael Sappol, *A Traffic of Dead Bodies: Anatomy and Embodied Social Identity in Nineteenth-Century America* (Princeton: Princeton University Press, 2002), 168–211; Lamar Riley Murphy, *Enter the Physician: The Transformation of Domestic Medicine, 1760–1860* (Tuscaloosa: University of Alabama Press, 1991), 140–85; Foster James Flint, "An Historical Study of School Health Education in Massachusetts from the Colonial Period to the First World War" (EdD diss., Boston University, 1954), 43–45; Cyrus Peirce, *The First State Normal School in America: The Journals of Cyrus Peirce and Mary Swift* (1926; repr., New York: Arno Press, 1969).

10. John H. Griscom, *First Lessons in Human Physiology; To Which Are Added Brief Rules of Health. For the Use of Schools*, 2nd ed. (New York: Roe Lockwood and Son, 1846), 121.

11. Ibid., 63, 18.

12. Noel, "Schooling the Body," 75–167, 173–74.

13. Lydia Folger Fowler, *Familiar Lessons on Physiology: Designed for the Use of Children and Youth in Schools and Families*, 2 vols. (New York: Fowlers and Wells, 1848), 1:13; William B. Fowle, *A Key to Fowle's Diagrams, for the Illustration of Human Physiology; Being Also a Familiar Treatise on Human Anatomy and Human Physiology, Adapted to the Education of Children in Schools and Families* (Boston: Fitz, Hobbs, 1850), 180.

14. Griscom, *First Lessons*, 141–42; Jane B. Donegan, *"Hydropathic Highway to Health": Women and Water-Cure in Antebellum America* (New York: Greenwood Press, 1986), 135–61.

15. Kim Tolley, "Science for Ladies, Classics for Gentlemen," *History of Education Quarterly* 36 (1996): 129; Madeleine B. Stern, *Heads and Headlines* (Norman: University of Oklahoma Press, 1971), 8–14; John A. Nietz, *Old Textbooks* (Pittsburgh: University of Pittsburgh Press, 1961), 292; Noel, "Schooling the Body," 169–74.

16. George Hayward, *Outlines of Human Physiology; Designed for the Use of the Higher Classes in Common Schools* (Boston: Marsh, Capen, and Lyon, 1834); Paul Starr, *The Social Transformation of American Medicine* (New York: Basic Books, 1982), 3–64.

17. William W. Cutler III, "Cathedral of Culture: The Schoolhouse in American Educational Thought and Practice since 1820," *History of Education Quarterly* 29 (1989): 2.

18. William C. Woodbridge, "Communication on the Size and Ventilation of School-Rooms," in *The Introductory Discourse and the Lectures Delivered before the American Institute of Instruction, in Boston, August, 1831. Including the Journal of Proceedings* (Boston: Hilliard, Gray, 1832), 261–71.

19. Horace Mann, *Report of the Secretary of the Board of Education, on the*

Subject of School Houses, Supplementary to His First Annual Report (Boston: Dutton and Wentworth, 1838), 5–10, 25, 24–25, 12, 57–64.

20. George B. Emerson and Alonzo Potter, *The School and Schoolmaster. A Manual for the Use of Teachers, Employers, Trustees, Inspectors, &c., &c., Of Common Schools. In Two Parts* (New York: Harper and Bros., 1842), 529–31, 530 n., 534–38, 537 n.; Horace Mann, *Tenth Annual Report to the Board* (Boston: Dutton and Wentworth, 1847), 68; Flint, "Historical Study," 52–63.

21. John Lee Comstock, *Outlines of Physiology, Both Comparative and Human* . . . (New York: Robinson, Pratt, 1844), 267–68, 249, and see 249–75.

22. Benjamin Rush, "Thoughts upon the Mode of Education Proper in a Republic," in *Essays on Education in the Early Republic*, ed. Frederick Rudolph (Cambridge, MA: Harvard University Press, 1965), 15–16.

23. Roxanne Marie Albertson, "Physical Education in New England Schools and Academies from 1789–1860: Concepts and Practices" (PhD diss., University of Oregon, 1974), 171–76 and passim; John Spencer Bassett, "The Round Hill School," *Proceedings of the American Antiquarian Society* 27 (1917): 18–62.

24. Barbara Welter, "The Cult of True Womanhood, 1820–1860," *American Quarterly* 18 (1966): 151–74; Fowle, *Key to Fowle's Diagrams*, 97–98.

25. J. V. C. Smith, *The Class Book of Anatomy, Explanatory of the First Principles of Human Organization, as the Basis of Physical Education. Designed for Schools and Families*, 9th, improved stereotype ed. (Boston: Robert S. Davis, 1845), 39; Jane Taylor, *Primary Lessons in Physiology: For Children*, new ed. (New York: George F. Cooledge and Brother, 1848), 111; Reynell Coates, *Physiology for Schools* (Philadelphia: Marshall, Williams and Butler, 1840), 228, 274.

26. Quoted in Comstock, *Outlines of Physiology*, 265–66; William B. Fowle, "Gymnastics for Girls," *American Journal of Education* 1 (1826): 698; Fowle, *Key to Fowle's Diagrams*, 88.

27. *The Young Girl's Book of Healthful Amusements and Exercises* (New York: J. S. Redfield, [1840?]), 17, and see 17–23; Alma Lutz, *Emma Willard, Daughter of Democracy* (Boston: Houghton Mifflin, 1929), 27; Catharine Beecher, *A Treatise on Domestic Economy* (1841; repr., New York: Schocken Books, 1977), 255, and see 254, 256.

28. Albertson, "Physical Education," 130–35; Todd, *Physical Culture*, 120, 152–53.

29. Elizabeth Alden Green, *Mary Lyon and Mount Holyoke: Opening the Gates* (Hanover, NH: University Press of New England, 1979), 80, 81, 173–81, 210, 220, 271–74, 280, 296; Persis Harlow McCurdy, "The History of Physical Training at Mount Holyoke College," *American Physical Education Review* 14 (1909): 139–41; Albertson, "Physical Education," 108–10; Margaret Duncan Greene, "The Growth of Physical Education for Women in the United States in the Early Nineteenth Century" (EdD diss., University of California at Los Angeles, 1950), 89–100, 261–63; Todd, *Physical Culture*, 122–28.

30. Quotation in McCurdy, "History of Physical Training," 144; quotation from

Susan Lennan to Emily Whitten, January 8, 1852, in Green, *Mary Lyon,* 335, and see 212, 327, 341; Edward Hitchcock, *The Power of Christian Benevolence Illustrated in the Life and Labors of Mary Lyon* (New York: American Tract Society, 1858), 212–15 and passim.

31. Albertson, "Physical Education," 56, 87–91, 121–23, 135–40; James McLachlan, *American Boarding Schools: A Historical Study* (New York: Charles Scribner's Sons, 1970), 71–101, 112, 241.

Part V

||||||||||||||||||||||||||||||||||||||||||||||||||||

Documents

Historians of children and youth sometimes have to make choices between writing about children as representations of adult notions about childhood and writing about them as historical actors in their own right. Those who choose the former often produce books and articles about the ways in which adults acted toward children or about how they believed children should behave. They often examine institutions designed to shape children into good citizens—such as schools and orphanages—or explore advice books, children's literature, schoolbooks, and descriptions of children's activities in newspapers or other sources created by adults. Most of the essays in this collection—like most books on children and youth in general—fit into this category.

But several of the essays—not to mention the brief introductions to each section—draw heavily on sources produced by children (or at least by adults writing about their childhoods) and offer glimpses of children as *people* rather than *objects* or *ideals*. Memoirs and autobiographies are obvious sources for getting at the points of view of children, but among the primary sources that present the children's points of view are letters written by youngsters to their parents, pension applications by old men who were boy soldiers, and graduation speeches by young women.

The three documents that follow feature three very different children: an affluent New England girl recording impressions of her first trips away from home; a pioneering editor recalling his long-ago, hardscrabble boyhood in upstate New York; and an African American describing the hardships and heartbreaks of the slave life he had left at the age of twenty— about a decade before writing about them. Jenny Trumbull's diaries are the most direct source, of course; she is not writing for posterity, and the events she describes have just happened—she has not had time to reflect on their meaning. Joseph T. Buckingham was in his seventies when he wrote about his childhood; time no doubt dimmed some of his memories and made others more pleasant. William Wells Brown's narrative was written while the events of his tragic youth were still fresh in his mind but were intended to convince readers that slavery must be abolished. Despite the biases and limitations of these sources—and all primary sources are biased or limited in some way—they can, if read carefully, open a window into the lives of children in the early republic on their terms, unfiltered by adults.

A Teenager Goes Visiting
The Diaries of Louisa Jane Trumbull (1835, 1837)

Holly V. Izard and Caroline Fuller Sloat

"It is now ten days since I wrote in my journal and very many things have happened in that time, which are great events in my life," Louisa Jane (Jenny) Trumbull wrote in her diary during the first month that she had ever spent far from home by herself. An "initiating" overnight visit to in-town relations several weeks earlier had elicited different emotions, for then she noted: "This week's experience has convinced me that it is a possible thing that I may be homesick. After all there is no place like home, be it ever so homely."

The following excerpts from the second and fourth volumes of the diaries kept by Louisa Jane (Jenny) Trumbull of Worcester, Massachusetts, record several sleep-away visits that she made on her own in the summer of 1835, four months before her thirteenth birthday, and again in the summer of 1837, when she was approaching fifteen. Entries in her first diary, begun in 1829 at the age of seven, indicate that visits such as these were considered a step toward maturity. She had regularly noted when her older siblings left home for visits or for boarding school, and now her own overnight visits were signs that the time for her to learn independence had come. They also exemplified part of her mother's plan for her children, which included keeping a diary as a means of remembering the "common occurrences" of life that would otherwise be lost to time, valuing education, and creating and nurturing strong bonds between immediate and extended family members.[1] From this daughter's perspective, Louisa Clap Trumbull (1798–1885) was a powerful force in the lives of her children. And in spite of twelve pregnancies between 1816 and

1841 and the ever-present burdens of the infants and toddlers, Mrs. Trumbull remained dedicated to the schooling and informal education of her daughters as they grew older.

While Jenny chatters on about her daily life and the people she encounters at home, at church, and in her walks about the bustling community in the pages of her diaries, the impressions that she writes down shift over the years from those of a youngster whose observations include a child's activities and the overheard conversations of adults to reflections that are increasingly her own. After trial runs visiting her father's cousins at increasing distances from home but still in town, Jenny had been invited to stay with his relations in Jamaica Plain and Milton, Massachusetts. There she came to understand and appreciate the endless variety of personalities that made up her large extended family. She learned through discovering a book about them that the Forbes family, to which the Trumbulls were related, belonged to the Massachusetts mercantile elite.[2] Yet as grand as the estates that she visited and carriages she rode in were, she saw that some family members valued teaching Sunday school and attending to needy neighbors. (Jenny described a visit to a poor black family.) She made detailed observations on seeing Boston for the first time, purchasing her first pair of stays (a symbol of young womanhood), shopping for gifts to bring home, and socializing with wealthy and elite family members at their estates. Continuing a practice begun in her first diary, she documented her reading, which advanced to increasingly mature books. During these years she also grasped the toll that childbirth exacted on her mother's health and, to her chagrin, on family quietude. Finally, feelings of homesickness were replaced with the pure and unfettered enjoyment that visiting promised. If the marriage of Jenny's oldest sister, Elizabeth, to William Sever Lincoln, the son of one of Worcester's leading families (his father was governor of Massachusetts), represented what her mother hoped for each of her daughters, then Jenny's visits to Milton were an effort to introduce her to a wider circle of acquaintances and create the ability to adapt to different milieus. The diary excerpts have been chosen to show how Jenny gained confidence and became independent.

Jenny was born on October 12, 1822, fourth of twelve children in the family of George and Louisa Clap Trumbull of Worcester, Massachusetts. She was given the names of her mother and her mother's best friend, Jane Bancroft, and was called Jenny in her youth and Jane as she matured. As well connected as the Worcester Trumbull family was, they represented the poorer cousins of its elite and well-traveled members in Worcester, Salem, Milton, and greater Boston. Though Jenny was not aware of it during the years covered in her diaries, her family lived in a house that had been purchased for them by her grandmother's wealthy sister, Sarah Paine Perkins, and subsequently deeded to three generations of Trumbull women (specifically excluding her sister's husband and son, who had demonstrated a lack of business acumen). Through the efforts of this same great-aunt, Trumbull girls received "gifts" of outgrown clothing from older relatives and Trumbull boys obtained employment.

The Paine family was at the center of an extensive and highly intertwined extended network of relations within which Jenny and her family operated. They were the most prominent and one of the wealthiest families in Worcester, and they were thickly connected to seaboard elites. For a time, Jenny's family lived with her paternal grandparents, Elizabeth Paine Trumbull (1766–1832) and Joseph Trumbull (1756–1824). As Jenny had been just two when her grandfather Trumbull died, she knew only the family matriarch, "Grandmother Trumbull." This grandmother was very close to her sister Sarah Paine Perkins (1764–1841), widow of James Perkins (1761–1822), who, with his brother Thomas Handasyd Perkins (1754–1856), had founded a lucrative West India trading enterprise and then entered the China trade; eventually, they ranked among the merchant princes of Boston and drew other members of the family into the business. "Aunt" Perkins (as Jenny called her great-aunt) figured prominently in the young girl's diaries, as the sisters frequently visited back and forth. Children of Sarah's widowed sister-in-law, Margaret Perkins Forbes (1775–1856)—Emma, Margaret, Fanny, and sometimes Bennet—often accompanied their aunt to Worcester, staying with either the Trumbulls or the Paines. Like Sarah Perkins, Margaret Forbes was a very wealthy widow, as her husband had made a fortune as a merchant and sea captain. Mrs. Forbes and her children were also quite worldly, having lived in France for about fifteen or twenty years. Jenny's diary entries suggest that in the early 1830s the Forbes children and possibly their mother actually lived with their Aunt Sarah Perkins when she took up summer residence at Pine Bank in Jamaica Plain. (Jenny noted that the girls were "not at home" when Grandmother Trumbull died there in 1832, although they quickly returned and cut off locks of hair to make everyone keepsakes; even after their mother's new estate was built in Milton in 1833—now the Forbes House Museum—the Forbes girls had their own rooms at Pine Bank.) Jenny frequently mentioned her cousin Sarah P. Perkins (1818–93) and her brothers, children of Aunt Perkins's deceased son James, whose mother had left children behind with their grandmother when she remarried in the later 1820s and moved to New Jersey. (She and her Episcopal bishop second husband also figure in the diaries, not always in a complimentary way.) Sarah and Elizabeth Paine's sister Hannah Paine Bradish (1755–1841), a regular fixture in Jenny's life, had settled in Worcester in widowhood with courting-age granddaughters in tow but had raised her own family on a slave plantation in Natchez, Mississippi, where her husband and son were active in the Perkins West India trade network. Another sister, Harriet Paine Rose, who had married an English planter and borne nine children on a slave plantation in Antigua, lived in Worcester for several years after her husband died with her two surviving daughters, her sister-in-law, and a woman formerly a slave. To her annoyance, Jenny was continually thrown together with her rather odd older cousin Josephine. Sarah and Elizabeth's oldest brother, William Paine, who occupied the family estate in Worcester in maturity, had married and raised his family primarily in Salem, and his children had scattered far and wide. Jenny knew him only as a feeble old gentleman but frequently interacted with his son Frederick William—heir to the estate—and his family. Like many of the men in this kin network, her Uncle Frederick made his fortune and saw the world under the auspices of the Perkins merchant princes. Other surnames that appear in Jenny's entries during her visits, such as Sturgis and Cushing (international merchants and traders), Abbott (headmaster of Exeter Academy), and Robbins (Perkins trader-turned-woolens dealer), are also part of this constellation of highly prominent relations.

Immersed as Jenny was in this influential circle of kith and kin and in a socially and culturally complex tapestry of international businessmen, wealthy and independent-minded widows, a former slave brought from the West Indies, and Chinese men, her familial reference points certainly set her apart from most of her peers. Yet her diary entries also reveal fairly universal benchmarks and experiences in the passage from childhood to young womanhood. The portrait of Jenny Trumbull that emerges by the end of her fourth (and last surviving) diary is of an independent, educated, and well-read young woman who knew the ways of polite society and socialized easily with some of the most influential New Englanders of her day.

Interspersed with selections from Jenny's diaries are extracts or summaries taken from her mother's diaries, which overlap or give insight into passages from Jenny's.[3] They are italicized.

Saturday morning, April 4th 1835. In keeping a journal I at first did it because my sisters kept one. Afterwards I wrote because it was the wish of my mother and now it is done not only to serve as means of being employed about something useful and proper, but because it is a source of pleasure to me. . . .

May 9th 1835. Josephine Rose and Dr. Chandler settled about their engagement last fall when she visited Worcester. I shall be glad when she is married and fairly settled down amongst us. She is a clever girl and I like her very much but she is not overstocked with sense. This is not her fault, however, and nothing should be ever said about any of our imperfections save those which it is in our power to make way with. And Josey cannot help this surely.[4]

Friday afternoon, May 22nd 1835. On Wednesday . . . George [her brother] carried me to Cousin Sarah's in the chaise, and . . . I have been there ever since. Returned this morning at eight o'clock, father came for me. I have had a delightful visit and they have all been very kind and attentive to me. . . . Monday I go to Mrs. Hill's and the rest of the week I spend with Cousin Nancy. I anticipate much enjoyment from my visit.[5]

Saturday morning May 30th 1835. I have been here (at Cousin Frederick's) all this week & have had a very pleasant visit indeed. Cousin Nancy [his wife] has been all kindness to me & Cousin Frederick also. We have played checkers a great deal and now I can play quite decently. . . . I wish to see all our family very much and I probably shall see them this evening as I propose going home this afternoon. After [her younger sister] Sarah went away on Wednesday I really felt quite homesick and had quite a good cry, but I on the whole have been very well contented. I feel much better than I did when I came here, the change I suppose is one reason. And every day I have walked more or less. This I am convinced has done me much good. . . . I suppose we shall go to Greenfield in about a fortnight.

I shall admire to go, but this week's experience has convinced me that it is a possible thing that I may be homesick. After all there is no place like home be it ever so homely. I feel as if I had been absent from home a month instead of a week and I wish more than I can express once more to behold them.[6]

In a retrospective entry on April 9, 1835, Jenny's mother Louisa Trumbull confided to her diary:

The events of the few past months are so full of interest I can with difficulty find words to relate them. My poor husband after toiling and saving for twenty years has by unforeseen events lost his all and we are now left poor with nine children dependent upon our exertions. When the truth burst upon him the shock was tremendous . . . [and] produced a violent fit of gout which confined him for more than a week to the house, during which time his suffering was intense part of the time. Joseph, Charley, Susan & Isabella all have had the whooping cough. . . . Many nights they could not rest from the violence of the cough. . . . Caroline made a visit in Boston of a month, took musick lessons with the hope she might instruct at a future time. George has been with us all winter and has rendered his father great assistance in the Bank, part of the time in his father's absence he performed the whole duty. . . .

More from Jenny's diary:

Wednesday evening, June 3rd 1835. . . . Emma [Forbes] today came and called to see us this evening.[7] She invited me to go to Milton on a visit of a month. I accepted of course and on Saturday I leave Worcester for the first time without my mother. I anticipate much pleasure from my visit. I shall not probably write again in this until I arrive in Milton. . . .

Milton, June 10th, Thursday morning. Well I am really here and settled. On Saturday morning last at six o'clock I stepped into Aunt Perkins's barouche and bade adieu to . . . dear friends. . . . We arrived at Westborough at half past seven where I saw my baggage and Mr. Burt deposited on the top of the stage.[8] We arrived at Framingham at half past nine where Emma insisted upon my lying down. We dined at half past eleven, Emma saying she advised it to be called a late breakfast. We had a tolerable dinner consisting of as tough beef and veal as ever a knife encountered. Asparagus good, potatoes indifferent, fine butter bread and cheese, iced water, fine custards as I ever eat, a pie. At one we set off again. Stopped at Needham and had a glass of water that was hotter than fire and finally arrived at Pine Bank at half after three. Here I had another lay down upon Margaret's bed. George Cabot drank tea here and I was very much pleased with him. He is very handsome. But eighteen years old yet engaged to Sarah P. Perkins.[9] . . . Sunday morning I wrote to my much loved Mother. . . . Monday morning sewed and read. In the afternoon Mrs. Danforth and her daughter took tea here. . . . Yesterday Aunt and Sarah P. Perkins spent the day here. After they had gone, Emma, Mrs. Gorham, Mrs. Forbes, and myself went to ride. We went to Quincy and had a very pleasant ride. This morning Joseph Cabot came here. At about ten, Mrs. Forbes, Emma, this same Joe, Willy Willis, and I set out for a ride. We went to Brush Hill to see Mrs. James Robbins.[10] Came home, dined. After dinner I had a nap, then wrote to mother, now in Journal. This morning had a letter from Mother, all were well. Expect to see [sister] Lizzy and William [Lincoln] either this or next week. My hand begins to ache.

Monday morning, June 14th. All has gone on well since I last wrote. . . . Saturday Mrs. G[orham], Emma, and I set out for a ride. We went to the Tide mill in Dorchester to take a salt bath but the bathing house was destroyed so we rode on. I saw a ship, a sight I never saw before. Also the glorious sea. There was a good air and the sea breeze seemed to instill a vigour in my limbs and throughout my frame. When we got home, dined. . . .

Sunday, beautiful day. Went to church in the morning. Very warm. Came home. Dined, went to church again. . . . Am a member of Emma's class at Sunday school so I stayed and recited. Came home and found Bennet and his wife, also two Spanish gentlemen.[11] Both could speak French, but only one English. Much amused. Drank tea. . . . Have not heard again from home, I am getting rather impatient. Liz I hope to see tomorrow. . . . I know not when we shall go into town. I hope soon for I really want some stays. Miss Lake is to cut me some as she is a professed stay maker. Surrounded as I am by kind friends I still wish to see my own loved family. However I am not homesick and hope and trust I shall not be. . . . I have not spent a cent of my money yet, but shall without doubt spend it all in purchasing materials for my stays. I suppose I have written all I have got to write so I think it would be not a bad plan certainly for me to lay down my pen and resume my work.

Tuesday evening, June 16th 1835. . . . Emma went with me a mile and a half (on our feet) this morning. I got much tired but laid down immediately after dinner and did not arise till nearly five, when I found Mrs.

John Forbes had arrived. She is a dear little woman and I begin to love her already. George Cabot and Sarah P. Perkins rode out on horseback and drank tea; indeed, they have not left here yet. Mr. and Mrs. Cunningham also drank tea here. No news from home. I wrote to Aunt Bradish two pages and Mother one yesterday.[12] Sarah P. says I am going to Nahant and they are going when it is warm enough although I see no prospect as yet of our ever having warm weather. . . . Oh, would I could have a letter from home! If it were but one line I should be thankful for it, provided it contained news of the health of those I love so well. And even if it contained bad news I hate to be in suspense. Oh write to me!

Friday morning June 13th. Here I am again seated at Cousin Emma's writing desk intending to write in this journal and I hope I shall be able to expect something. . . . Wednesday afternoon went with Emma to give a black woman three dollars. We found her house and herself in a very comfortable, tidy state but she had a daughter very sick. The money was sent by the members of the Village Benevolent Society. As Emma is the treasurer she gives the money. The poor woman seemed very grateful. She had seven children, five of whom died within the last eighteen months. And a short time since her husband fell from his wagon or was turned over and broke his leg. We feel the comforts God has given us and know how to value our blessings more perfectly when we have such a picture as this presented to our view.

Thursday morning got up, breakfasted, then dressed at nine. Emma and Margaret on the front, and Sarah and I on the back seat of the carryall drove from the door of Mrs. Forbes' house [Milton Hill]. We arrived at Pine Bank at half past ten after a delightful ride. . . . After dinner . . . Sally [Sarah P. Perkins] took me all over the grounds. Oh how beautiful, how perfect it was. We went down by the waterside and sat an hour or two, then went round the grounds again and got the man to clean out the boat. Then Sally and I stepped into it, rowed round a little while and came up to the shore and took in Mrs. Sarah Forbes [wife John Murray Forbes]. We rowed all around the lake and it was truly sublime. The water was very calm. Came back just in time for tea. . . .

Tuesday morning, June 30th. It is now ten days since I wrote in my journal and very many things have happened in that time, which are great events in my life. On Tuesday morning last Aunt and Madge [Margaret] drove up in the barouche and said they had come to carry me home with them. I went. . . . Wednesday morning Madge and I rode into town. So I have seen Boston. I have seen the state house. It is a magnificent edifice in its magnificence. It is in Beacon Street. I have seen St. Paul's church, grand in its grandeur. It is in Tremont Street. I have seen Trinity Church, sublime in its sublimity. I have seen Boston Common, lovely in its loveliness. I have seen Masonic Temple. Trinity church is in Summer Street.

I went to Mrs. Foster's and bought myself a pair of stays which cost me 9 shillings. Then to Mrs. Barnard's to see Lucy Stone. I found her better but still weak and feeble. She went with me to Mrs. Bennet Forbes's in Temple Court. I also went to see Mrs. and Betsey Sturgis.[13] They insisted on my going there two or three days before I went home and spend the time with them and starting for Worcester from their door. I shall certainly go. . . . Thursday morning Aunt Perkins went into town with me again. We made no calls as Aunt P. went shopping. She bought me four cambrick handkerchiefs. . . . Friday morning nothing of importance occurred. In the afternoon Aunt and I seated ourselves in the barouche and drove to Watertown. We first went to Mr. Cushing's but did not see the greenhouse. We saw a Chinese with black hair braided and hanging to his feet. Mrs. Cushing said they had a younger son whose hair was not longer than to reach his shoulders so he took a piece of black ribbon and tying it on made it to drag on the ground.[14] From there to Mrs. Gardiner's where we stayed only a few minutes, from there to Dr. Follen's where we drank tea and had a very pleasant time too.[15]

Wednesday morning, Milton, July 1st 1835. . . . Monday evening I played billiards with Emma. She beat me of course. It was my first attempt but I hope it will not be the last. I admire the game very much indeed. I shall probably be in Worcester *next* Wednesday morning.

The railroad between Boston and Worcester is to be open throughout on Monday [July 4] and the gentlemen of Boston are invited to go down and dine with their Worcester friends. . . . They leave Boston at half past nine Monday morning and reach Worcester in three hours. They will stay there two or three hours and ride back in the afternoon. I may go to Worcester in the railroad car. . . . I have enjoyed my visit here highly and shall always look back to it with unfeigned pleasure. Mrs. Forbes you can hardly know and not love.

Milton, July the second, Thursday morning, AD, eighteen hundred and thirty-five. . . . Wrote a long letter home yesterday in the morning. I have not heard from home for some time. . . . Last evening Mrs. Smith, Ida and Amelia Russell, [and] the two Spanish gentlemen spent the evening here. . . .

Milton, Tuesday morning, July the 7th 1835. . . . Aunt [Perkins] gave me five dollars to pay my expenses home and left a frisette [fringe of hair] for Aunt Bradish which I am to carry to her. . . . This morning Fanny has gone to Nahant and Emma to Boston. William [Lincoln, her sister's fiancé] and E. are coming Wednesday and going home Saturday and I go with them. I go to Mrs. Sturgis's Thursday morning or Wednesday night. I have not written in my journal for a long time I see. I played billiards 4th of July. I am happy to say I am very well and happy. Emma and all of them in fact are as kind as possible to me and I feel their goodness more than I can express in words. Aunt Perkins seemed very well Thursday indeed. I have been weeding in [Emma's sister] Mary's garden today and like it much. I feel very nicely indeed. Hope to hear from home.

Thursday, July 25th 1835, Worcester. Well! I am in Worcester once more, I am rejoiced to say, for pleasant as was the time I passed from home I feel as if I was glad to see all my dear friends once more. I have been at home some time, it being a fortnight tomorrow since I arrived. We came up in the railroad cars and I liked them very much. . . . I drank tea yesterday with Hester Newton who had quite a large party. I enjoyed myself very much.[16] . . . Wednesday I drank tea at Mrs. [Governor] Lincoln's with Elizabeth. In the morning we made several calls and did some shopping. . . .

Mrs. Trumbull's reflections on Jenny's return:

The 7th Elizabeth, Caroline & Mr. Lincoln went to Boston to accompany Jenny home after an absence of five weeks. Poor dear child, many anxious hours have I watched for your breathing the past winter, and now the happy tidings of recovery are sweet indeed. [Mrs. Trumbull obsessed about her children's health, having lost one child suddenly and unexpectedly as a toddler.] I cannot express all my sensations when thinking of this precious child, ever affectionate, considerate, conscientious to a nicety, thoughtful of the wants and suffering of all the human family, anxious to do her duty, and faithful, industrious, and scrupulously saving, yet generous and noble spirited without the shadow of selfishness. God grant she may be spared to bless us in our journey.

In this summary entry Mrs. Trumbull also mentioned that her husband had been confined to the house for a week in July with an attack of gout and that, once again, their son George had taken full charge of his business at the bank. Like her daughter, she noted the opening of the Boston-&-Worcester Railroad and the great expectations it had raised for an "increase of business and importance of our town."

Almost two years passed before Jenny found herself again visiting seaboard relations. During the interim she wrote of family doings— noting her beloved older sister Elizabeth's marriage to William Lincoln (the governor's son) on October 22, 1835, describing a visit to their lodgings in Millbury and her own new clothing for different seasons, discussing Cattle Show festivities and an "incendiary" who had set fire to the Baptist Church, recording highlights of her school curriculum and teachers, confiding her annoyance at the expectation of yet another baby, worrying over her mother's poor health following the birth, observing (without comment) another of her father's career changes, and more. She noted hopefully an invitation to visit Mrs. Abbott in Exeter in the summer of 1836, writing: "Cousin Nancy [Paine] says if I am a rational being I shall go for I shall have a most capital time. Of this I have no doubt." As wife of the headmaster of Exeter Academy, Mrs. Abbott would have introduced Jenny to another circle of educated and worldly gentlemen and ladies, but Mrs. Trumbull apparently decided she could not spare her teenaged daughter with three very young children to tend to and her two eldest gone. Then, in the spring of 1837—three months after the arrival of the eleventh baby and the same week her older brother returned home, having lost his job in New York City because of the financial panic—Jenny, now approaching fifteen, was off again to Milton Hill and Pine Bank.

May 4th 1837. Aunt Perkins a fortnight since invited me to make her a little visit at Pine Bank. This invitation I was truly happy to accept. . . . Monday found me seated in the cars under the care of Mr. Burnside. It was cloudy when we set out and half an hour before we reached Boston it rained very hard. Mr. Burnside put me into a hack in which were two Irish people and one American man. The hackman was preparing to start when I asked him if my trunk was on. He said no, and went for it. I felt rather unpleasantly to be riding in a hack in Boston with no one to protect me. However the distance was short. It was so unpleasant Aunt did not send in for me as she had intended. I remained at Mrs. Sturgis's [in Boston] that day and night. . . .

Yesterday I read to Aunt from Grund's *America*. It is very interesting. He speaks very highly of the Americans, particularly the ladies. He thinks them patterns of wives and mothers. I am of opinion he praises us rather too much. He says the dress, furniture, and carriages of our people are remarkable for their republican plainness. This is a mistake, for in New York the servants of the wealthier citizens wear liveries. This certainly is not precisely republican simplicity. Again he says a miss of respectable parents is expected to be well acquainted with Latin and Greek, besides the English branches, to which the more gifted add Hebrew and the higher branches of mathematics. He expatiates largely on the beauty of the ladies and recommends the attention of poets and painters to their beautiful feet and ankles.

I have been this morning with Cousin Emma [who is at Pine Bank] over the grounds. Everything is beautiful. I have been very happy this morning sewing in Queen Margaret's chamber. I have been very lazy the three past days, however I have enjoyed myself very much and when I am from home I think that is the main point to be kept in view. I shall do more, however, in a few days. At present I wish for nothing more than to look around this paradise on earth. . . .

Pine Bank, May 28th 1837, Sunday morning. Wednesday afternoon Misses Elizabeth, Sarah, and Charlotte Forbes with Misses Susan and Catherine Lyman drank tea here.[17] Thursday it rained but Calvin went into town for Cousin Sarah [Perkins]. She had not arrived [from visiting her mother in Burlington, New Jersey]. Emma read alone to Aunt *The Cry of the Last Minstrel* and *The Ancient Mariner*. Friday Aunt and Cousin Emma went for Sarah. She did not come. In the afternoon Mrs. Bennet Forbes called here and said they would not be here until this (Sunday) morning. . . . I have written a long letter home, the first one since I left home. I have not yet heard from Mother. . . . I have been very happy the past week, although the weather has been very unpleasant, but that we were satisfied with by having a good fire pleasant company. Not forgetting the books we have read. We have now a book of traditions of old families, among which are those of the Forbes's.

I yesterday saw Cousin Sarah's portrait. It is very like her and a beautiful picture. Cousin Nancy Paine said the figure was very bad and I was not prepared to like it so extremely. I know nothing of painting of course. Cousin Margaret says she should infer from the picture that Cousin S. was a very tall damsel.

L.J.T.

Milton Hill, June 15th 1837. I intended going home last Wednesday. Aunt and Sarah were going to Worcester and the plan was for me to go with them. Instead of that, Emma was so kind as to ask me out here. So last Tuesday afternoon Aunt brought me out. She stopped for an hour on our way at a dentist's and got her teeth tightened and suffered a great deal of course. . . . Emma had a letter from Sarah a day or two since. . . . They had a pleasant ride down, having a nice book with them. They found Aunt Bradish better than they had any right to expect. They were staying at our house as Mrs. Blake had injured her hand.[18]

Wednesday last I went with Cousin Mary and the two Lymans to Brush Hill and spent a very pleasant day with Mrs. Robbins. I got well acquainted with the Lymans and liked them very much indeed. Susan the eldest is a beauty and Kitty is a merry little thing as ever breathed.

Thursday Mrs. Lyman and Mrs. Robbins spent the day here, and Mrs. Carey and Miss Martha Lyman drank tea. Friday and Saturday nothing very remarkable happened save Friday the Lymans went to Brush Hill and Emma and Mrs. Forbes went with them and drank tea there. Saturday Mrs. Carey and her husband drank tea here. Sunday morning I did not go to church but took a short walk with Cousin Margaret. At noon Bennet and Mr. Edward Lyman took their luncheon here and drank tea at night. I went to meeting in the afternoon. Mr. Allger of Chelsea held forth. And at night I took a walk and found some very nice sweet-scented grass. Monday morning Fanny and myself went to ride in an open wagon and had a charming time. In the afternoon Mr. and Mrs. Carey and their two children drank tea here.

Last Saturday Mr. Cushing came bringing Margaret some beautiful strawberries. Tuesday Fanny drove out Mrs. Forbes, Margaret, and myself in the carryall and had a very nice ride. Wednesday morning Fanny and I went to walk. I had a pleasant walk but I felt rather tired. Then in the afternoon Mr. John Forbes and his wife came home. They have been to Philadelphia, New York, etc. Stopped in Worcester Tuesday night. They said Aunt came home Tuesday. Annie Robbins came here yesterday with her father and is to stay until Saturday. She is an only child and very much indulged. She is very fat and not over-interesting in her manners. She has gone this afternoon (Thursday) with Emma to Pine Bank. . . .

The day Sarah [Perkins] went to Worcester, her engagement came out with Mr. Henry Cleveland. I have seen him almost every day while I was at Pine Bank, that is to say after Sarah came home, but I was decided in my own mind not to hint anything in my letters home or to anyone else, as it was none of my business and I was to know nothing until I was told. The day Aunt went away Winifred [hired help] brought over my work box and she said Mr. Cleveland was going to Worcester on Saturday and was to take Sarah's clean clothes. That day we heard of the engagement. He keeps school in Boston. He is about thirty years of age. Sarah was nineteen last January.[19]

I expect letters from home by Emma tonight. I have been and am very happy here. . . . I never enjoyed myself more, or as much from home as I have the three weeks past. I have heard once from home, all were as usual. I long to see dear little Bell with her bright blue eyes and her curls, but I have been thinking it was possible Mother cut off the latter since I have been from home. If she has I shall not get over it for some time.[20]

Pine Bank, June 25th 1837. Sunday afternoon. Emma brought me a letter as I had hoped. Aunt came out that afternoon to tea. Mother said I might stay until Mrs. Sturgis went to Worcester, which would be in the course of a few weeks. They enjoyed Aunt's visit and both Sarah and Mr. Cleveland very much. She adds "Mr. C. has won all our hearts and we hope to see him with Sarah again in the course of the summer." All were well, Bell quite happy under [sister] Cally's government. Hannah Rich was at our house during Aunt's stay and relieved Mother much by her assistance.[21] . . . Bennet Forbes called to see her the Wednesday before. There is a prospect of Miss Mary Springs (a ward of Dr. Robbin's [of Milton]) being with [teacher] Dr. Park this summer. It will depend upon their being willing to pay a high price, the present pressure of times having alarmed the Dr., he has lent a willing ear to the plan fearing his ends might not meet this year. All were well. No more now.

That ended Jenny's own narrative of experiences as she moved toward personal independence amid her wealthy and worldly seaboard relations. Over the next couple of years, Mrs. Trumbull wrote of her daughter Jane's visits to her Aunt Ripley in Greenfield and once to a Chandler relation in Lancaster—places her sisters Sarah and Caroline also visited at other times—but not to Milton Hill or Pine Bank. Jenny's Great-Aunt Perkins, who was caring for a granddaughter of similar age from 1830 to early 1838, had probably facilitated in arranging the earlier visits to the magnificent country estates. And it may have been under her supervision that the visits swept in the great circle of family that they did, though the ties were certainly enduringly thick between seaboard and Worcester relations. Sarah Paine Perkins was, after all, a matriarch of exceeding wealth and influence. Many gentlemen in the family network found employ and made their fortunes in the international trade businesses founded by her husband James Perkins and his brother Thomas Handasyd Perkins. After Widow Perkins died in 1841, the "glue" that held the seaboard visiting was gone. Her Perkins grandchildren in Boston all married and/or moved away. Very likely, the single Forbes daughters—Emma, Margaret, and Fanny—became preoccupied with their brothers' growing broods of children. And Jenny herself moved to Illinois to be with Elizabeth and her young sons.

Always close to her older sister, after Elizabeth and William Lincoln moved to Alton, Illinois (where he became city attorney), Jenny responded to an appeal for help in 1844. A year later, Elizabeth's health dictated a return to Worcester, but Jenny, now Jane, stayed, planning to marry Henry Lea, an established Alton merchant nineteen years her senior. The couple married in Worcester on September 2, 1845, then "went westward in September after visiting Mr. Lea's friends on the way."²² Their son and only child was born in 1846. They remained in Alton until Mr. Lea retired and moved the family to his former home in Delaware. After he died early in 1881, Jane returned to Massachusetts and lived with her son James Henry (Harry) Lea and his family in Fairhaven where she died on January 30, 1890.

These diary entries, written over a few years when Jenny Trumbull moved into young womanhood while living amid gentlemen and ladies of extraordinary wealth and cultivation, open an entrancing adolescent world.

NOTES

1. March 1829, Louisa Clap Trumbull, Journal 1, March 1829–June 1833, Manuscript Collection, American Antiquarian Society, Worcester, MA.

2. While the title of the book Jenny read is not known, see Sarah Hughes Forbes, ed., *Letters and Recollections of John Murray Forbes*, 2 vols. (Boston: Houghton Mifflin, 1899).

3. Four of Louisa Jane Trumbull's childhood diaries survive and are held in the collection of the American Antiquarian Society. Holly Izard has transcribed and annotated each of these diaries, and the first volume has been published with an introductory essay, "Worcester through a Child's Eyes: The Diaries of Louisa Jane Trumbull, 1829–1837," *Proceedings of the American Antiquarian Society* 113 (2003): 303–498. The other volumes are available in the society's reading room. Louisa

Clap Trumbull's diaries, 1829–79, are also available as manuscripts and annotated transcriptions at the American Antiquarian Society.

4. Josephine Rose (1815–66), daughter of Joseph Warner (1773–1826) and Harriet Paine Rose (1779–1860). Her fiancé, also a relation, was assistant superintendent of the State Lunatic Asylum in Worcester at the time and would later advance to superintendent. For a detailed annotation of many of the individuals mentioned in the course of the diaries, see Izard, "Worcester."

5. Her father's cousin Sarah Chandler Paine (1794–1840), was the daughter of Judge Nathaniel Paine (1759–1840), another of Elizabeth and Sarah Paine's siblings. Mrs. Hill was Francis Mary Clark (1811–96), who married the Reverend Alonzo Hill, a Harvard graduate and junior minister of the Unitarian Church, on December 29, 1830. Jenny spent the day with Mrs. Hill fairly regularly and, it appears, helped her with sewing tasks. "Cousin Nancy" was Anne Cushing Sturgis Paine (1797–1890) of Boston, wife of Frederick William Paine (1788–1869), who very likely met her while working for her uncles, James and Thomas Handasyd Perkins.

6. Next in age to Jenny, Sarah Trumbull (1824–47) was two years younger. Louisa Clap Trumbull's mother and two of her sisters (Lucy Clap and Susan Ripley) lived in Greenfield, and there was a lot of visiting back and forth.

7. Emma Forbes (1815/19–47) was the youngest daughter of Ralph Bennet (1773–1824) and Margaret Perkins Forbes (1775–1856) of Milton and France. The Forbes home where Jenny was to visit was built in 1833 for the widowed Margaret, financed by her children in honor of their older brother Thomas, who had perished in a typhoon in China in 1829. It is now the Forbes House Museum.

8. Simeon Burt was a prominent Worcester attorney. When traveling without a parent, the Trumbull children were generally charged to the care of an adult family friend. In this case Jenny was with Great-Aunt Perkins, but her entry suggests that Mr. Burt had some role in watching for their well-being.

9. Margaret Forbes (1800–before 1860) was Emma's oldest sister. George Cabot (1817–50) was a recent Harvard graduate, like many of the gentlemen mentioned in Jenny's diaries. Sarah Paine Perkins (1818–93) was the daughter of James Perkins Jr. (1792–1822) and his wife, Elizabeth Green Callahan.

10. Mrs. Gorham (first name not known) was the daughter of Exeter Academy headmaster Benjamin Abbott and his wife, Mary Perkins, a sister of Mrs. Forbes and Great-Aunt Perkins's sister-in-law. Joseph Sebastian Cabot (1796–1874) was the son of Jenny's Aunt Esther Orne Cabot Tucker (1774–1854) and her first husband, Joseph Cabot of Salem. He was also a Harvard graduate who began his adult life as an agent for the Perkins brothers. Mary Frances Harris Robbins was married to James Robbins, a wealthy gentleman who had gotten his start in the Perkins China trade.

11. This is China trade merchant Robert Bennet (Bennet) Forbes (1804–89), Emma's older brother, and his wife, Rose Green Smith Forbes (1798–1885). Having

been raised in France, he spoke French fluently and could therefore converse easily with the Spanish gentlemen Jenny mentioned.

12. Sarah Swain Hathaway (1813–1900) was the wife of Bennet Forbes's younger brother John Murray Forbes (1813–98), who was also engaged in the China trade. Francis Cunningham was a minister, whose preaching Jenny admired. (He would later marry her father's cousin Mary Forbes.)

13. Temple Court was the Boston townhouse where Bennet and Rose Forbes resided. Elizabeth Perkins Sturgis (1756–1843) was the widow of international trader Russell Sturgis (1750–1826); Betsey (1788–1873) was their daughter.

14. John Perkins Cushing (1787–1862), who was raised by his Uncle Thomas Handasyd Perkins after his mother's untimely death, represented the Perkins's trading firm in Canton from 1803 to 1830. When he returned to Boston he brought Chinese manservants with him, arousing intense local interest. He was married to Mary Louisa Gardiner, only child of the Reverend John S. Gardiner, rector of Trinity Church in Boston. The couple's homes were a fashionable dwelling on Summer Street and a country estate built on two hundred acres in Watertown, which Cushing named "Bellmont" (now part of Belmont). This estate included an extravagant conservatory, which he opened to the public.

15. Charles Follen (1796–1840) was a German intellectual who immigrated to America in 1825 and in 1830 was appointed the first professor of German at Harvard University. Elite merchants, including Thomas Handasyd Perkins, funded this position with the expectation that Harvard would eventually take over. However, Follen's outspoken support of abolitionist William Lloyd Garrison led to his termination in the spring of 1835. The same group of gentlemen arranged for him to tutor the Perkins boys who had been left with their Grandmother Perkins. On June 1, 1835, Jenny noted the comings and goings of her cousin Sarah Perkins and several other relations and added: "The boys are with Dr. and Mrs. Follen in Watertown. Dr. F. has all his expenses paid, his carriage and horses, besides two thousand dollars a year for taking care of them."

16. Hester Newton (1823–99), daughter of Rejoice and Rebecca Lincoln Newton, was Jenny's childhood best friend. Hester's father was among the leading attorneys in Worcester; her mother was Governor Levi Lincoln's sister.

17. The Lymans were relations through the Robbins and Murray families.

18. Elizabeth Chandler Blake (1775–1839), widow of Attorney Francis Blake (1774–1817), lived with Jenny's Great-Aunt Bradish as both a helpmate and friend. Her well-respected husband had died at forty-three without building financial security for his family.

19. Sarah Perkins's engagement to George Cabot had broken off (she feared he was out for her money) and she married Harvard-educated Henry Russell Cleveland (1808–43). After the couple visited Worcester in 1837, Louisa Clap Trumbull described Cleveland as a "worthy young gentleman" and an "excellent . . . young man."

20. Jenny's youngest sister, Isabella Frink Trumbull, just three years old at this time.

21. Hannah Rich (1819–38), daughter of Peter Rich Jr. and wife Lucy Simmons Rich, was African American. Her family lived near the Trumbulls on Summer Street in a neighborhood of people of color. This is one of just two appearances by nonwhite servants in the Trumbull diaries.

22. Retrospective entry, January 1864, Louisa Clap Trumbull Journal 2, June 1833–December 30, 1879.

"Though the Means Were Scanty"

Excerpts from Joseph T. Buckingham's Personal Memoirs and Recollections of Editorial Life *(1852)*

Vincent DiGirolamo

No life is fully representative of its time, but some have the capacity to illuminate the distinctive themes or prevailing tensions of an era. The self-styled "Editorial Life" of Joseph T. Buckingham is one such example. Born during the War of Independence, Buckingham belonged to that first generation of Americans who grew up with the Republic and strove to live up to its egalitarian ideals in an age still rocked by political turmoil, economic strife, and intellectual ferment. His account of those early years—both his own and the nation's—sheds light on some of the most common experiences of youth in early America, namely their encounters with death, poverty, charity, education, apprenticeship, and religion.

Published in 1852, Buckingham's 1,200-page autobiography describes his rise from abject poverty to artisanal independence to journalistic and political prominence as an ascent open to all men of character in early nineteenth-century America. In the end, financial security eluded him, as it did many young men on the make in the emerging market economy, but that failure just makes his story all the more poignant, not to say representative.[1]

Born Joseph Buckingham Tinker in Windham, Connecticut, in 1779, he dropped his humble surname in 1804 at age twenty-one in favor of the more dignified Buckingham to facilitate his rise to respectability. His father, Nehemiah Tinker, was a Revolutionary War veteran who incurred great debt on behalf of the Continental army.

He and his wife, Mary Huntington, together produced ten children, eight of whom survived to adulthood. They made a meager living fixing shoes and keeping a tavern until 1783, when forty-three-year-old Nehemiah died, plunging the family into an economic freefall that culminated in the intervention of town charity officials and Joseph's twelve-year indenture to a local farmer. Buckingham describes these years between seven and sixteen as a not wholly unpleasant blend of physical labor, literary enchantment, and religious instruction. Indeed, his memoirs testify to the persistence of Puritan beliefs and evangelical fervor that swept through the colonies during the Great Awakening of the 1740s.

On entering adolescence, Buckingham became a direct beneficiary of the expanded use of print. Upon the expiration of his indenture in 1795, he apprenticed himself to printers in Walpole, New Hampshire, and Greenfield and Northampton, Massachusetts, where he learned all aspects of the printer's trade and producing newspapers. Buckingham's formal schooling was minimal, but he was a voracious reader. He once apologized proudly that the print shop was his academy and that he had "no diploma from any other university than that, of which Gutenberg, Laurentius, and Faust, were the founders."[2]

As an adult, Buckingham pursued journalism and fatherhood with equal vigor. He married Melinda Alvord in 1805 at age twenty-six and started a family that would grow to thirteen children. This was a rather large family for the time; the average size of American families dropped 25 percent between 1800 and 1860, from between seven and eight children to between five and six.[3] Meanwhile, Buckingham began publishing *Polyanthos,* a monthly theatrical sheet, and in 1809 the *Ordeal,* a short-lived Federalist weekly. Unfortunately, too much speculative publishing caused him to lose his printing office. He taught school briefly and then worked as an overseer at a printing firm where the partners allowed him to use the equipment for his own ventures. Between 1813 and 1828 he published two religious periodicals, *Christian Disciple* and *Friend of Peace,* and the *New-England Galaxy,* a literary weekly underwritten by the Freemasons. His biting editorials incited several libel suits, but he managed to squirm out of them all.[4]

Buckingham's most successful publication was the *Courier,* a liberal Whig daily that he edited in Boston between 1824 and 1848.

Among its most popular features were regular letters from New York by abolitionist Lydia Maria Child, which introduced the personal column as a standard feature in American journalism.[5] Buckingham also launched a literary monthly, the *New England Magazine,* with his son in 1831, and was active in civic affairs. He served as president of the Massachusetts Charitable Mechanics Association, held office in the Bunker Hill Monument Association, and was elected to the Massachusetts state legislature intermittently between 1828 and 1851. He died at age eighty-one in Cambridge, Massachusetts on April 11, 1861, the day Confederates demanded the surrender of Fort Sumter and thus the dissolution of the Union Buckingham had revered all his life.

Buckingham's memoirs were well received when they appeared in 1852, but it was the early chapters on his youth that garnered the most praise. "The tale of poverty which Mr. Buckingham tells, is one of the most pathetic we ever read," wrote *Graham's American Monthly Magazine.* "The description of the struggles of his mother, left after his father's death with a large family, to support herself and her children, is more powerful than anything of the kind we remember in romance. The trusting piety, which mingled with all her miseries and lightened their load, is touchingly delineated. Indeed, the first fifty pages of the book are worthy to be placed in the front rank of biographical literature."[6] Modern readers may judge for themselves whether this appraisal still holds.

I was born on the twenty-first day of December, 1779, and was the tenth in numerical order in a family of eight sons and two daughters. One of the sons, and a daughter, born two years after me, died in infancy. By request of a relative and intimate friend of my mother's, I was baptized by the name of Joseph Buckingham.

At the time of my father's death, my eldest brother was at sea in a merchant vessel, and my eldest sister was married. My mother, with eight children, continued to occupy the tavern; but the income afforded slender means for the support and education of so numerous a family; and this income, insufficient as it was, was diminished by the expenses of an unsuccessful law-suit, which the administrator on my father's estate prosecuted against one of the individuals who had reaped the benefit of his transactions as a contractor of supplies for the army.

I have no other recollection of my father *living,* than an indistinct idea of sitting on his knee, and hearing him sing for my diversion; but, of the father *dead,* the picture is fresh and vivid. The sensation that I felt, when carried into the room where the body was laid out in its shroud, I shall never forget. The room was darkened; whether by the closing of window curtains or by a cloudy atmosphere, I cannot tell. The body lay on a smooth board, which was placed on a table. The closed eye and the pale lip, even the plaits on the stock around the neck, (such as were then worn by men and buckled on the back of the neck,) now form as perfect an image in my memory, as the fold in the sheet of paper on which I am writing. Of the funeral, too, my recollection is almost as distinct as the remembrance of the events of the last week. The bier is standing before the door. The coffin is placed on it and covered with a black pall. A procession is formed and goes to the meeting-house. The bell tolls. The funeral prayer is said. The procession is again formed, and proceeds to the burying ground. The family crowd around the grave. The coffin is laid in its appointed place. Mr. Huntington, my mother's brother, takes me in his arms and holds me over it, so that I may see the coffin. The earth is thrown upon it. I hear the rattling of the gravel upon its lid. I feel now, as I have always felt, when I have called up the remembrance of this scene, the chill which then curdled my blood, and the fluttering of the heart, that then almost suspended the power to breathe.

The death of my father, under the circumstances I have related, was, of course, but the prelude to further domestic calamity. My mother was naturally of a delicate constitution, and had been broken down by frequent and severe attacks of rheumatic fever. She continued, however, to keep the tavern for some months—perhaps a year. At length, the establishment was abandoned, and the family necessarily dispersed. The second son went to sea; the next was apprenticed to a saddler; the third to a shoemaker; and for the next two, places were provided, at which they were supplied with food and clothing for such services as they were able to perform, till they should be of an age suitable to go out as apprentices. The furniture of the tavern was sold to pay off debts; and my mother, with a few articles, indispensable in housekeeping, and with two young children, me and a sister two years older, hired a couple of rooms in the house which her husband had built in the days of his prosperity, and which she had once expected to call her own for life. Here amidst occasional sickness, and constant destitution and sorrow, she supported her two remaining children, by the labor of her hands, chiefly needle-work.

But the depth of her destitution and distress she had not yet reached. There were still some demands against her late husband's estate pressing for payment. How long she continued with us in this house, I cannot tell, but I think I could not have been more than four years and a half old, when another portion of her scanty stock of furniture was taken from her by an officer of the law. With one bed, a case of drawers, two or three chairs, and a few cooking utensils, she left the rooms she had occupied and took refuge in the adjoining building, which my father had erected some twenty years before for a workshop. She held me and my sister by the hand, while a constable sold, at the door, the only andirons, shovel and tongs, chairs, beds, table, &c. which she had reserved when she left the tavern; leaving her one bed, one table, three chairs, the old case of drawers, a frying-pan and tea-kettle, and probably the articles absolutely necessary to enable a woman and two children to eat their food with decency;—but of this I am not positive. I went to a wheelwright's shop on the opposite side of the street, and gathered some chips to build a fire in our new habitation. The place of andirons was supplied with stones, taken from the street, and the service of shovel and tongs was performed by a spoke from a broken wheel,—the gift of our neighbor the wheelwright.

At this time we had no dependence for subsistence but the labor of my mother. She was often sick and unable to work. When in a condition to labor, she was employed in sewing for a neighbor who was a tailor, or in *"binding* and *closing"* women's shoes, which were then made principally of cloth, for another neighbor. This was a business in which she was expert, having done much of it when her husband carried on the manufacture. I was sometimes employed in sticking card-teeth, for a manufacturer of cards.[7] But, with all these poor resources, we must have suffered with cold and hunger but for the charity of a few friends.

I have no recollection of any time when I could not read. Probably I had attended a school in the summer after my father's death, but of this I have no remembrance. While we were living in this state of abject poverty, some one gave me a few coppers on a training day,[8] with which I bought a New-England Primer, and no speculator who makes his thousands by a dash of the pen ever felt richer than I did with my purchase. To my mother I was indebted for constant daily instruction, and I may say, without boasting, that her pupil repaid her attention, and at this moment feels an emotion of gratitude, which time has not destroyed or enfeebled. My elder brothers, when they came home to see us, (Heavens, what a home!) sometimes brought me a picture-book, and I was the owner of Robinson Crusoe, Goody Two-shoes, Tom Thumb, and perhaps half-a-dozen other books of a similar character. I have a confused idea of going to a woman's school in the summer after I was four years old; but, as the district schools were then kept but two months in the winter and two in the summer, two months was the longest term that I could have attended, and probably I was not there half of the time.[9]

In December, 1784, the month in which I was five years old, I went to a master's school, and, on being asked if I could read, I said I could read in the Bible. The master placed me on his chair and presented a Bible opened at the fifth chapter of Acts. I read the story of Ananias and Sapphira falling down dead for telling a lie. He patted me on the head and commended my reading. It was that winter, I believe, that Noah Webster's Spelling Book was first introduced into the schools. I could not read with the class, to which I properly belonged, because they read from that book; *mine* was an old Dilworth, and my mother had not the means to buy a Webster.[10]

But the instruction of my mother was not confined alone to teaching me to read. She was a firm believer in the doctrines of the Puritans, and she took pains to impress on my young mind the principles of the Westminster Assembly's Catechism,—the whole of which I could repeat, probably before I had read it.[11] It was her constant practice to pray with us daily. In the morning before we ate our breakfast, we (my sister and I) read each a chapter (or a part of one) in the Bible, and she always followed the reading with a prayer. In the evening, after she had placed us in the bed, (we had but one, and I was placed at the foot,) she knelt at the bed-side and poured out her heart to the widow's God—sometimes in thankfulness for unlooked-for favors, and, at others, in supplicating agonies for relief, which almost prevented utterance.

Once, on a Saturday evening, after I had gone over the customary exercise of repeating the catechism and certain hymns, and while my mother was on her knees at the side of the bed; there was a knocking at the door. She rose and opened it. The deacon of the church had sent by his servant the crust of several loaves of bread which were prepared for the celebration of the sacrament of the Lord's Supper that was to be observed the next day,—a small quantity of tea and sugar, and some other articles of food, and as much wood as could be placed on a small sled.

* * *

Necessity at length compelled my mother to ask assistance of the selectmen of the town; and, but for the aid obtained from them and the charity of friends, both she and her two children might have perished in the winter of 1785–6. I was without stockings or shoes through that winter, and otherwise but thinly clad. A load of wood had been dropped and cut up at the door by order of the selectmen, and I went out, barefooted, in the snow to pick up the chips. This and other similar exposures produced chilblains that were most grievously painful, and probably planted in my physical system the seeds, which later years ripened into rheumatism. The *staple* of our subsistence, for the greater part of the winter, was bread and molasses. Thus we lived till the summer, when a relative at Worthington, Mass. adopted my sister as one of his family, and a place was provided for me by the selectmen. I was put into the family of a respectable farmer, three miles from the principal village, and, by their authority, bound by indenture to live with him, till I should become sixteen years old.

* * *

The place provided for me was the family of one of the most respectable farmers of the town. His name was JOHN WELSH. He lived about three miles from the village, or *the town,* as that part where the meeting-house, court-house, taverns, and stores were situated, was called by way of distinction. To this good old man I was, as I have said, bound by the selectmen, acting in their capacity as overseers of the poor, to live till I should be sixteen years of age. It was on the eleventh day of July, 1786,—a day that has seldom been unnoticed in my retrospect of almost seventy anniversaries,—that I was prepared for separation from my only parent. The small parcel of clothing which I did not wear was tied up in a handkerchief. With admonitions, blessings, and tears, my mother bade me farewell and placed me in the care of my brother,—the apprentice to the saddler,—to be conducted to my new abode. The pang of separation was soothed by the novelty of the prospect, and the idea of having a permanent home, where I anticipated plenty and comfort, gave me inexpressible delight. A part of the road was new to me. The meadows and the forests, which we passed, were never before so green, the sun never shone with such brilliancy, the sky was never so blue and clear, and the beautiful yellow butterflies, that sported round the wet places by the way-side, never before looked so gay and happy. Alas! I knew not then how soon my dream of happiness might be dissipated, nor how fatal to my anticipations, would be the parting from my brother when I should be left among strangers. When that moment arrived, I felt an unutterable aversion to his departure without me, and the separation was not effected without force. The indulgence and tenderness, with which I was treated, soon produced forgetfulness of my grief, and I became perfectly contented and happy.

This family consisted of Mr. Welsh and his wife, both of whom were over sixty years of age; two daughters, past thirty; and a son about twenty-five. I was immediately instructed in the performance of such labors as were suitable to my age and strength, but was never taxed beyond that capacity. During the whole term that I lived with them, from the age of six and a half to sixteen, I felt not the loss of parents. When my mother came to see me, which was three or four times a year, it is true that the parting was accompanied with a sigh or a tear, but the emotion of sorrow soon passed away. To this period of my life I never look back but with feelings of gratitude. Though never suffered to be idle, no hardship was ever imposed; and I am not sure that I was not treated, in some respects, with more indulgence than if I had been a grand-child of the worthy old couple.

From my earliest recollection I was fond of books, and my propensity to reading was indulged to as great an extent as circumstances admitted. At that time, a farmer in Connecticut was not expected to keep much of a library. The Bible and Dr. Watts's Psalms and Hymns were indispensable in every family, and ours was not without them. There were, also, on the "book shelf," a volume or two of Sermons, Doddridge's "Rise and Progress of Religion," and a very few other books and pamphlets, chiefly of a religious character.[12] For a number of years, and until the old lady died, I read every day, at least one chapter, and often two or three chapters in the Bible. This was a daily exercise immediately after dinner, when the good old couple sat down to smoke their pipe. They probably thought it their *duty* to demand this of me; but I believe it was a pleasure to them to hear me, as I am sure it was to me to be permitted to read. I have no doubt that I read the Bible through *in course* at least a dozen times before I was sixteen years old, with no other omissions than the jaw-breaking chapters of the Chronicles. The historical parts I had read much oftener, and the incidents and the language became almost as familiar as the grace which the old gentleman said before and after meals,—neither of which ever varied a word during the nine years and a half that I lived with him.

* * *

At the period of which I am writing, the district schools in Connecticut were kept no more than four months in a year—two in the winter by a man, and two in the summer by a woman. That which was taught by the female was for girls and for children of both sexes, who were just learning the alphabet and the first lessons in spelling. I had outgrown this school both in age and acquirement, and never went to a female school or teacher, after I left my mother. The school-house in our district was more than a mile from our house, and during the winter term, the weather was often cold and boisterous. I went to school only in pleasant weather, and never more than half a day at a time till the winter when I attained my fourteenth year. Admitting that I went half a day on every alternate day for the two months, which is a calculation that I know exceeds the truth, it would amount to no more than twelve days in a year. When I was fourteen I began to *cipher* [study arithmetic] and during that and the next winter, my attendance at the school was more constant,— amounting in the aggregate, perhaps, to a couple of months. And there ended my *education*, as far as *schooling* was concerned. But I had the good fortune to live with a family, where reading and writing were not deemed unimportant, and where I learned nearly as much as boys of my age who were more constantly at school. Nothing but reading, writing and arithmetic were then taught as branches of common-school education. Of geography I knew but little, and of English grammar nothing, till after I began my apprenticeship. It was a blessing that I had a disposition for reading, and that I had the *privilege* of indulging it, though the means were scanty.

The family was a religious one. No labor, except works of absolute necessity, was ever performed on Saturday evening, after sunset. My last exercise on this evening of preparation for the Sabbath was the repeating of the Westminster Catechism, and such Psalms or Hymns as I might have committed to memory in the course of the week. There was a time when I could recite Watts's version of the Psalms from beginning to end, together with many of his Hymns and Lyric Poems. Among these, the *Indian Philosopher, Few Happy Matches, True Riches,* and *Happy Frailty,* were my favorite recitations. The poem entitled *God's Dominion and Decrees* excited me very much. It contained this stanza,

> Chained to his throne a volume lies,
> With all the fates of men,
> With every angel's form and size,
> Drawn by the eternal pen.

I was greatly puzzled to make out the picture of this volume in my imagination, and was anxious to know how Dr. Watts could have found out what it contained, since he afterwards said,

Not Gabriel asks the reason why,
Nor God the reason gives,
Nor dares the favorite angel pry
Between the folded leaves.

But I was still more rapt in astonishment, on reading the famous poem by the Rev. Michael Wigglesworth, entitled *The Day of Doom*.[13] The representation, in that poem, of the crowd of infants pleading for relief from punishment for Adam's transgression, caused me many an hour of intense mental agony. But I had access, for amusement, (not on Sunday or Saturday night) to another set of works, such as I have never seen since, and to which I was indebted for much useful instruction. We had on our book-shelf a regular file of *Almanacks*, for near or quite fifty years. Some of them were dated as far back as 1720, and some were made by "Nathaniel Ames, *Philomath*."[14] These periodicals I read often, and with never-relaxing interest. They contained many fragments of history, scraps of poetry, anecdotes, epigrams, &c. One of them had a long poetical account of Braddock's Defeat.[15] Others contained accounts of events which led to the Revolutionary War. One in particular made a deep impression on my mind. The title page had on it a large picture of a female, representing America, in a recumbent position, held down by men representing members of the British ministry, while Lord North was pouring Tea down her throat from an immense teapot. From his pocket was represented as falling out a roll of parchment, labeled "Boston Port Bill." The Articles of Confederation between the colonies, Petitions to the King, the Declaration of Independence, and many other papers connected with the history and politics of the country, were preserved in these useful annuals, and afforded me ample food for study. But what excited my especial wonder was the calculations of the eclipses, and prognostications concerning the weather. To me these old periodicals were sources of delight and instruction. I would now give more for that file of old almanacks, than for the most splendid of the *souvenirs* that modern taste and skill can produce— merely to enjoy the reminiscences and associations which they would awaken.

* * *

I pass over several years of monotonous, but not unhappy or unprofitable life. My physical wants were provided for; there was no lack of moral instruction; and no labor was imposed beyond what the formation of industrious habits required. It was a part of my duty as well as my privilege to go to meeting on Sundays, and generally to visit my mother during the intermission between the morning and evening services.

About this time, my brother Alexander completed his apprenticeship, and set up the business of shoemaking in Windham. He hired a part of a house in which he and our mother went to house-keeping. Thanksgiving day came soon after, and presented an opportunity to indulge in its peculiar enjoyments. The two younger sons; of which I of course was one, who lived at a distance from each other, *went home to keep Thanksgiving.* WENT HOME! what thrilling sensations of rapture does that thought communicate to the heart! The festive preparations were completed; the table was spread; around it stood a mother and three sons, who had not been assembled together before within the remembrance of the youngest of the group. The grateful and pious mother lifted her soul and voice to the widow's God, and uttered a blessing on that kindness, which had not broken the bruised reed, and which had known all her sorrows, and permitted her once more to see so many of her orphan children assembled around her. Her expressions of gratitude were not finished when the sentiment of affection and thanksgiving, which swelled in her heart, overpowered her strength; her bosom heaved, as if in strong convulsion; her utterance was choked; the lips could not relieve with words the soul-felt emotion; she faltered, and would have fallen, had not the elder son caught her in his arms. Tears at length came to her relief, and her agitation was succeeded by those grateful and affectionate sensations, which find no parallel but in a mother's heart. It is now near sixty years since this incident took place. The scene is as bright and life-like in my imagination as it was at the moment of its occurrence. Eternity cannot obliterate the impression from my memory; and if it could, I would not willingly accept of eternal life on such condition; for, I would never forget that that widow was MY MOTHER. She has long since put off her mortal clothing, and has, I trust, joined that innumerable company that are clad in white raiment, and receive palms in their hands from HIM whom they have confessed in the world.

NOTES

1. See Gary J. Kornblith, "Becoming Joseph T. Buckingham: The Struggle for Artisanal Independence in Early Nineteenth-Century Boston," in *American*

Artisans: Crafting Social Identity, 1750–1850, ed. Howard B. Rock, Paul A. Gilje, and Robert Asher (Baltimore: Johns Hopkins University Press, 1995), 123–34, and Joyce Appleby, *Inheriting the Revolution: The First Generation of Americans* (Cambridge, MA: Harvard University Press, 2000), 165, 209, 211.

2. Joseph T. Buckingham, *Specimens of Newspaper Literature: With Personal Memoirs, Anecdotes, and Reminiscences* (Boston: Redding, 1850), 1:ix.

3. Margo Horn, "Childhood and Children," in *Encyclopedia of American Social History,* ed. Mary Kupiec Cayton, Elliott J. Gorn, and Peter W. Williams (New York: Scribners, 1993), 2026.

4. Ronald J. Zboray, "Buckingham, Joseph Tinker," American National Biography online, www.anb.org/articles/16/16-00215.html (accessed October 31, 2007).

5. Frederic Hudson, *Journalism in the United States, From 1690 to 1872* (New York: Harper and Brothers, 1873), 384–86.

6. *Graham's American Monthly Magazine* 41 (1852): 554. The excerpts are from Joseph T. Buckingham, *Personal Memoirs and Recollections of Editorial Life,* 2 vols. (Boston: Ticknor, Reed, and Fields, 1852), 2:5–12,14–24.

7. Card teeth are the wire bristles in brushes, or cards, used for combing wool, cotton, or flax to align fibers and remove tangles before spinning.

8. Training days were the days when militias were required to muster; they were often observed as holidays, with parades and sporting events.

9. Open to all children in the community, New England district schools were supported by district taxes, state funds, and "rates," or tuition, from those parents who could afford it.

10. In 1783 Noah Webster published *A Grammatical Institute, of the English Language, Comprising an Easy, Concise, and Systematic Method of Education, Designed for the Use of English Schools in America* with the aim of introducing a system of pronunciation that would unify the new nation. A revised edition, *The American Spelling Book,* appeared in 1787 and became the standard text.

11. Puritans advocated simplicity in doctrine and worship and strictness in religious discipline. First published in 1692, Thomas Watson's *A Body of Divinity Contained in Sermons upon the Westminster Assembly's Catechism* condensed scriptural teachings into a series of memorizable short questions and answers.

12. The "Father of English Hymnody," Dr. Isaac Watts was a renowned scholar and noncomformist to the Church of England who wrote more than seven hundred hymns, including "Joy to the World." His *Hymns and Spiritual Songs* was first published in London in 1707–9. Watts's friend and fellow noncomformist Philip Doddridge published "The Rise and Progress of Religion in the Soul" in 1745, which he dedicated to Watts.

13. In 1662 Michael Wigglesworth's "The Day of Doom, or a Description of the Great and Last Judgment," became America's first bestseller. It was especially popular in rural New England before the Revolution. Buckingham published his own religious guide, *Devotional Exercises for Common Schools,* in 1842.

14. Almanacs were annual publications containing calendars, astronomical data, and other useful information. Nathaniel Ames (1708–64) was a physician and tavern keeper in Dedham, Massachusetts, who began publishing his almanac in 1725. It had a circulation of sixty thousand copies and was continued by his son until 1795. Ames's self-conferred title Philomath means "lover of learning" in Greek.

15. "Braddock's defeat" refers to British General Edward Braddock's fatal effort to capture Fort Duquesne early in the French and Indian War.

A Stolen Life

Excerpts from the Narrative of William W. Brown, a Fugitive Slave, Written by Himself *(1847)*

James Marten

"Each time a child was born in bondage," writes the historian Marie Jenkins Schwartz, "the process of enslavement began anew, as owners attempted to teach these children how to be a slave and parents struggled to give them a sense of self and belonging which denied the owner complete control over their lives."[1] A century and a half earlier, William Wells Brown said about the same thing; his master, he wrote in his autobiography, "stole me as soon as I was born." Brown's narrative of his first eighteen years—which occupies roughly the first seventy pages of the autobiography he wrote as a free man while in his early thirties—is a chronicle of freedoms denied and hopes shattered.

Though slaves held virtually no power over their own lives and masters literally held the power of life and death over their human property, the institution of slavery was much more complicated than it might seem. For instance, most slave children, historians suggest, enjoyed hints of real childhoods: the youngest had time to play and sometimes owned homemade dolls and toys. They were loved and nurtured by a mother or father or other family member. On large plantations, at least, they were worked gradually into the never-ending cycle of work, at first performing light cleaning duties, caring for younger children, or working in gardens. By the age of eleven of twelve they might be classified as "full hands" and be sent to the fields.[2]

Even this condensed version of a child's life cycle is absent from Brown's memoir. Published by an antislavery organization several years after Brown finally escaped from bondage, the autobiography, like dozens of other memoirs of former slaves published in the decades prior to the Civil War by abolitionist societies, indicts the institution of slavery for its particular cruelty to children and for its destruction of slave families and homes. Born in Kentucky, probably in 1814 (although Brown was never sure of his exact birth year), Brown spent nearly twenty-one years as a slave. As his memoir indicates, Brown had a varied life as a slave child. He was moved frequently, working on different occasions as a servant, a skilled laborer, and a field hand. Because he often worked on riverboats, he saw more of the world than most slaves. His early life was shaped by two constants: the instability of his personal life and his determination to escape. He was owned by or worked for planters and riverboat captains, as well as a slave trader, a newspaper editor, and a tavern owner. By the end of the time period covered in this excerpt from his autobiography, Brown had experienced more cruelty and seen more varieties of slavery than most bondspeople ever would. All of the events detailed in the excerpt below took place before Brown turned eighteen.[3]

I was born in Lexington, Ky. The man who stole me as soon as I was born, recorded the births of all the infants which he claimed to be born his property, in a book which he kept for that purpose. My mother's name was Elizabeth. She had seven children, viz: Solomon, Leander, Benjamin, Joseph, Millford, Elizabeth, and myself. No two of us were children of the same father. My father's name, as I learned from my mother, was George Higgins. He was a white man, a relative of my master, and connected with some of the first families in Kentucky.

My master owned about forty slaves, twenty-five of whom were field hands. He removed from Kentucky to Missouri, when I was quite young, and settled thirty or forty miles above St. Charles, on the Missouri, where, in addition to his practice as a physician, he carried on milling, merchandizing and farming. He had a large farm, the principal productions of which were tobacco and hemp. The slave cabins were situated on the back part of the farm, with the house of the overseer, whose name was Grove Cook, in their midst. He had the entire charge of the farm, and having no family, was allowed a woman to keep house for him, whose business it was to deal out the provisions for the hands.

A woman was also kept at the quarters to do the cooking for the field hands, who were summoned to their unrequited toil every morning at four o'clock, by the ringing of a bell, hung on a post near the house of the overseer. They were allowed half an hour to eat their breakfast, and get to the field. At half past four, a horn was blown by the overseer, which was the signal to commence work; and every one that was not on the spot at the time, had to receive ten lashes from the negro-whip, with which the overseer always went armed. The handle was about three feet long, with the butt-end filled with lead, and the lash six or seven feet in length, made of cowhide, with platted wire on the end of it. This whip was put in requisition very frequently and freely, and a small offence on the part of a slave furnished an occasion for its use. During the time that Mr. Cook was overseer, I was a house servant—a situation preferable to that of a field hand, as I was better fed, better clothed, and not obliged to rise at the ringing of the bell, but about half an hour after. I have often laid and heard the crack of the whip, and the screams of the slave. My mother was a field hand, and one morning was ten or fifteen minutes behind the others in getting into the field. As soon as she reached the spot where they were at work, the overseer commenced whipping her. She cried, "Oh! pray—Oh! pray—Oh! pray"—these are generally the words of slaves, when imploring mercy at the hands of their oppressors. I heard her voice, and knew it, and jumped out of my bunk, and went to the door. Though the field was some distance from the house, I could hear every crack of the whip, and every groan and cry of my poor mother. I remained at the door, not daring to venture any farther. The cold chills ran over me, and I wept aloud. After giving her ten lashes, the sound of the whip ceased, and I returned to my bed, and found no consolation but in my tears. It was not yet daylight.

* * *

Soon afterwards, my master removed to the city of St. Louis, and purchased a farm four miles from there, which he placed under the charge of an overseer by the name of Friend Haskell. He was a regular Yankee from New England. The Yankees are noted for making the most cruel overseers.

My mother was hired out in the city, and I was also hired out there to Major Freeland, who kept a public house. He was formerly from Virginia, and was a horse-racer, cock-fighter, gambler, and withal an inveterate drunkard. There were ten or twelve servants in the house, and when he was present, it was cut and slash—knock down and drag out. In his fits of anger, he would take up a chair, and throw it at a servant; and in his more rational moments, when he wished to chastise one, he would tie them up in the smoke-house, and whip them; after which, he would cause a fire to be made of tobacco stems, and smoke them. This he called "Virginia play."

I complained to my master of the treatment which I received from Major Freeland; but it made no difference. He cared nothing about it, so long as he received the money for my labor. After living with Major Freeland five or six months, I ran away, and went into the woods back of the city; and when night came on, I made my way to my master's farm, but was afraid to be seen, knowing that if Mr. Haskell, the overseer, should discover me, I should be again carried back to Major Freeland; so I kept in the woods. One day, while in the woods, I heard the barking and howling of dogs, and in a short time they came so near, that I knew them to be the bloodhounds of Major Benjamin O'Fallon. He kept five or six, to hunt runaway slaves with.

As soon as I was convinced that it was them, I knew there was no chance of escape. I took refuge in the top of a tree, and the hounds were soon at its base, and there remained until the hunters came up in a half or three quarters of an hour afterwards. There were two men with the dogs, who, as soon as they came up, ordered me to descend. I came down, was tied, and taken to St. Louis jail. Major Freeland soon made his appearance, and took me out, and ordered me to follow him, which I did. After we returned home, I was tied up in the smoke-house, and was very severely whipped. After the Major had flogged me to his satisfaction, he sent out his son Robert, a young man eighteen or twenty years of age, to see that I was well smoked. He made a fire of tobacco stems, which soon set me to coughing and sneezing. This, Robert told me, was the way his father used to do to his slaves in Virginia. After giving me what they conceived to be a decent smoking, I was untied and again set to work.

Robert Freeland was a "chip off the old block." Though quite young, it was not unfrequently that he came home in a state of intoxication. He is now, I believe, a popular commander of a steamboat on the Mississippi river. Major Freeland soon after failed in business, and I was put on board the steamboat Missouri, which plied between St. Louis and Galena. The commander of the boat was William B. Culver. I remained on her during the sailing season, which was the most pleasant time for me that I had ever experienced. At the close of navigation, I was hired to Mr. John Colburn, keeper of the Missouri Hotel. He was from one of the Free States; but a more inveterate hater of the negro, I do not believe ever walked on God's green earth. This hotel was at that time one of the largest in the city, and there were employed in it twenty or thirty servants, mostly slaves.

Mr. Colburn was very abusive, not only to the servants, but to his wife also, who was an excellent woman, and one from whom I never knew a servant to receive a harsh word; but never did I know a kind one to a servant from her husband. Among the slaves employed in the hotel, was one by the name of Aaron, who belonged to Mr. John F. Darby, a lawyer. Aaron was the knife-cleaner. One day, one of the knives was put on the table, not as clean as it might have been. Mr. Colburn, for this offence, tied Aaron up in the wood-house, and gave him over fifty lashes on the bare back with a cowhide, after which, he made me wash him down with rum. This seemed to put him into more agony than the whipping. After being untied, he went home to his master, and complained of the treatment which he had received. Mr. Darby would give no heed to anything he had to say, but sent him directly back. Colburn, learning that he had been to his master with complaints, tied him up again, and gave him a more severe whipping than before. The poor fellow's back was literally cut to pieces; so much so, that he was not able to work for ten or twelve days.

. . . If all the slave-drivers had been called together, I do not think a more cruel man than John Colburn,—and he too a northern man,—could have been found among them.

While living at the Missouri Hotel, a circumstance occurred which caused me great unhappiness. My master sold my mother, and all her children, except myself. They were sold to different persons in the city of St. Louis.

* * *

I was soon after taken from Mr. Colburn's, and hired to Elijah P. Lovejoy, who was at that time publisher and editor of the "St. Louis Times." My work, while with him, was mainly in the printing office, waiting on the hands, working the press, &c. Mr. Lovejoy was a very good man, and decidedly the best master that I had ever had. I am chiefly indebted to him, and to my employment in the printing office, for what little learning I obtained while in slavery.

Though slavery is thought, by some, to be mild in Missouri, when compared with the cotton, sugar and rice growing States, yet no part of our slave-holding country, is more noted for the barbarity of its inhabitants, than St. Louis. It was here that Col. Harney, a United States officer, whipped a slave woman to death. It was here that Francis McIntosh, a free colored man from Pittsburgh, was taken from the steamboat Flora, and burned at the stake. During a residence of eight years in this city, numerous cases of extreme cruelty came under my own observation;—to record them all, would occupy more space than could possibly be allowed in this little volume. I shall, therefore, give but a few more, in addition to what I have already related.

Capt. J. B. Brunt, who resided near my master, had a slave named John. He was his body servant, carriage driver, &c. On one occasion, while driving his master through the city,—the streets being very muddy, and the horses going at a rapid rate,—some mud spattered upon a gentleman by the name of Robert More. More was determined to be revenged. Some three or four months after this occurrence, he purchased John, for the express purpose, as he said, "to tame the d—d nigger." After the purchase, he took him to a blacksmith's shop, and had a ball and chain fastened to his leg, and then put him to driving a yoke of oxen, and kept him at hard labor, until the iron around his leg was so worn into the flesh, that it was thought mortification would ensue. In addition to this, John told me that his master whipped him regularly three times a week for the first two months:—and all this to "tame him." A more noble looking man than he, was not to be found in all St. Louis, before he fell into the hands of More; and a more degraded and spirit-crushed looking being was never seen on a southern plantation, after he had been subjected to this "taming" process for three months. The last time that I saw him, he had nearly lost the entire use of his limbs.

While living with Mr. Lovejoy, I was often sent on errands to the office of the "Missouri Republican," published by Mr. Edward Charles. Once, while returning to the office with type, I was attacked by several large boys, sons of slave-holders, who pelted me with snow-balls. Having the heavy form of type in my hands, I could not make my escape by running; so I laid down the type and gave them battle. They gathered around me, pelting me with stones and sticks, until they overpowered me, and would have captured me, if I had not resorted to my heels. Upon my retreat, they took possession of the type; and what to do to regain it I could not devise. Knowing Mr. Lovejoy to be a very humane man, I went to the office, and laid the case before him. He told me to remain in the office. He took one of the apprentices with him, and went after the type, and soon returned with it; but on his return informed me that Samuel McKinney had told him that he would whip me, because I had hurt his boy. Soon after, McKinney was seen making his way to the office by one of the printers, who informed me of the fact, and I made my escape through the back door.

McKinney not being able to find me on his arrival, left the office in a great rage, swearing that he would whip me to death. A few days after, as I was walking along Main Street, he seized me by the collar, and struck me over the head five or six times with a large cane, which caused the blood to gush from my nose and ears in such a manner that my clothes were completely saturated with blood. After beating me to his satisfaction, he let me go, and I returned to the office so weak from the loss of blood, that Mr. Lovejoy sent me home to my master. It was five weeks before I was able to walk again. During this time, it was necessary to have some one to supply my place at the office, and I lost the situation.

After my recovery, I was hired to Capt. Otis Reynolds, as a waiter on board the steamboat Enterprize, owned by Messrs. John and Edward Walsh, commission merchants at St. Louis. This boat was then running on the upper Mississippi. My employment on board was to wait on gentlemen, and the captain being a good man, the situation was a pleasant one to me;—but in passing from place to place, and seeing new faces every day, and knowing that they could go where they pleased, I soon became unhappy, and several times thought of leaving the boat at some landing place, and trying to make my escape to Canada, which I had heard much about as a place where the slave might live, be free, and be protected.

But whenever such thoughts would come into my mind, my resolution would soon be shaken by the remembrance that my dear mother was a slave in St. Louis, and I could not bear the idea of leaving her in that condition. She had often taken me upon her knee, and told me how she had carried me upon her back to the field when I was an infant—how often she had been whipped for leaving her work to nurse me—and how happy I would appear when she would take me into her arms. When these thoughts came over me, I would resolve never to leave the land of slavery without my mother. I thought that to leave her in slavery, after she had undergone and suffered so much for me, would be proving recreant to the duty which I owed to her. Besides this, I had three brothers and a sister there,—two of my brothers having died.

My mother, my brothers Joseph and Millford, and my sister Elizabeth, belonged to Mr. Isaac Mansfield, formerly from one of the Free States, (Massachusetts, I believe.) He was a tinner by trade, and carried on a large manufacturing establishment. Of all my relatives, mother was first, and sister next. One evening, while visiting them, I made some allusion to a proposed journey to Canada, and sister took her seat by my side, and taking my hand in hers, said, with tears in her eyes,—

"Brother, you are not going to leave mother and your dear sister here without a friend, are you?"

I looked into her face, as the tears coursed swiftly down her cheeks, and bursting into tears myself, said—

"No, I will never desert you and mother."

She clasped my hand in hers, and said—

"Brother, you have often declared that you would not end your days in slavery. I see no possible way in which you can escape with us; and now, brother, you are on a steamboat where there is some chance for you to escape to a land of liberty. I beseech you not to let us hinder you. If we cannot get our liberty, we do not wish to be the means of keeping you from a land of freedom."

I could restrain my feelings no longer, and an outburst of my own feelings, caused her to cease speaking upon that subject. In opposition to their wishes, I pledged myself not to leave them in the hand of the oppressor. I took leave of them, and returned to the boat, and laid down in my bunk; but "sleep departed from my eyes, and slumber from my eyelids."

* * *

Toward the latter part of the summer, Captain Reynolds left the boat, and I was sent home. I was then placed on the farm under Mr. Haskell, the overseer. As I had been some time out of the field, and not accustomed to work in the burning sun, it was very hard; but I was compelled to keep up with the best of the hands.

I found a great difference between the work in a steamboat cabin and that in a corn-field.

My master, who was then living in the city, soon after removed to the farm, when I was taken out of the field to work in the house as a waiter. Though his wife was very peevish, and hard to please, I much preferred to be under her control than the overseer's.

* * *

I was sent home, and was glad enough to leave the service of one who was tearing the husband from the wife, the child from the mother, and the sister from the brother,—but a trial more severe and heart-rending than any which I had yet met with awaited me. My dear sister had been sold to a man who was going to Natchez, and was lying in jail awaiting the hour of his departure. She had expressed her determination to die, rather than go to the far south, and she was put in jail for safe keeping. I went to the jail the same day that I arrived, but as the jailor was not in, I could not see her.

I went home to my master, in the country, and the first day after my return, he came where I was at work, and spoke to me very politely. I knew from his appearance that something was the matter. After talking about my several journeys to New Orleans with Mr. Walker, he told me that he was hard pressed for money, and as he had sold my mother and all her children except me, he thought it would be better to sell me than any other one, and that as I had been used to living in the city, he thought it probable that I would prefer it to a country life. I raised up my head, and looked him full in the face. When my eyes caught his, he immediately looked to the ground. After a short pause, I said,

"Master, mother has often told me that you are a near relative of mine, and I have often heard you admit the fact; and after you have hired me out, and received, as I once heard you say, nine hundred dollars for my services,—after receiving this large sum, will you sell me to be carried to New Orleans or some other place?"

"No," said he, "I do not intend to sell you to a negro trader. If I had wished to have done that, I might have sold you to Mr. Walker for a large sum, but I would not sell you to a negro trader. You may go to the city, and find you a good master."

"But," said I, "I cannot find a good master in the whole city of St. Louis."

"Why?" said he.

"Because there are no good masters in the State."

"Do you not call me a good master?"

"If you were, you would not sell me."

"Now I will give you one week to find a master in, and surely you can do it in that time."

The price set by my evangelical master upon my soul and body was the trifling sum of five hundred dollars. I tried to enter into some arrangement by which I might purchase my freedom; but he would enter into no such arrangement.

I set out for the city with the understanding that I was to return in a week with some one to become my new master. Soon after reaching the city, I went to the jail, to learn if I could once more see my sister; but could not gain admission. I then went to mother, and learned from her that the owner of my sister intended to start for Natchez in a few days.

I went to the jail again the next day, and Mr. Simonds, the keeper, allowed me to see my sister for the last time. I cannot give a just description of the scene at that parting interview. Never, never can be erased from my heart the occurrences of that day! When I entered the room where she was, she was seated in one corner, alone. There were four other women in the same room, belonging to the same man. He had purchased them, he said, for his own use. She was seated with her face towards the door where I entered, yet she did not look up until I walked up to her. As soon as she observed me, she sprung up, threw her arms around my neck, leaned her head upon my breast, and, without uttering a word, burst into tears. As soon as she recovered herself sufficiently to speak, she advised me to take mother, and try to get out of slavery. She said there was no hope for herself,—that she must live and die a slave. After giving her some advice, and taking from my finger a ring and placing it upon hers, I bade her farewell forever, and returned to my mother, and then and there made up my mind to leave for Canada as soon as possible.

I had been in the city nearly two days, and as I was to be absent only a week, I thought best to get on my journey as soon as possible. In conversing with mother, I found her unwilling to make the attempt to reach a land of liberty, but she counselled me to get my liberty if I could. She said, as all her children were in slavery, she did not wish to leave them. I could not bear the idea of leaving her among those pirates, when there was a prospect of being able to get away from them. After much persuasion, I succeeded in inducing her to make the attempt to get away.

The time fixed for our departure was the next night. I had with me a little money that I had received, from time to time, from gentlemen for whom I had done errands. I took my scanty means and purchased some dried beef, crackers and cheese, which I carried to mother, who had provided herself with a bag to carry it in. I occasionally thought of my old master, and of my mission to the city to find a new one. I waited with the most intense anxiety for the appointed time to leave the land of slavery, in search of a land of liberty.

The time at length arrived, and we left the city just as the clock struck nine. We proceeded to the upper part of the city, where I had been two or three times during the day, and selected a skiff to carry us across the river. The boat was not mine, nor did I know to whom it did belong; neither did I care. The boat was fastened with a small pole, which, with the aid of a rail, I soon loosened from its moorings. After hunting round and finding a board to use as an oar, I turned to the city, and bidding it a long farewell, pushed off my boat. The current running very swift, we had not reached the middle of the stream before we were directly opposite the city.

We were soon upon the Illinois shore, and, leaping from the boat, turned it adrift, and the last I saw of it, it was going down the river at good speed. We took the main road to Alton, and passed through just at daylight, when we made for the woods, where we remained during the day. Our reason for going into the woods was, that we expected that Mr. Mansfield (the man who owned my mother) would start in pursuit of her as soon as he discovered that she was missing. He also knew that I had been in the city looking for a new master, and we thought probably he would go out to my master's to see if he could find my mother, and in so doing, Dr. Young might be led to suspect that I had gone to Canada to find a purchaser.

We remained in the woods during the day, and as soon as darkness overshadowed the earth, we started again on our gloomy way, having no guide but the NORTH STAR. We continued to travel by night, and secrete ourselves in woods by day; and every night, before emerging from our hiding-place, we would anxiously look for our friend and leader,—the NORTH STAR.

His and his mother's dash to the North Star failed, and both were returned to slavery. A few years later, however, he finally escaped to freedom in 1834. He adopted the name of a Quaker who had helped him survive for a few weeks in wintry Ohio, worked on a Lake Erie steamer, and aided a number of fugitive slaves to escape. He made his living for a number of years as a journalist and as a lecturer on antislavery and temperance, which inspired him to write his *Narrative*. He also wrote plays and novels; *Clotel; or, The President's Daughter: A Narrative of Slave Life in the United States*, published in 1853, was the first novel written by an African American. Among his other writings were a history of African Americans during the Revolutionary War and another autobiography, *My Southern Home*. He died in Massachusetts in 1884.

NOTES

1. Marie Jenkins Schwartz, *Born in Bondage: Growing Up Enslaved in the Antebellum South* (Cambridge, MA: Harvard University Press, 2000), 18; William Wells Brown, *Narrative of William W. Brown, a Fugitive Slave, Written by Himself* (Boston: Anti-Slavery Office, 1847), 13. The following excerpts are from pages 13–16, 21–35, and 63–69 of Brown's *Narrative*.

2. The most complete studies of slave children in the United States are Schwartz, *Born in Bondage,* and Wilma King, *Stolen Childhood: Slave Youth in Nineteenth-Century America* (Bloomington: Indiana University Press, 1998).

3. William Edward Farrison, *William Wells Brown, Author and Reformer* (Chicago: University of Chicago Press, 1969), 3–68.

Questions for Consideration

1. Much is made in this volume about the idea that studying the history of children and youth during the era of the new republic can help us understand both subjects better. Find examples of events or ideas related to the political and economic events of the first few decades of the United States that we can understand better by researching the lives of children. What elements of children's lives can be explored more thoroughly with a knowledge of the philosophies and assumptions of the new republic?

2. Summarize what Americans believed were the most important features of being an American during this period. What values did they apply to the political, moral, social and economic facets of their society? How did they apply these values and assumptions to the lives of their children? Which children were most and least likely to be influenced by these ideas?

3. Many of the authors cite a book by Jacqueline S. Reinier called *From Virtue to Character: American Childhood, 1775–1840*. What does it mean to suggest that expectations for children evolved during this period from expecting them to be "virtuous" to expecting them to demonstrate "character?"

4. How was the life of the "typical" child in 1840 different from the life of the "typical" child in 1776? What forces caused those changes? What elements in the lives of the children and youth remained the same during this time?

5. If this was the era in which "normal" childhood developed—at least the kind of childhood that most middle-class Americans would identify as "normal"—describe that childhood on the basis of the articles and documents in this anthology. What elements of that childhood resemble the childhoods of today?

6. What were the main factors that caused variety in the lives of American children during this era? In other words, how did the childhood and youth of African Americans and Native Americans differ from those of

Anglo Americans? Examine the way in which those factors influenced family dynamics, education, the life cycle, social and economic expectations, and the differences between boys and girls.

7. How did a boy or girl know that he or she was "grown up" during this period in history? What "coming of age" rituals and experiences did youth have? How did those experiences differ depending on ethnicity, race, gender, and economic standing?

8. A term often used by historians in discussing children in the past is *agency*—the idea that children have choices and participate in decisions that affect them. What examples of children's agency can you find in these essays and documents?

9. During the period of the new republic, child rearing evolved from a moral imperative to a patriotic duty. What does that mean? How did that change in focus affect children and youth?

10. Native American and African American children came out of very different traditions. In what ways were they and their parents forced to share Anglo-Americans assumptions about childhood? How were they denied the chance to absorb "American" ideas about children? Which elements of "American" child rearing did they reject?

Suggested Readings

The communities of scholars who conduct research in children's history and in the history of the new republic have not necessarily considered themselves part of the same historiographical family. A recent anthology of essays on the past and future historiography of the early republic, edited by former editors of the *Journal of the Early Republic*, enthusiastically reports the "explosion of scholarly activities that have marked our field in the last decade or so" but fails to mention a single book or issue related to children or youth.[1]

As the foregoing suggests, the historiography on the period of the early republic rose to prominence after an outpouring of books on republican ideology appeared in the late 1960s, 1970s, and 1980s, starting with Bernard Bailyn's *The Ideological Origins of the American Revolution*. Bailyn and his colleagues framed many of the questions that would guide virtually every historian writing on the new republic, but none sought to include specific ideas about childhood or specific experiences of children. That was not their purpose, of course, but it is worth noting that a number of writers on republicanism did stress that education was, in the words of Gordon Wood, "the most obvious republican instrument for eliminating . . . prejudices and inculcating virtue in a people."[2] Indeed, the earliest work by professional historians on children's history came from educational historians, who have naturally gravitated toward the period. The title of Carl F. Kaestle's *Pillars of the Republic* suggests the centrality of education to the founders' vision, while the second volume of Lawrence A. Cremin's massive history of American education covers the periods of the Revolution and early republic. Steve J. Novak shows how the spirit of the times leaked into college culture in *The Rights of Youth: American Colleges and Student Revolt*. Early national education clearly had a religious component, as Ann Boylan shows in *Sunday School: The Formation of an American Institution, 1790–1880*. Ann Kuhn's *The Mother's Role in*

Childhood Education shows the importance placed on the home education of children during the decades after 1800.

Other notable works on the history of children during the five decades or so after the American Revolution include Bernard Wishy's 1968 *The Child and the Republic: The Dawn of Modern American Child Nurture*, which was part of the first generation of books to confront ideas about and the experiences of American children. Joseph Kett's 1977 *Rites of Passage: Adolescence in America, 1790 to the Present* remains on everyone's short list of seminal works on the history of children and youth. And although it is not specifically about children, David J. Rothman's pathbreaking *The Discovery of the Asylum: Social Order and Disorder in the New Republic* suggested ways in which efforts by postrevolutionary reformers foreshadowed the work of "child-savers" later in the century.

A number of historians of children and youth have dipped into the period to explore how emerging ideas about the Republic and about children converged. Holly Brewer, in *By Birth or Consent: Children, Law, and the Anglo-American Revolution in Authority*, examines the effects of political events of the period on legal issues related to the family, while Karin Calvert includes the material culture of the period in the wider net she casts in *Children in the House*. Two books that look at attitudes about children and the family in different parts of the country are rooted in the early republic, even though they extend to the eve of the Civil War: Sylvia D. Hoffert's *Private Matters: American Attitudes toward Childbearing and Infant Nurture in the Urban North, 1800–1860* and Jane Turner Censer's *North Carolina Planters and Their Children*.

Three broad works on American children's history published in the last dozen years take different approaches to the period, while emphasizing the transformations that rocked the social, economic, and political systems. Steven Mintz's *Huck's Raft*, perhaps the most complete survey of the three, devotes several chapters to the early republic, focusing especially on education, slavery, and origins of the middle class. Joseph E. Illick's *American Childhoods* is a much more focused look at class and ethnic differences; he stresses the effects of early industrialization on children and youth. Harvey Graff's *Conflicting Paths* traces common patterns of growing up shaped by economic change, religion, and westward expansion. Other sweeping accounts of the history of children and youth that also offer material on this period are Annette Atkins, *We Grew Up Together: Brothers and Sisters in Nineteenth-Century America*; Penny Colman, *Girls: A History of Growing Up Female in America*; Thomas Hine, *Rise and Fall of the American Teenager*; and Lynne Vallone, *Disciplines of Virtue: Girls' Culture in the Eighteenth and Nineteenth Centuries.*

NOTES

1. John Larson and Michael Morrison, eds., *Whither the Early Republic: A Forum on the Future of the Field* (Philadelphia: University of Pennsylvania Press, 2005), 2.
2. Gordon S. Wood, *The Creation of the American Republic, 1776–1787* (Chapel Hill: University of North Carolina Press, 1969), 426.

The following bibliography offers a sampling of books that provide political, economic, and social contexts to the lives of children and youth and a representative selection of books on topics related specifically to children and youth. Full citations are also provided for sources cited partially in the essays.

Politics, Economy and Society in the Early Republic

Anderson, Fred. *A People's Army: Massachusetts Soldiers and Society in the Seven Years' War.* Chapel Hill: University of North Carolina Press, 1984.

Appleby, Joyce. *Inheriting the Revolution: The First Generation of Americans.* Cambridge, MA: Harvard University Press, 2000.

Bailyn, Bernard. *The Ideological Origins of the American Revolution.* Cambridge, MA: Harvard University Press, 1967.

Bellows, Barbara L. *Benevolence among Slaveholders: Assisting the Poor in Charleston, 1670–1860.* Baton Rouge: Louisiana State University Press, 1993.

Boydston, Jeanne. *Home and Work: Housework, Wages, and the Ideology of Labor in the Early Republic.* New York: Oxford University Press, 1990.

Brown, Richard D. *Knowledge Is Power: The Diffusion of Information in Early America, 1700–1865.* New York: Oxford University Press, 1989.

—— *The Strength of a People: The Idea of an Informed Citizenry in America, 1650–1870.* Chapel Hill: University of North Carolina Press, 1996.

Cox, Caroline. *A Proper Sense of Honor: Service and Sacrifice in George Washington's Army.* Chapel Hill: University of North Carolina Press, 2004.

Dublin, Thomas. *Women at Work: The Transformation of Work and Community in Lowell, Massachusetts, 1826–1860.* New York: Knopf, 1979.

Ellis, Joseph J. *Founding Brothers: The Revolutionary Generation.* New York: Knopf, 2000.

Elson, Ruth Miller Elson. *Guardians of Tradition: American Schoolbooks of the Nineteenth Century.* Lincoln: University of Nebraska Press, 1964.

Fitzgerald, Frances. *America Revised: History Schoolbooks in the Twentieth Century.* New York: Vintage Books, 1980.

Foster, Lawrence. *Religion and Sexuality: The Shakers, the Mormons, and the Oneida Community.* Urbana: University of Illinois Press, 1984.

———. *Women, Family, and Utopia: Communal Experiments of the Shakers, the Oneida Community, and the Mormons.* Syracuse: Syracuse University Press, 1991.

Gilmore, William J. *Reading Becomes a Necessity of Life: Material and Cultural Life in Rural New England, 1780–1835.* Knoxville: University of Tennessee Press, 1989.

Gordon-Reed, Annette. *Thomas Jefferson and Sally Hemings: An American Controversy.* Charlottesville: University Press of Virginia, 1997.

Hutchins, Catherine E., ed. *Everyday Life in the Early Republic.* Winterthur, DE: Winterthur Museum, 1994.

Jensen, Joan M. *Loosening the Bonds: Mid-Atlantic Farm Women, 1750–1850.* New Haven: Yale University Press, 1986.

Johnson, Paul E. *A Shopkeeper's Millennium: Society and Revivals in Rochester, New York, 1815–1837.* New York: Hill and Wang, 1978.

Kelley, Mary. *Learning to Stand and Speak: Women, Education, and Public Life in America's Republic.* Chapel Hill: University of North Carolina Press, 2006.

Kettner, James H. *The Development of American Citizenship, 1608–1870.* Chapel Hill: University of North Carolina Press, 1978.

Larkin, Jack. *The Reshaping of Everyday Life, 1790–1840.* New York: Harper and Row, 1988.

Larson, John Lauritz, and Michael A. Morrison, eds. *Whither the Early Republic: A Forum on the Future of the Field.* Philadelphia: University of Pennsylvania Press, 2005.

May, Henry F. *The Enlightenment in America.* New York: Oxford University Press, 1976.

McCoy, Drew R. *The Elusive Republic: Political Economy in Jeffersonian America.* Chapel Hill: University of North Carolina Press, 1980.

Nash, Margaret A. *Women's Education in the United States, 1780–1840.* New York: Palgrave Macmillan, 2005.

Purcell, Sarah J. *Sealed with Blood: War, Sacrifice, and Memory in Revolutionary America.* Philadelphia: University of Pennsylvania Press, 2002.

Rothman, David J. *The Discovery of the Asylum: Social Order and Disorder in the New Republic.* Boston: Little, Brown, 1971.

Selby, John E. *The Revolution in Virginia, 1775–1783.* Charlottesville: University Press of Virginia, 1988.

Stansell, Christine. *City of Women: Sex and Class in New York, 1789–1860.* Urbana: University of Illinois Press, 1987.

Ulrich, Laurel Thatcher. *A Midwife's Tale: The Life of Martha Ballard, Based on Her Diary, 1785–1812.* Random House: New York, 1990.

Waldstreicher, David. *In the Midst of Perpetual Fetes: The Making of American Nationalism.* Chapel Hill: University of North Carolina, 1997.

Wilentz, Sean. *Chants Democratic: New York City and the Rise of the American Working Class, 1788–1850.* New York: Oxford University Press, 1984.

Wood, Gordon S. *The Creation of the American Republic, 1776–1787.* Chapel Hill: University of North Carolina Press, 1969.

——— . *The Radicalism of the American Revolution.* New York: Vintage Books, 1993.

Children and Families in the Early Republic and Beyond

Adams, David Wallace. *Education for Extinction: American Indians and the Boarding School Experience, 1875–1928.* Lawrence: University Press of Kansas, 1995.

Atkins, Annette. *We Grew Up Together: Brothers and Sisters in Nineteenth-Century America.* Urbana: University of Illinois Press, 2001.

Bardaglio, Peter W. *Reconstructing the Household: Families, Sex, and the Law in the Nineteenth-Century South.* Chapel Hill: University of North Carolina Press.

Berkin, Carol. *Revolutionary Mothers: Women in the Struggle for America's Independence.* New York: Knopf, 2005.

Boylan, Ann. *Sunday School: The Formation of an American Institution, 1790–1880.* New Haven: Yale University Press, 1988.

Brewer, Holly. *By Birth or Consent: Children, Law, and the Anglo-American Revolution in Authority.* Chapel Hill: University of North Carolina Press, 2005.

Buel, Joy Day, and Richard Buel Jr. *The Way of Duty: A Woman and Her Family in Revolutionary America.* New York: W. W. Norton, 1995.

Calvert, Karin. *Children in the House: The Material Culture of Early Childhood, 1600–1900.* Boston: Northeastern University Press, 1992.

Censer, Jane Turner. *North Carolina Planters and Their Children, 1800–1860.* Baton Rouge: Louisiana State University Press, 1984.

Child, Brenda. *Boarding School Seasons: American Indian Families, 1900–1940.* Lincoln: University of Nebraska Press, 1998.

Colman, Penny. *Girls: A History of Growing Up Female in America.* New York: Scholastic Reference, 2000.

Cott, Nancy F. *The Bonds of Womanhood: "Woman's Sphere" in New England, 1780–1835.* New Haven: Yale University Press, 1977.

Cremin, Lawrence A. *American Education: The National Experience, 1783–1876.* New York: Harper and Row, 1980.

Graff, Harvey. *Conflicting Paths: Growing Up in America.* Cambridge, MA: Harvard University Press, 1995.

Greven, Philip. *The Protestant Temperament: Patterns of Child-Rearing, Religious Experience, and the Self in Early America.* New York: Knopf, 1977.

——. *Spare the Child: The Religious Roots of Punishment and the Psychological Impact of Physical Abuse.* New York: Knopf, 1991.

Hacsi, Thomas A. *Second Home: Orphan Asylums and Poor Families in America.* Cambridge, MA: Harvard University Press, 1997.

Hawes, Joseph M., and N. Ray Hiner, eds. *American Childhood: A Research Guide and Historical Handbook.* Westport, CT: Greenwood Press, 1985.

Heininger, Mary Lynn Stevens, et al. *A Century of Childhood, 1820–1920.* Rochester, NY: Margaret Woodbury Strong Museum, 1984.

Hine, Thomas. *Rise and Fall of the American Teenager.* New York: Bard, 1999.

Hoffert, Sylvia D. *Private Matters: American Attitudes toward Childbearing and Infant Nurture in the Urban North, 1800–1860.* Urbana: University of Illinois Press, 1989.

Hoffman, Ronald, and P. J. Albert, eds. *Women in the Age of the American Revolution.* Charlottesville: University of Virginia Press, 1989.

Illick, Joseph E. *American Childhoods.* Philadelphia: University of Pennsylvania Press, 2002.

Jabour, Anya, ed. *Major Problems in the History of American Families and Children.* Boston: Houghton Mifflin, 2005.

——. *Marriage in the Early Republic: Elizabeth and William Wirt and the Companionate Ideal.* Baltimore: Johns Hopkins University Press, 1996.

Jones, Jacqueline. *Labor of Love, Labor of Sorrow: Black Women, Work, and the Family from Slavery to the Present.* New York: Basic Books, 1985

Kaestle, Carl F. *Pillars of the Republic: Common Schools and American Society, 1780–1860.* New York: Hill and Wang, 1983.

Kerber, Linda K. *Women of the Republic: Ideology and Intellect in Revolutionary America.* Chapel Hill: University of North Carolina Press, 1980.

Kerrison, Catherine. *Claiming the Pen: Women and Intellectual Life in the Early American South.* Ithaca: Cornell University Press, 2006.

Kett, Joseph F. *Rites of Passage: Adolescence in America, 1790 to the Present.* New York: Basic Books, 1977.

Kierner, Cynthia A. *Beyond the Household: Women's Place in the Early South, 1700–1835.* Ithaca: Cornell University Press, 1998.

King, Wilma. *Stolen Childhood: Slave Youth in Nineteenth-Century America.* Bloomington: Indiana University Press, 1998.

Kuhn, Anne L. *The Mother's Role in Childhood Education: New England Concepts.* New Haven: Yale University Press, 1947.

Ladner, Joyce. "Racism and Tradition: Black Womanhood in Historical Perspective." In *Black Woman Cross Culturally,* edited by Filomena Chioma Steady. Cambridge, MA: Schenkman, 1981.

Leavitt, Judith Walzer. *Brought to Bed: Childbearing in America, 1750–1950.* New York: Oxford University Press, 1986.

Lewis, Jan. *The Pursuit of Happiness: Family and Values in Jefferson's Virginia.* Cambridge: Cambridge University Press, 1983.

MacLeod, Anne Scott. *American Childhood: Essays on Children's Literature of the Nineteenth and Twentieth Centuries.* Athens: University of Georgia Press, 1994.

Mason, Mary Ann. *From Father's Property to Children's Rights: The History of Child Custody in the United States.* New York: Columbia University Press, 1994.

Mihesuah, Devon A. *Cultivating the Rosebuds: The Education of Women at the Cherokee Female Seminary, 1851–1909.* Urbana: University of Illinois Press, 1993.

Mintz, Steven. *Huck's Raft: A History of American Childhood.* Cambridge, MA: Harvard University Press, 2004.

Mintz, Steven, and Susan Kellogg. *Domestic Revolutions: A Social History of American Family Life.* New York: Free Press, 1988.

Norton, Mary Beth. *Liberty's Daughters: The Revolutionary Experience of American Women, 1750–1800.* Boston: Little, Brown, 1980.

Novak, Steve J. *The Rights of Youth: American Colleges and Student Revolt.* Cambridge, MA: Harvard University Press, 1977.

Pollack, Linda A. "Parent-Child Relations." In *Family Life in Early Modern Times, 1500–1789,* edited by David I. Kertzer and Marzio Barbagli. New Haven: Yale University Press, 2001.

Reinier, Jacqueline S. *From Virtue to Character: American Childhood, 1775–1840.* New York: Twayne, 1996.

Rorabaugh, W. J. *The Craft Apprentice: From Franklin to the Machine Age in America.* New York: Oxford University Press, 1986.

Ryan, Mary P. *Cradle of the Middle Class: The Family in Oneida County, New York, 1790–1981.* New York: Cambridge University Press, 1981.

Saxton, Martha. *Being Good: Women's Moral Values in Early America.* New York: Hill and Wang, 2004.

Schwartz, Marie Jenkins. *Born in Bondage: Growing Up Enslaved in the Antebellum South.* Cambridge, MA: Harvard University Press, 2000.

Smith, Daniel Blake. *Inside the Great House: Planter Family Life in Eighteenth-Century Chesapeake Society.* Ithaca: Cornell University Press, 1980.

Stanton, Lucia. *Free Some Day: The African American Families of Monticello.* Charlottesville, VA: Thomas Jefferson Foundation, 2000.

Stevenson, Brenda. *Life in Black and White: Family and Community in the Slave South.* New York: Oxford University Press, 1996.

Strasser, Susan. *Never Done: A History of American Housework.* New York: Pantheon Books, 1982.

Tyack, David, and Elisabeth Hansot. *Managers of Virtue: Public School Leadership in America, 1820–1980.* New York: Basic Books, 1982.

Vallone, Lynne. *Disciplines of Virtue: Girls' Culture in the Eighteenth and Nineteenth Centuries.* New Haven: Yale University Press, 1995.

White, Deborah Gray. *Ar'n't I a Woman? Female Slaves in the Plantation South.* New York: W. W. Norton, 1985.

Wishy, Bernard. *The Child and the Republic: The Dawn of American Child Nurture.* Philadelphia: University of Pennsylvania Press, 1968.

Zipf, Karin L. *Labor of Innocents: Forced Apprenticeship in North Carolina, 1715–1919.* Baton Rouge: Louisiana State University Press, 2005.

About the Contributors

Gretchen A. Adams is Assistant Professor of History at Texas Tech University (TTU), where she won the TTU Alumni Association's New Faculty Award in 2005. She is author of *The Specter of Salem: Politics and Memory in Nineteenth-Century America* (2008) and associate editor of *The Records of the Salem Witch Hunt* (2008).

Paul S. Boyer is Merle Curti Professor of History Emeritus at the University of Wisconsin. Among his many books are *Salem Possessed: The Social Origins of Witchcraft* (1974, coauthored with Stephen Nissenbaum); *Urban Masses and Moral Order in America, 1820–1920* (1978); *By the Bomb's Early Light: American Thought and Culture at the Dawn of the Atomic Age* (2nd ed., 1994); *When Time Shall Be No More: Prophecy Belief in Modern American Culture* (1992); and the coauthored textbook *The Enduring Vision: A History of the American People* (6th ed., 2007).

Todd M. Brenneman is a PhD candidate in the Religion Department at Florida State University. He is author of entries in the *Encyclopedia of Slave Resistance and Rebellion* and the forthcoming *Encyclopedia of Christian Civilization* and of "Out of the Mouths of Babes: Religion and Spirituality among Children and Teens," in *Faith in America*, ed. Charles Lippy (2006).

Caroline Cox is Associate Professor of History at the University of the Pacific and author of *A Proper Sense of Honor: Service and Sacrifice in George Washington's Army* (2004) and coauthor of *Opening Up North America, 1497–1800* (2005). She is currently working on a manuscript entitled *Boy Soldiers: War and Society in Revolutionary America*.

Vincent DiGirolamo is Assistant Professor of History at Baruch College, City University of New York. His essays and documentary work have

appeared in *Labor History, Radical History Review,* and the *Journal of Social History* and on PBS. He is chief historical adviser to the online teaching resource "Young America: Experiences of Youth in U.S. History," and
creator of the Web module "The Big Strike: Labor Unrest in the Great
Depression." His book *Crying the News: A History of America's Newsboys*
is forthcoming from Oxford University Press.

A. Kristen Foster is Assistant Professor of History at Marquette Univer-
sity. She is author of *Moral Visions and Material Ambitions: Philadelphia
Struggles to Define the Republic, 1776–1836* (2004), assistant editor of
Voices from Vietnam (1997), and coeditor of *More than a Contest Between
Armies: Essays on the Civil War Era* (2007).

Andrew K. Frank is Assistant Professor of History at Florida State University. He is author of *Creeks and Southerners: Biculturalism on the Early
American Frontier* (2005) and *The Routledge Historical Atlas of the American South* (1999) and editor of *The American Revolution: People and Perspectives* (2007). He is currently working on a manuscript titled *The Second Conquest: Indians, Settlers and Slaves on the Florida Frontier.*

Holly V. Izard is Curator of Collections at the Worcester Historical Museum. Her 1996 dissertation at Boston University was entitled "Another
Place in Time: The Material and Social Worlds of Sturbridge, Massachusetts, from Settlement to 1850." She has published articles in a number
of journals, including the *Proceedings of the American Antiquarian Society, Winterthur Portfolio, William and Mary Quarterly,* and *Agricultural
History.*

Cynthia A. Kierner is Professor of History at George Mason University.
She is author of *The Contrast: Manners, Morals, and Authority in the Early
American Republic* (2007); *Scandal at Bizarre: Rumor and Reputation in
Jefferson's America* (2004); and *Beyond the Household: Women's Place in
the Early South, 1700–1834* (1998). Her current project is a biography of
Martha Jefferson Randolph. She was President of the Southern Associa-
tion for Women Historians in 2006–7.

James Marten is Professor and Chair of the History Department at Marquette University. Among his books are *The Children's Civil War* (1998),

which was chosen as a *Choice Magazine* "outstanding academic title," and the edited anthologies *Children in Colonial America* (2006) and *Children and War: A Historical Anthology* (2002), both published by NYU Press. He is a founder and Secretary-Treasurer of the Society for the History of Children and Youth.

Rebecca R. Noel is Assistant Professor of History at Plymouth State University. Her Boston University dissertation was entitled "Schooling the Body: The Intersection of Educational and Medical Reform in New England, 1800–1860." She is author of "Salem as the Nation's Schoolhouse," in *Salem: Place, Myth, and Memory,* ed. Dane Morrison and Nancy Lusignan Schultz (2004), and "Cultures of Boys' Play in Mid-Nineteenth-Century New England: The Case of James Edward Wright," in *The Worlds of Children, 1620–1920,* ed. Peter Benes (2004).

Martha Saxton is Associate Professor of History at Amherst College. She is author of *Being Good: Women's Moral Values in Early America* (2003); *Louisa May Alcott,* (1977, 1995); and the forthcoming *The Widow Washington.* She is also coeditor of the *Journal for the History of Childhood and Youth*

Caroline Fuller Sloat is Director of Scholarly Publications at the American Antiquarian Society. She has been editor of the *Proceedings of the American Antiquarian Society* since 1993. She coordinates the five-volume series A History of the Book in America, a joint project with the University of North Carolina Press, and is also editor of *The Book: Newsletter of the Program of the History of the Book in American Culture.*

Nancy Zey is Assistant Professor of History at Sam Houston State University. Her 2007 dissertation at the University of Texas at Austin is entitled "'Rescuing Some Youthful Minds': Benevolent Women and the Rise of the Orphan Asylum as Civic Household in Early Republic Natchez." She is author of the forthcoming "'Every Thing but a Parent's Love': The Family Life of Orphan Asylums in the Lower Mississippi Valley," in *Southern Families: Perspectives on Domesticity in the Old South,* ed. Craig Thompson Friend and Anya Jabour, University of Georgia Press. She is also a list editor for H-Education and a columnist for the *Society for the History of Children and Youth Newsletter.*

Index